# WINNING WAYS:

## HOW TO SUCCEED IN THE GYM AND OUT

Winning Ways: How to Succeed In the Gym and Out
© 2004 Randall J. Strossen, Ph.D.

Cataloging in Publication Data
Strossen, Randall—
Winning ways: how to succeed in the gym and out
1. Sports—Psychological aspects    2. Weight training      I. Title
2004      796.01      2004115160
ISBN 0-926888-13-7

Published in the United States of America.
IronMind Enterprises, Inc., P. O. Box 1228, Nevada City, CA 95959 USA

Book design: Tony Agpoon Design, Sausalito, California

Printed in the U.S.A. First Edition
10 9 8 7 6 5 4 3

RANDALL J. STROSSEN, PH.D.

# WINNING WAYS:

# HOW TO SUCCEED IN THE GYM AND OUT

IronMind Enterprises, Inc.
Nevada City, California

This book is dedicated to:

my Uncle Lenny,
who introduced me to lifting weights over 40 years ago;

the University of Wisconsin–Madison and Stanford University,
where I was privileged to study psychology;

John Balik,
who began running my monthly sports psychology column in *IRONMAN* magazine in 1988 and has never tired of it (yet!);

my countless lifting friends from Anchorage to Almaty—
you are the faces on the theories; and

Elizabeth M. Hammond,
without whom this book would never have been completed.

Thank you!

Other IronMind Enterprises, Inc. publications:

*SUPER SQUATS: How to Gain 30 Pounds of Muscle in 6 Weeks* by Randall J. Strossen, Ph.D.

*The Complete Keys to Progress* by John McCallum, edited by Randall J. Strossen, Ph.D.

*Mastery of Hand Strength* by John Brookfield

*IronMind: Stronger Minds, Stronger Bodies* by Randall J. Strossen, Ph.D.

*MILO: A Journal for Serious Strength Athletes*,
Randall J. Strossen, Ph.D., Publisher and Editor-in-chief

*Powerlifting Basics, Texas-style: The Adventures of Lope Delk* by Paul Kelso

*Of Stones and Strength* by Steve Jeck and Peter Martin

*Sons of Samson, Volume 2 Profiles* by David Webster

*Rock Iron Steel: The Book of Strength* by Steve Justa

*Paul Anderson: The Mightiest Minister* by Randall J. Strossen, Ph.D.

*Louis Cyr: Amazing Canadian* by Ben Weider, CM

*Training with Cables for Strength* by John Brookfield

*The Grip Master's Manual* by John Brookfield

*Dexterity Ball Training for Hands Course* by John Brookfield

*Captains of Crush® Grippers: What They Are and How to Close Them*
by Randall J. Strossen, Ph.D., J. B. Kinney and Nathan Holle

To order additional copies of *Winning Ways: How to Succeed In the Gym and Out*
or for a catalog of IronMind Enterprises, Inc. publications and products, please contact:

IronMind Enterprises, Inc.
P.O. Box 1228
Nevada City, CA 95959 USA
tel: (530) 265-6725
fax: (530) 265-4876
web site: www.ironmind.com
e-mail: sales@ironmind.com

STRONGER MINDS, STRONGER BODIES™

# About the Author

**R**andall J. Strossen, Ph.D., a leading figure in the Iron Game, is one of the field's best-known authors and photojournalists.

After earning his Ph.D. in psychology from Stanford University, Dr. Strossen began his career as a marketing researcher for Bank of America, and in 1988, he founded IronMind, a name synonymous with strength around the world. For over 12 years, Dr. Strossen wrote the monthly sports psychology column for *IRONMAN* magazine, the publication that decades earlier had carried an account of his own success with the classic 20-rep squat program. Of the original 145 columns, the first 60 were published in 1994 as *IronMind: Stronger Minds, Stronger Bodies*. The final 85 are presented here in *Winning Ways: How to Succeed In the Gym and Out*.

Dr. Strossen is the author of over 200 articles and three additional books: *SUPER SQUATS: How to Gain 30 Pounds of Muscle in 6 Weeks*; *Paul Anderson: The Mightiest Minister;* and *Captains of Crush Grippers: What They Are and How to Close Them* (with J. B. Kinney and Nathan Holle). He is also the publisher of *MILO: A Journal for Serious Strength Athletes*.

# Contents

# Preface

Everyone jokes about the physician's ubiquitous advice to "take two aspirins and go to bed," but when you have something that simple that works so well, it's easy to make very heavy use of it, possibly to the point of over-reliance.

I've long felt that the psychological counterpart to this medical advice comes in the form of mental rehearsal, wherein the admittedly potent tool of visualization in some quarters is the be-all, end-all of psychological interventions aimed at enhancing performance. Given that I was educated as an experimental social psychologist, I had a different take on things and began to focus on diverse social psychological phenomena that apply to how well we perform in the gym and in the larger world—and that approach is one of the characteristics that set this book apart from most others in the field of sports psychology, performance enhancement, and life management.

Besides being fresh, I think you will find that the topics, psychological principles, and self-help tools discussed in *Winning Ways: How To Succeed In the Gym and Out* really are remarkably potent. I hope that, after reading this book, you will fully embrace the idea that just as we each have the ability to make ourselves and those around us quite miserable, we also have the ability to aim high, accomplish great things, and give both ourselves and the larger world something positive by virtue of our presence.

*Winning Ways* is all about making the most of things, so here's to your own successes—PRs in the gym and a great many satisfying accomplishments outside.

Randall J. Strossen, Ph.D.
IronMind Enterprises, Inc.
Nevada City, California

# 1: Long Journey, Short Steps

| **How to:** | Handle big, overwhelming tasks |
| --- | --- |
| **Key idea:** | ⭐ *Chunking* – chopping unmanageable problems into bite-sized pieces to get you started and sustain your effort to the very end |

Al Reese was like a lot of other guys. He went to school, he worked, and he lifted weights in between, all of which made his life pretty busy. Al was also like a lot of other guys in that too often he found himself procrastinating when it came time to study or train, and he sometimes just plain threw in the towel because the battles seemed too overwhelming to even begin to fight.

"Think about it," he would say to himself. "After I spend an hour doing calculus problems, my reward is to memorize more irregular German verbs. And then there's poly sci, and on and on— I'm looking at three hours of homework so that maybe in a few years I can graduate. Then it'll be graduate school and more of the same. Why bother to start?" When it came to his training, Al went through the same process.

Of course, when Al was on a six-days-a-week, 25-sets-per-body part, multiple-split routine, it was easy to understand his aversion to even beginning a workout, but what about when he used a basic, total-body, three-days-a-week program?

Talk about simple. All he had to do for his thighs, for example, was one lousy set of 20 reps in the squat, but even that was getting to Al: "When I get to the twelfth rep, I'll be in agony— which will only get worse as the set goes on. Steve Holman doesn't call them '9-1-1 squats' for nothing. I think I'll just sit this one out." So off Al would head for the couch.

Al's similarity to a lot of other guys ended at this point, however, because one day, instead of heading for the couch in front of his television set, he headed for the couch of his local sports psychologist to see if the fellow could shed a little light on Al's situation.

Al found the psychologist in his garage—although, other than the fact that there was a car under a cover and squeezed into one corner and a small workbench stuck in another corner, there was little to suggest that it was really a garage. It looked more like an attempt to defy the principle of physics which states that only one body of mass can occupy a given point in space at a given point in time. This guy had managed to jam more stuff into a garage than Al had ever seen before, and not content with his towering accomplishment, he was trying to cram in even more. "Different strokes," Al thought.

The psychologist told Al to make himself comfortable and waved him over to a flat bench. Al sat down, wondering whether he would soon be buried under the piles of stuff that surrounded him, but being pretty desperate for some help with his problem, he decided to take the risk and stay.

"So it's almost as if I get overwhelmed by what I have to do and then never even get started," Al explained as he concluded his story. "Things just spiral downward from there."

The psychologist had been listening to Al, and even though the doctor's eyes had occasionally wandered while Al was speaking, there was something in his manner that left no doubt that he had a handle on what was bugging Al. The psychologist grabbed a piece of cardboard from a pile by his side, pulled a pen from his pocket and scribbled "Ea-tmo-repr-ote-int-oge-tbi-g-ger" on it. He handed the cryptic message to Al and said, "If I gave you five seconds to memorize this, you probably couldn't, right?" Al nodded, but he was starting to wonder if maybe this psychologist needed a little help himself.

"But suppose," continued the doctor, "I arranged the letters like this." He scribbled "Eat more protein to get bigger" on another piece of cardboard. "No problem, right?" Al nodded again, but he still didn't see the point.

"This is an example of what cognitive psychologists often call chunking," explained the doctor, "and it shows how the structure of information makes a tremendous difference in terms of what we can memorize. We're going to apply a parallel principle to help you chop your otherwise unmanageable problems into bite-size pieces and make even your biggest challenges seem small enough to give you the confidence and sense of accomplishment necessary to both get you started and sustain your effort to the very end. Your accomplishments will soar as a result of your properly using this technique."

"All that plus a Ginzu knife, I bet," thought Al, but he had nothing to lose, so he figured that he might as well listen to the guy.

"Whenever you face a daunting task," continued the psychologist, "you should begin by structuring it—not just for meaning, as you do to help your memory, but to arrange it into digestible pieces. The biggest mistake you can make when tackling a big mountain, literally or figuratively, is to try to charge up its side. If you've ever watched mountaineers working their way up the side of a big peak, you've noticed that they seem to be moving in slow motion. This is because they use what's called the rest step. They literally pause for a moment each time they take a step. This might sound like a great way to move at a snail's pace, but it actually makes the most efficient use of your energy—physical and psychological—allowing you to not only keep going, but also to reach the summit . . . and as quickly as possible, too."

The psychologist could see that he had Al's attention, but he knew that he had to bring it down to terms that Al could relate to or the lesson might be lost.

"Not that you have to go to Nepal to put this idea into practice," the doctor continued. "Believe it or not, some people have such an aversion to cutting their toenails that the only way they can get started is to tell themselves that they just have to cut one of them. They pause and then tell themselves that they just need to cut one more. Before long, by combining the manageably small steps, they've actually finished the Herculean feat of cutting all ten toenails."

It made Al smile to know that someone in the world had trouble getting through a task that left him unfazed, but he hoped the psychologist would wrap up with an Iron Game-related example. He did.

"Suppose you're doing a set of 20-rep squats," the psychologist went on. "Everyone and his mother knows that the set is going to be tough and that anything you can do to reduce the mental trials and tribulations will help you move more weight. And moving more weight will mean more gains, so your ticket to success is to structure this task in a way that keeps what we might call your anticipatory anxiety to a minimum."

Al nodded in agreement.

"Here's what you do," said the psychologist. "Don't start off by telling yourself that you have to do 20 reps—that will kill you before you even get started. Pretend you only have to do five reps because, let's face it, if you plan to do 20 reps with a weight, you'd better be able to knock off the first five without the sort of effort that has you hallucinating. When you get to five, count backward for another five reps: 5, 4, 3, 2, 1. You've now done 10 reps, but by counting them this way you've made the psychological burden much lighter than if you'd just rattled off 1 to 10 with another 10 staring you in the eyes.

"Next, bang out another five, counting from 1 to 5. By now you really will be hurting, but you'll also be within spitting range of your final goal, so if you have any motivation at all, you can squeeze out the last five reps—counting them any way you like at this point. This system might sound simple, but it works."

Al nodded his approval, and the psychologist could sense that the wheels in Al's head were turning, already applying the technique to a variety of situations.

"Remember to use this approach for anything large that stumps you—school, work, or whatever," the doctor said. "Don't just use it for your training."

Al was sold. He thanked the psychologist and headed off to the gym, planning to have his best workout in a long, long time.

Meanwhile the psychologist faced 125 cubic feet of additional stuff he wanted to cram into the garage. "No problem," he said to himself. "I can put my coffee cup over here . . . ."

# 2: Mad But with a Mission

| How to: | Psych up using focused anger |
|---|---|
| **Key idea:** | ❧ *Synthetic anger* – consciously, and therefore artificially, thinking about being angry and putting yourself in that state |

Mention the 1930s to most Americans who have a sense of history, and they'll conjure up images of the Great Depression, like unemployment lines, soup kitchens, and people selling apples on street corners. Mention the 1930s to bodybuilders and lifters who have a sense of history, however, and they'll most likely think of Mark Berry and the way he revolutionized the business of getting big and strong by advocating heavy work on the basic exercises—most notably the squat.

As is commonly done today, Berry reinforced his message by pointing to live examples that proved the wisdom of his recommendations. Unlike what happens with some folks both past and present, however, he didn't fake his testimonials. He didn't have to, because Berry's success stories were so astounding that they rocked the Iron Game to its foundations. Imagine, for example, J.C. Hise, who piled on 29 pounds of muscular bulk in a mere month under conditions that today would be regarded as extremely primitive at best.

And then there was William Boone, who was related somehow to Daniel Boone and who, not to be outdone by Hise, carved out his own set of high-powered gains. Now, William was no shrinking violet, and having acquired a penchant for his father's cigars at a young age, he enjoyed testing the patience of his high school principal by driving up to the school with a cigar in his mouth and then—to the delight of his schoolmates—lifting the front end of his Model T.

William once wrote of himself, "I started training with weights in 1929 at [the] age of 14 because of my inability to hold up my end of fistfights with boys 17 to 20 years of age. Needless to say, by the time I was 17, I had whipped all of those same boys and was the champ of Homer, Louisiana, after five fights with one 20-year-old, 195-pound fellow. In the last one I outted him in about 30 seconds."

Not that William was some sort of mindless ruffian. In fact, his training techniques reflected an unusual degree of intelligence and analytical ability, not to mention a rare level of creativity. Fairly early on in his career, William observed that he couldn't lift much unless he first got what he called "synthetic mad," a process that might be dryly described as achieving a heightened state of physiological and psychological arousal.

Decades after Boone began putting focused anger to work for himself, sports psychologists around the world confirmed that this type of what they call preparatory arousal is exactly what gives strength athletes a big performance boost. Perhaps the most extensive research in this area so far was conducted by Filip Genov, a Bulgarian who demonstrated performance increases in everything from dynamometer tests, which measure hand strength, to standing broad jumps and short sprints when the subjects were properly aroused immediately before performing. Genov also showed that these psych-up times increase as the task becomes more difficult. For example, he found a pattern among top weightlifters in which they take increasingly more time to psych up as they move from their first attempt to their second to their third.

As I suggested, the changes that take place during this process aren't just psychological. Physiologically, for example, your heart rate, respiration rate, and muscle tone increase, and there are changes in hormonal levels as well.

So how do you put this process to work for you? Take a lesson from William Boone and think "synthetic mad"; that is, consciously—and therefore artificially—think about being angry and put yourself in that state. Athletes often like to pace rapidly back and forth while accelerating their breathing and selectively tensing their muscles. You might invoke a mental image of someone or something that makes you go ballistic—maybe the person who put the door ding in your new car while it was parked at the gym or the boss you'd like to donate to a Haitian voodoo ceremony.

Consider this to be your pre-fight ritual, if you will, and there's no need to make it complicated. For example, one of the most successful self-psychers I've seen simply takes a series of 20 or so rapid breaths while silently repeating a litany of every four-letter word he knows. This fellow is none other than William Boone himself, and I've watched him, in his late seventies, get psyched up and then—on his first attempt—rip a 665-pound deadlift so hard that I thought he was going to power-clean the bar.

This brings up an interesting question. Everyone and his or her mother knows that stress kills, so why would it ever be beneficial to systematically raise your stress levels by consciously creat-ing internal anger? The answer is that you wouldn't want to do it too much. In fact, you should use this technique sparingly and only for particular purposes. The point is not, for example, to create lots of generally angry young men.

There's a fellow who's a friend of a friend, whom I'll call Eddy. Eddy stands about 5'-4" and weighs around 150 pounds. He subscribes to *Soldier of Fortune*, and he owns—and sometimes wears—a pair of gloves that are lined with lead shot. He collects combat knives and—surprise, surprise—likes guns, especially handguns. If he has a dog, it's probably a pit bull or a Rottweiler. Eddy tends to look for trouble across the board; for example, if he knows he's going to shake hands with you, he starts to wind up when he's still about 50 yards out—one of those guys who like to watch you wince when they mash your hand.

Eddy represents what I'm not talking about here. What I am talking about is selectively inducing this state of "synthetic mad" for the specific purpose of lifting more weight—right then and there—with a generally cool demeanor both preceding and following the calculated anger. If you strive to create this state as a general frame of mind, your training progress—not to mention your general happiness—will take a decided turn to the south.

The 1991 World Weightlifting champion and 1992 Olympic silver medalist in the 110-kilo class is a fellow named Artur Akoev. One of the things you immediately notice about Artur when he lifts is that he appears so angry that you can almost see smoke and steam rising from his body. This guy gives personal meaning to the phrases "seething anger" and "white-hot anger." At the '91 World Championships I had a chance to tell him what I had observed and to ask if he was really as angry as he appeared. He looked at me as if I were remarkably stupid and said, "Of course!"

Maybe that's why he was lifting big, big weights and I was taking pictures.

# 3: Words to Grow By

| **How to:** | Use self-encouragement to help you grow |
| --- | --- |
| **Key ideas:** | ❧ *Self-encouragement* – giving yourself verbal pats on the back. |
| | ❧ *Effort control* – a valuable self-coaching tool that will help you get through tough moments on your path to success |
| | ❧ *Segment goals* – information you pass along to yourself on your way through a difficult task |
| | ❧ *Positive self-talk* – general statements, like "Great work," that make you feel good and lead to good results |

What would a good training session be without some words of encouragement? Unlikely, for starters—and certainly less exciting. The truth is that the right words will help you grow.

Does that mean there's such a thing as anabolic words? While that phrase might be a little strong, the fact is, there really are words to grow by.

As we all know, negative words have no place in your vocabulary—unless you really want to prove that you cannot gain no matter what you do. In terms of positive words, sports psychologist Brent Rushall outlined four major categories that are relevant to your efforts in the gym: self-encouragement, effort control, segment goals, and positive self-talk. Let's walk through them in the context of the most demanding—and the most rewarding—exercise of all, the squat.

"Self-encouragement" is just what it sounds like—giving yourself verbal pats on the back. This is a good way to get yourself going early in a set and creates a basis for some momentum to carry you into the hard part. Starting with the lift-off, you might say, "This weight feels pretty light" and words to that effect, and follow up with, "I'm going to have a great set." What you're doing is priming the pump. You should view self-encouragement as one of the most basic building blocks in a program of constructive growth-enhancing talk and use it to help yourself get going early in your workout or set so you can build up some steam to carry yourself into the difficult stages.

"Effort control" helps you deal with different stages in your performance, especially the tough moments. For example, when you're ready to drop into your squat, you might think, "This first rep is going to feel heavy, but if I just stick with it, I'll get warmed up and the reps will get easier." Or in between reps you might say to yourself, "Just relax as much as possible and suck in all the air you can." Or you might remind yourself when setting up for the next rep, "Just stay tight on the way down and blast up when you hit bottom."

Think of effort control as a tool that will help you focus on and complete a critical step on your path to success. It is, therefore, a valuable self-coaching tool.

"Segment goals" deal with information you pass on to yourself along the way. For example, if you've knocked off the first 10 reps in a set of 20, you might say to yourself, "Way to go—you're coming down the home stretch now," giving yourself some solid reinforcement for the distance you've already covered. Don't be afraid to let this feedback take the form of self-coaching; for example, "Remember, chest high, back arched."

This is also a good time to correct any breakdowns in your technique. "Lead with your head" and "Your hips are coming up too fast" are examples of how your self-talk can be instructive and help you finish a lift, making necessary adjustments along the way. In general, use segment goals to master and execute the key stages of your lifts.

"Positive self-talk" includes all those general statements like "I feel good," "Great work," "That rep was a piece of cake," and "This workout is going to make me grow." If you aren't already in the habit of making positive self-talk an automatic, ongoing part of your day, the time to start is right now. The best thing about using a lot of positive self-talk is that once you initiate the process, it tends to keep itself going automatically. Positive self-talk makes you feel good, which leads to good results, which makes you say nice things to yourself and feel good, and so on.

Now that you're armed with a basic framework of how to structure what you say to yourself when you're training, it's time to shed some light on specific words to grow by.

Relevant early research directed by social psychologist Donald Meichenbaum demonstrated that little kids boosted their performance speeds when they said or thought the words "Faster, faster" during an experimental task. This idea may seem simple, but it has significant implications for us. From these elementary roots we can build a program for identifying and using words that can further enhance your growth. In fact, we'll show you a particularly powerful way to use your mouth to prime your muscles.

Based on Meichenbaum's research, Rushall hypothesized that words that actually describe performance mood will enhance achievement and, therefore, should be included in task-specific statements. In other words, besides telling yourself things like "Maintain your groove," which is a task-specific statement, you should also use performance-mood words, saying things like "*Explode* under it" and "*Ram* the bar up."

Rushall tried out this approach using a hand dynamometer test for grip strength in three situations:

1) Where the subjects received no instructions about self-talk.
2) Where the subjects were instructed to make sterile statements, for example, "exert force."
3) Where the subjects were instructed to choose and use a compatible mood word, for example, "crush" or "grind."

Repeated trials, balanced presentation order, averaged scores, and other scientific niceties were observed, so we can have confidence in Rushall's results. Here's what he found.

The first two groups performed about the same, which indicates that it's not particularly helpful to talk to yourself in neutral language. The third group did much better, however, which implies that if you want some verbal support for moving bigger weights, you should choose words that have a little kick to them. For example, "Apply effort" just won't cut it; you want to tell yourself to "blast," "rip" or "smash." According to Rushall, it's important to pick words that meet the following criteria:

1) They have movement content.
2) They are emotionally charged.
3) They are meaningful to the person who's using them.

If all this talk about growth-enhancing language is completely new to you, it's time to put together a mental training program that supports your workouts with a little exercise between your ears. For example, start with the category of positive self-talk. Are you using this technique even though you never really thought about it? Or do you tend to do the opposite, telling yourself things like, "Man, this weight is killing me!" If you need help to learn this technique, get an index card, write a few positive statements on it, and read them about a dozen times a day. Keep doing it until you get the message and start saying positive things to yourself naturally. Do the same thing with self-encouragement.

To be able to use effort control and segment goals you need to understand two things: how the movement should be done and how you are performing it. For example, what are your strong points and your weak points? This is where a good coach or training partner comes in handy. But don't worry—even if you train alone, you can apply these techniques. Just analyze the lifts, put your form in the context of the ideal, and away you'll go. Build in mental markers, which are body cues that tell you where you are compared to your ideal position, and have some language ready to reinforce what you're doing right and correct what you're doing wrong.

For the last element in building your words-to-grow-by program, start looking around for the emotionally charged word or words that will squeeze a little extra adrenaline into your system. Think of these words as octane boosters. Try out some different ones, and remember that what works on one exercise might not be the best for another. In addition, these words may be highly personal. What charges your battery might not do a thing for your training partner. If you need help in coming up with possibilities, go to a thesaurus and look up some words that you think might do the trick—and try out some of the synonyms listed.

Now that you know the drill, *jump* on it.

# 4: Ricky and the Rut

**How to:** | Change patterns or habits that keep you from making gains

**Key ideas:** | ❧ *Habituation* – getting used to certain stimuli so that you no longer respond to them as strongly as you once did
❧ *Sensory adaptation* – one form of habituation, such as when your eyes adapt to changes in light without your knowing it

One thing that you could say about Ricky Edwards was, he was reliable. Take his training, for example. He never missed a workout. In fact, he always showed up at the same gym at the same time of the day. He always followed his routine to the letter, and his routines always followed a consistent pattern. He could even be counted on in terms of the T-shirts he trained in. Ricky was dependable right down to what he weighed and what he lifted—because that never changed either. And it might not have been a problem except that Ricky wanted to get bigger and he wanted to get stronger.

Ricky was reliable all right, but more to the point, he was in a rut. A deep rut. While he was primarily concerned with his biceps, he realized that much of what was holding him back was lodged in his brain, so he sought out a certain sports psychologist who was known to specialize in applying mind sciences to bodybuilding and lifting problems.

When Ricky arrived, the psychologist was on the phone, trying to persuade a long-distance carrier that he was perfectly satisfied with its service—even if its telephones themselves left something to be desired. The psychologist didn't seem to be making much progress, but he was spared further exasperation when the line suddenly went dead. He looked upward, raised his hands in gratitude and said "Thank you," before turning his attention to the young man in front of him.

Ricky briefed the good doctor, who cleared his throat and told Ricky, in so many words, that the problem was solvable.

"Let's face it," the doctor began, "we all have little patterns in our lives. They might be as benign as starting the day with our favorite newspaper or as destructive as remaining in a deeply dysfunctional relationship. There's something very comfortable about patterns, but when it comes to making training progress, too much comfort is the kiss of death. Let's take a look at what research psychologists call 'habituation,' see how it applies to training, and then develop some strategies for turning the tables to stimulate new gains in size and strength.

"When we become accustomed to a certain stimulus, we no longer respond to it as strongly as we once did. What happens is a process called habituation, and it is a powerful factor. We not only get used to things that are as ordinary as a specific temperature range or as unfamiliar as the causes of seasickness, but we also adapt to stimuli that are as alien as moderately intense electric shock. So electric shocks that initially produce cries of pain and attempts to escape, not to mention increased heart rate and blood pressure, can eventually lose their impact." The psychologist paused because he'd noticed that whenever he started talking about administering electric shocks, his clients began eyeing him with suspicion and subtly checking out the couch for telltale signs of hidden wires. So far Ricky hadn't reacted.

"Habituation patterns aren't always what you might expect," the psychologist continued. "For example, if you move close to a train track, the noise of the train—reasonably enough—will keep you awake at first. Later you won't notice it, but if the train doesn't come through as scheduled one night, there's a good chance that you'll be awakened."

The doctor glanced at Ricky again to see if he'd lost him yet. "This kid must be pretty desperate," he thought. "He's still listening." So the good doctor kept talking.

"One form of habituation is what psychologists call 'sensory adaptation,' and it's an excellent way to appreciate the raw power of getting used to something even if you're unaware of it. Seldom do we go directly from a very bright environment to a very dark one or vice versa, but when we do, we see just what we've been taking for granted. If you go directly from the bright outdoors to a darkened room, the result is so powerful that it blinds you until your eyes adjust to the new environment; and if you reverse the order, going from a dark environment to a very bright one, the experience will probably be so painful that you'll have to close your eyes.

"Without going to this extreme," the doctor continued, "we want to capitalize on what we'll call the growth-enhancing benefits of a novel stimulus. In more common terms, we want to shock you into new growth, which we do by 'dishabituating' you, and the key to this is to introduce some novelty into your training.

"If you're thinking about shaking up your workouts, the first thing that will probably come to mind is that you should change the routine itself. This could involve changing any combination of the following: your exercises, the order in which you do them, the sets and/or the reps. These changes can be as simple as no longer supersetting certain movements. Even subtle changes can produce dramatic differences in the way your body responds.

"Here's your chance to be creative," the psychologist concluded. "For example, some very accomplished lifters have stimulated new progress through such unorthodox techniques as loading the bar differently, using different plate combinations to alter the appearance of a given weight. I've seen world-class lifters literally change their perspectives by turning around and facing a different direction on the lifting platform. It can be something as simple as getting new workout clothes, going to a different gym, or just training at a different time.

"More sophisticated ways to introduce novelty into your training often involve cycling either your reps and sets or your exercises. In fact, the point of cycling reps and sets is to adjust your training volume and intensity over time to avoid excessive neural, hormonal, muscular, and psychological adaptation. You want to keep your entire system fresh, and one way to do this is to keep altering, according to a plan, the reps and sets you do. This is why one of the most effective ways to increase your strength is to plan cycles of successively lower repetitions, beginning for example with a cycle based on sets of five reps and ending three cycles later with a routine composed of singles."

The psychologist considered pointing out that this latter approach was based on what is called Matveyev's Principle, but he thought that might be a little much for Ricky, who looked as if he was getting the message.

"By far, the most powerful way to jolt yourself out of a rut is to switch to a radically different program, one that has goals that are aggressive, achievable, and measurable," the good doctor said. "Say, for example, that you've been locked into routines based on five sets of five, and, even though you want to get bigger and stronger, you weigh the same as you did a year ago, and your bench hasn't moved. What you need to do is to try something fairly revolutionary—such as going on a basic growth-enhancing routine with the idea of outgrowing a set or two of clothes in the next month or so. You should end up not just much bigger, but also capable of handling your current PRs with consummate ease."

The psychologist paused because he could see that Ricky's mind was racing, already applying what they had just discussed. In fact, Ricky stood up at that point, thanked the psychologist, and headed off to what seemed to be certain progress—big gains.

The psychologist, who generally tried to practice what he preached, wasn't always perfect, however. Noticing that it was high noon—the magical hour when he always trained, no matter what—that's exactly what he did.

# 5:  Medals of the Mind

| How to: | Change the way you think about lifting |
|---|---|

| Key ideas: | ✎ *Increased volume and intensity* – greater loads challenge the athlete's biological system, which will bring higher training effects and higher performances |
|---|---|

Once a dominant international force in weightlifting, the United States had last won an Olympic medal in that sport in full competition in 1976, when Lee James did us proud by finishing second to then-Soviet lifting legend David Rigert. The U.S. Weightlifting Federation [now USA Weightlifting] made no bones about it—its officials had had it with the drought and wanted to see at least one American win a medal at the 2000 Olympics; a crucial step along the path was our performance at the 1996 Olympics.

A critical element in our 1996 Olympics game plan revolved around a high-powered Romanian import, one Dragomir Cioroslan, who is the U.S. national coach. Make no mistake about it, Dragomir had his hands full. Not only did he face the challenge of rebuilding the team, but he had to do it while the entire sport was going through a major transition. If you haven't already guessed, a key tool in Dragomir's arsenal was changing the way his lifters think. Here's the situation.

Nineteen ninety-three will go down as a watershed year in the history of Olympic-style weightlifting. Sweeping rule changes affected everything from permissible attire to the once-sacrosanct body weight classes, and lifters can even wear gloves in competition now (my goodness!). In addition to these internal changes, the sport has been altered forever by certain world events—specifically, the break-up of the Soviet Union, long a juggernaut in the sport, into 12 independent republics. Now the Americans face the very real possibility of being beaten by not just one or two lifters from the USSR, but by a handful in many weight classes.

The perennial battle against banned substances took yet another turn in 1993 as weightlifting administrators began looking to the new blood test as a means of laying the issue to rest. And if all of the above weren't putting enough pressure on the U.S. weightlifting community, the sport's showcase event—the Olympics—was being staged in our back yard, in Atlanta, in 1996, and with the prestige of hosting the Games comes the added incentive to perform at our best.

Cioroslan would seem to be a good candidate to help pull off a dramatic turnaround in U.S. weightlifting fortunes and put at least one of our lifters on the podium in Atlanta because his life has already had something of a Walt Disney twist to it. Imagine a puny, sickly child who spent long periods of time in the hospital and who was laughed at by the coach the first time he entered a gym. After all, the 15-year-old Dragomir was 4'-9" tall and weighed less than 75 pounds. He persisted, however, and even though he broke down from overtraining when he started, he stuck with it and began to make such progress that he not only wasn't laughed at anymore, but he was advised that he might one day become a champion—a miraculous notion to the once bedridden youth. His many accomplishments include an Olympic bronze medal in weightlifting and Romania's highest coaching credential, which he earned before coming to America in 1990 as head of the Resident Training Program for the American lifters living at the U.S. Olympic Training Center in Colorado Springs.

Already Cioroslan has made his mark in coaching U.S. weightlifters. With his help, ex-powerlifter Mark Henry made the 1992 Olympic team in one year, and another American Tim McRae, our highest finisher at the Barcelona Games, is improving steadily. U.S. Weightlifting Federation President Jim Schmitz called Dragomir's performance "truly outstanding."

During 15 years of training as an athlete and 10 more as a coach, Cioroslan has "been in contact with very many specialists and experts in the field of sport throughout the world, including the Russians, the Bulgarians, the [East] Germans—the major representatives of the sport," he said. He has also done his share of library research in looking for the key to athletic success. "The conclusion which I am able to formulate at this moment is obvious," he related. "Those athletes and coaches who increased tremendously in their volume and intensity in training were the most successful in international competition."

In order to apply this principle to his U.S. coaching assignment, Dragomir "had to break the mental limitations athletes had before." American lifters have traditionally trained three times a week, and Cioroslan's feeling is that "with only three days per week you cannot do more than conditioning-type work, and the performance obtained from that will not be competitive anymore at the international levels. . . . The need to increase constantly the volume and intensity is probably one of the major changes I brought to the United States."

Dragomir explained that his training philosophy is "based on the idea that higher loads of volume and intensity, by challenging the athlete's biological system, will bring with them higher training effects which will be translated into higher performance."

Let's talk for a minute about just what he means by "higher loads of volume and intensity."

Under Cioroslan's leadership, the resident weightlifters at the Olympic Training Center "train 12 times a week, consuming up to 30 to 33 hours of specific training a week and up to 1,200 training hours a year," he said. "We're training here 300 days a year without breaking up too much, without taking too much time off, and most of the athletes are responding by increasing their total results by up to 60 kilograms a year. And these are elite athletes."

Dragomir told of how, in a recent week, the training program called for the lifters to perform 700 repetitions over 12 sessions, all of which took about 33 hours, and how those repetitions were for weights that were 80 percent or more of the athletes' bests. He also reported that 95 percent of the athletes performed according to the plan. As radical as this type of training might sound, Cioroslan explained it very matter-of-factly. "It is well-known and proven by the sports scientists that . . . it is very difficult to have tremendous impact on the athlete's performance without this type of approach," he said.

Lest you think that this merely proves the power of banned substances, understand that Dragomir is an advocate of high-quality protein and vitamin-and-mineral supplements but nothing stronger. This is a 100 percent clean program, and Cioroslan holds it out as an example of what "it's possible to achieve using this type of training without any drug abuse."

Does he think that some people have given up too quickly and become crybabies about training clean? "Oh, absolutely," he said. "People who gave up the fight for training under clean conditions without using steroids . . . just gave up on the change of knowledge and the scientific approach to training sessions because if you look into the possibilities open to you by sports science, the methodology of training programs according to modern principles, you will find extraordinary resources to improve your biological performance, your mental performance, allowing adaptation to higher and higher effort. The only barriers will be your own mental limitations."

Indeed, controlling the mind is a major factor in Dragomir's approach, as he continually urges his athletes to, "concentrate, concentrate, concentrate . . . it's all in the mind . . . If you know you can do it, you can!"

And quite often they do.

# 6:  The Greed Factor

| **How to:** | Properly manage your progress, avoiding too much too fast |
|---|---|
| **Key idea:** | ✎ *Greed factor – aggressive strategy for training that leads to burn-out and injury* |

**B**efore his affairs suffered a major reversal, Wall Street investor Ivan Boesky glibly pronounced, "Greed is good."  Putting aside the ethics of this philosophy, one might wonder about the wisdom of it, since it landed Boesky and several of his compatriots in prison, and if we can believe him, sent him into bankruptcy as well.  The funny thing is that this same principle—the greed factor—appears in gyms every day, and just as it is with investors, the results can range from mildly disruptive to permanently disabling.

Let's take a look at the greed factor in operation and see what it does to people who are on the path to getting bigger and stronger.

Imagine this archetypal scene: A very young lifter and an old fossil of a coach are in the gym together, and the coach is starting to talk brave.  Let's name our lifter Louie and eavesdrop for a couple of minutes.

"Louie, you can do it," the coach coaches, and then he follows that with, "If you want to enough," "Show us what you're made of," and the all-time favorite, "Be a man."  By now poor Louie has no choice but to at least outwardly go along with the plan.  Inside he's shaking, but what can he do?  His coach is calling for a personal record attempt.

As good fortune would have it, Louie hits the PR and what does the coach do?  Does he slap Louie on the back and offer to buy him a beer or whatever?  No way.  He ups the ante by starting the tough talk all over again and calls for another increase.  Louie's locked in by now because his coach is going to keep raising the weight until Louie misses, and then the coach is likely to have Louie try it two or three more times—each time boxing him on the ears with all the usual catchphrases.

Incidentally, this scene—involving this lifter and this coach—occurs at least once a week, and not uncommonly, it defines nearly every workout.

Across town another lifter is training under the watchful eye of another coach.  The lifter hits his top scheduled sets with authority and tells his coach how light they felt.  "Can I go up?" he asks, and the coach lets him take a shot at a weight that is 2.5 kilos over his best, which also flies up.

The lifter asks—nearly begs—for another increase, but the coach shakes his head and just says, "Don't be greedy. Save something for another day."

At least at first glance the aggressive coach's strategy would appear to be on the road to something big, while the second coach's strategy would appear to be fine for little old ladies, but that's about all. The funny thing is that the first coach's lifters don't have nearly the success that the second coach's lifters have. In fact, the first coach's lifters suffer from burn-out, bomb-outs, and battered bodies, while the second coach's lifters hit the big lifts when it counts and make Olympic teams, among other accomplishments.

The second coach says that his philosophy can be summed up by an old joke, which we'll offer in a sanitized form: Two bulls, one young and one old, are standing on a hillside looking down at a flock of sheep. "Let's run down and meet a couple of them," the young bull urges. "Let's walk down and meet all of them," the old bull replies. And if you press the second coach, he explains that while you'd like the lifter to always want to try more, one of the key roles of a good coach is to know when to hold the lifter back and when to send him out full tilt.

Don't think you have to have a coach or aspirations of achieving world-class performances in order to fall into the clutches of the greed factor. Consider the most basic programs around, programs that are successfully applied in the most primitive of gyms by zillions of guys training alone. Consider, in particular, a program that calls for the lifter to start with a moderate weight but to add five pounds to the squat bar at every single workout, three times a week, for six weeks.

The first lifter follows the program as written and at the end of the first two weeks is up to weights that are hard but not yet crippling. The second lifter is already in PR territory—having started at close to his limit and then slapped on 20 pounds at a crack. In another two weeks the first lifter is in PR territory, is growing like a weed, and is wondering why it took him so long to try this program. The second lifter has quit, complaining of numerous aches, and has returned to his beliefs that he shouldn't train too hard or too frequently because he's genetically predisposed to be a shrimp.

After two more weeks the first lifter is way into PR territory, has outgrown his second set of clothes, and has all his friends wondering just what he's doing to get so big so fast. The second lifter is still close to his opening body weight and has already blown up on yet another program, even though he's now training only once every six days.

As with many other facets of training, successful management of the greed factor requires striking the proper balance. You have to check the impulse to strive for too much progress too fast, which raises a critical point.

The folks who succumb to the greed factor in training aren't evil in any way—quite the contrary. What usually drives them to excess is their genuine enthusiasm and desire for success. It's this focus on progress that ultimately trips them up, however, just as a child who tries to run before learning to walk stumbles. What they need to learn is that the race for more size and strength is better run with the measured pace of the tortoise than the hurry-up-and-wait pace of the hare.

Besides slowing down your progress, succumbing to the greed factor can empty your checking account faster than an exotic car can. Remember our discussion of Machiavellians in muscledom and how being greedy is the best way to get fleeced (see *IronMind: Stronger Minds, Stronger*

*Bodies*, Ch. 54, p. 153)? People who look for something for nothing are prime prospects for con men. Thus, for example, an all-too-familiar pattern in the muscle industry takes the form of the latest, greatest supplement—the steroid replacement—which is always being presented to the eager and the gullible. The same applies to equipment and information—although not quite so dramatically. Meanwhile, the lifter who exercises some restraint along with his or her muscles realizes that there are no real secrets, and that anything that's presented as a shortcut is probably just another way to get short-changed.

Remember that the idea of properly managing the greed factor applies to the full spectrum of successful training programs, which is good because there's more than one way to arrive at your goals. This idea—that no matter which route to progress you take, greed will block your path—has long been recognized in the investment world as well, where people who try to profit by betting that the market is moving north are called "bulls" and those who bet that things are heading south are called "bears." The collective wisdom of Wall Street proclaims, "Bulls can get rich and bears can get rich, but pigs don't."

# 7: Plotting Progress

| | |
|---|---|
| **How to:** | Work consistently and steadily toward a goal without getting off track |
| **Key ideas:** | ✒ *Attention span* – how long you can work steadily on a particular task or activity |
| | ✒ *Lack of focus* – inability to maintain interest in a program or activity for an extended period of time |

Roger Mason is an absolute bundle of enthusiasm and energy—he approaches his workouts with an almost frightening level of commitment. In fact, the way he attacks his training, you get the feeling that if only he'd been at the Alamo, things might have turned out differently. There's just one problem with his approach, however: he changes routines faster than most channel surfers can hit their TV remotes.

For example, he might be into singles and nothing but singles for a couple of weeks. Ask him about his training philosophy, and you'll get an impassioned speech about the wonders of one-rep maxes that culminates in the strong personal testimonial, "I have always felt that to get strong you have no choice but to handle the heaviest weights you can." A short time later it's nothing but sets of five—the absolute Way to Power—and if you ask about this one, you're sure to hear another emotionally appealing argument, such as, "Ask the Russians what they can squat, and they always quote what they can do for five reps."

And so it goes. Doing absolutely no power rack training ("Have you ever seen a power rack in a Bulgarian gym?") gives way to power rack training as the path to success ("Our guys just don't know how to use a power rack correctly"). Until you get used to the pattern, the changes can make your head spin.

This amazing elasticity in terms of training philosophy doesn't just apply to Roger's lifting routines. Consider his aerobic training. For two weeks he'll be on a mountain bike kick, going through several workouts that include at least 3,000 feet of climbing per day. You can be sure that you'll hear all about these—not just how tough they are, but also how mountain biking is the be-all, end-all of Roger's life and, by the way, this is something you should try too. Next comes a couple of weeks of silence, and if you ask Roger about his biking activities, you'll learn that he hurt his ankle, got saddle sores, or in some other way had a monkey wrench thrown into his cycling program.

Things might remain quiet for a while, but one day he'll call you to report that he just ran 20 kilometers, including some hills. He'll also tell you that he did the same thing yesterday and plans to do it again tomorrow. "You know," he'll say, "you really should get into running." Two weeks later, for whatever reason, he'll be out of it.

The pattern is similar throughout Roger's life. For example, as with a lot of other people, he hates his job. Give him half a chance and he'll fill your ear with tales of woe about what jerks his supervisors are, how they shaft him at every turn, and on and on. If you took him literally, you'd have to believe that Roger's job is killing him, so it's hardly surprising to hear him say one day that he plans to be out of there soon. Correction: Roger says that he'll definitely be out of there and very quickly. Unfortunately, the first time you heard that one was about five years ago, and since then you've heard it almost as many times as you've heard the phrase "steroid replacement." Roger keeps talking about changing courses—doing everything from opening a restaurant to moving to Alaska—but just as the ever-new, nearly-perfect steroid replacements keep chugging down the pike, Roger keeps showing up for the job he hates, complaining about it every step of the way.

Roger suffers from the twin problems of a short attention span and lack of focus. As you might guess, these two maladies keep him from ever making any significant progress in his life—in either his training or his career—so let's talk about how you can avoid them.

Your attention span boils down to how long you can work steadily on a particular task or activity, whether it's your training or your income taxes. Did you ever notice how a first- or second-grader might be hard-pressed to do the same thing for five minutes, but a college student can work steadily for hours at a crack? This example is important not just because it illustrates how your ability to stay focused improves with maturity, but also because it implies how, with practice, you can train yourself to increase this ability. In addition, it demonstrates how the ability to stay on track is a prerequisite for success in nearly all walks of life.

Let's assume that you're convinced of the value of concentrated, steady effort and that you want some tips on how to increase your ability to work that way.

First of all, you need to define where you want to end up. In a sense, you have to do everything backward when plotting your course, starting with your end point and retracing your steps. "Easy to say but harder to do," you observe, recognizing that, for example, you are torn between winning the Mr. Olympia, getting a gold medal in weightlifting at the Atlanta Games, and trying to post a power lifting total that's 200 pounds above Ed Coan's best. Sure, in an ideal situation you'd have everything planned out from day one—kind of like those kids who "know" at age four that they plan to become medical doctors, thus giving their lives direction from preschool on. In the absence of such pinpoint targeting, take the pressure off yourself and pick a three-month goal, for example, and start laying out your game plan to reach your objective. Especially if you've been bouncing around almost from day to day the way Roger has, you need to commit to a definite goal that will require some systematic effort to reach.

Let's say that you decide to enter a power lifting contest in three months, with the goal of medaling. Looking at last year's results, you have an idea of what it's going to take to win, place, and show so you can set your training goals accordingly. Since your walking-around weight is between two body weight classes and you're what is politely called "tall" for either class, you decide to boost your body weight to the limit of the higher class. This becomes a sub-objective, or one that leads to your overall objective, which is to place in the contest, and serves as the basis for your training. If you prefer, consider this weight-gaining effort to be the first phase of your overall three-month program.

Continuing toward your goal, you shop the market and settle on an aggressive, bulk-building routine that should put you in the body weight range you've targeted in several weeks. Having a fairly short-term, specific goal—gaining, say, 15 pounds of solid body weight—is a powerful attention reinforcer, but you get an additional boost because the training program you have selected requires you to add five pounds to the squat bar at every single workout. The fact that these milestones are so concrete and come so quickly will be tremendously helpful in keeping you on track. Notice that one of the characteristics of Roger's misadventures is that he seems to pick workouts on a random basis—a technique that might work when you're playing the stock market, but not when you're looking to build size and strength as quickly as possible.

Once you get to your body weight goal, you turn to the second phase of your program, hitting a strength peak. Just as you used specific, short-term goals to keep yourself focused during the first phase, you do the same thing now. For example, you map out the remaining weeks leading to your contest so that you back down to the weights you plan to handle each week. This system applies equally well whether you use an elaborate program that carefully cycles your intensity levels based on percentages of your one-rep maximum or you simply try to add, say, five pounds to the bar every week or two. The point once again is that you take programmed steps toward a specific goal, which is drastically different from Roger's knee-jerk approach to training.

# 8: David and the Deficit

| How to: | Train for steady progress without overdoing it |
|---|---|
| **Key ideas:** | ❧ *Progressive resistance* – doing more in training today than you did yesterday<br>❧ *Overload* – subjecting your body to more than it's used to |

David Murray was the kind of guy who never approached anything halfway, so when the iron bug bit him, he took very definite steps to ensure, first, his immersion in the sport and, second, his success. Along with buying several sets of workout clothes, an armload of supplements, and a stack of books, he scheduled time with more than one highly touted personal trainer. In addition to thanking the folks who invented VISA cards, David assumed that he was laying the groundwork for what would be fast and steady progress.

Whatever he had—or didn't have—in the muscle department, David had plenty of potential when it came to brains, and he could sometimes spot patterns where others only saw a haze of details. In terms of training philosophies, one of the dominant philosophies—and one of the dominant patterns he picked up on from his many sources—was the need to keep pushing, to keep exceeding his previous work levels. David was not yet to the point where he could talk formally about volume and intensity, but he had gotten the idea: to make progress in the Iron Game, you must do more today than you did yesterday.

For a while things went swimmingly for David. His body weight, muscle mass, and strength levels increased very noticeably, and while he was no threat to the world-class lifters yet, he was headed in the right direction. When his progress slowed, David sat back, assessed the situation, reviewed what he'd done to date, and decided that to make more progress, he'd have to go back to the basics. For David this meant sitting down with a phone on his shoulder, a muscle mag in one hand, and a credit card in the other and restocking everything from rag tops to an herbal extract that was rumored to be the secret of the current Mr. Universe's awesome transformation.

In the gym David increased his training weights, reps, and sets while cutting his rest times. In fact, he was so taken with the idea of ever-exceeding yesterday's standards that he viewed each workout as a life-or-death struggle in which he fought the barbell with nothing less than eyeball-popping effort every inch of the way.

Once again David made progress for a while, but once again, the music stopped and his progress came to a halt. At this point David was ready to bet the bank and move to Los Angeles to work with a pricey personal trainer. He was also thinking about booking a berth on a muscle cruise, where he'd be able to mingle with stars and experts alike. Preparing for this latest round, David acquired another credit card, but suddenly there was no need for it—he was in too much pain to even think about working out.

For weeks he'd been aware of a sore shoulder, the result of getting five reps beyond failure by cheating more on each successive rep. The initial twinge hadn't gone unnoticed, but instead of doing anything as radical as dropping the offending movements or resting, David slogged on, bearing his pain as something of a badge of courage and dedication.

His wake-up call came one morning when David had so much shoulder pain that he couldn't even shave. That's when he noticed the reddish-purple spider web on the front of his shoulder, traces of internal bleeding in the area. Later that day he also got a call from his bank because his credit card payment was past due. "Funny thing," thought David, "there seems to be another pattern here."

While David's training was on ice, a gym buddy introduced him to an erstwhile coach who was known not only for his sometimes unorthodox views, but also for having helped produce some pretty staggering results on more than one occasion. What interested David was the fact that this fellow, who happened to be a psychologist, always stressed the need for fully employing your brain when training your body.

After listening to the story of David's trials and tribulations, the psychologist began by saying, "Nobody can short your determination, which is critical to success. Now let's check how you set your course.

"You are absolutely correct that each successive bodybuilding and lifting session depends on the principles of progressive resistance and overloading—which is just a polite way of saying that you must always do more than you're used to doing. The catch, however, is that you have to know how much more to do because this is not a case in which more is always better."

David nodded, thinking that while the guy wasn't saying anything radical, he did make sense.

"To take an extreme case," continued the psychologist, "suppose that you can squat 300 pounds. Is it going to do you any good to jump to 350 in one day? Of course not, even though it would appear that this might be consistent with your goal of doing more today than you did yesterday. The problem is that you not only have to be able to get through the heavier workload, but you must also be able to recover from it. In the most extreme case of violating this latter principle, you would injure yourself—the best way to absolutely stonewall your progress."

David ruefully rubbed his shoulder at this point, knowing that the psychologist was on track.

"Most people don't overdo their training to the point of being bedridden for days afterward or of seriously injuring themselves, but the tendency to continually overtax at least some body parts is amazingly prevalent," the psychologist said. "Sometimes the easiest way to understand things is by analogy, and we can use a financial analogy here to make sense of the training process. When you train, it's like borrowing money—what you borrow has to be repaid. Further, if you don't keep up with your payments, the interest keeps accumulating, increasing your total debt. In the ultimate financial case you go bankrupt, and in the ultimate physical case your body breaks down. Both instances leave you flat on your back."

"This guy does think a little differently from the muscle cruise set," David said to himself, "but this sounds reasonable." He nodded, and the psychologist went on.

"Just as it's sometimes wise to borrow money and sometimes necessary, it's a good thing to push yourself in your training. Even so, you have to manage the process very carefully because while you want to keep the pressure on yourself, ideally you'll never push things to the breaking point.

"This might sound very complicated," continued the psychologist, "but it's pretty simple in practice. The basic principle you need to follow is to not borrow more than you can repay. Steve Holman's book, *Mass-Training Tactics*, has a great Vince Gironda quote that pretty much sums things up: 'Never do today what you can't supersede tomorrow.'" The psychologist paused for a minute to let David digest that one. When he saw the light come on in his patient's eyes, he gave David some final advice.

"Train with the idea that the hardest workout in the world does you no good if you don't allow yourself time to rebuild and the idea that injury is the absolute worst outcome from your training. This is why you can't get greedy and why you can't borrow too much—because it will only help to defeat you. Plan your training cycles with patience. For example, it's far more productive to progressively increase your training weights over a four-to-six-week cycle than to compress the increase into a week or two."

David appeared to have gotten the message, so the psychologist concluded, "Remember that you're not running the country, so you can't just plan to build up runaway deficits."

# 9:  Two Weeks Weak

| How to: | Compete cleanly with an advantage over those using drugs |
| --- | --- |
| **Key ideas:** | ﹖ *Contrast effect* – what happens to performance going from a negative to a positive situation, and vice versa |
| | ﹖ *Social facilitation effect* – the way other people can make you stronger just by being there |

David Doright had some pretty heavy aspirations.  Not only did he plan to represent the United States weightlifting team at the Olympics, but he also planned to win a medal.  That was the reason he gave himself every advantage and did everything right.  He trained hard, ate well, got plenty of sleep, kept a positive outlook, and always tried to learn more.

One thing was bugging him, however.  David was a clean athlete, and he kept hearing rumors that the lifters in some other countries weren't being drug-tested randomly throughout the year the way he was.  Sure, he thought, those guys have to pass a drug test at the major meets like everyone else, but aren't they gaining a big advantage by being able to use steroids at other times during the year?

The question kept popping up in David's mind, and he started asking other people what they thought.  It turned out that there was a consensus of opinion on the subject.  Yes, by all appearances, some athletes were ignoring the rules about banned substances until shortly before a drug-tested competition.  Most people, particularly old-line coaches who had once been as adept as any at giving steroids to their athletes, felt that the matter was very straightforward— the guys who were dirty part of the year and then cleaned up for the test had a substantial advantage over the guys who were clean year-round.  At face value, at least, it was hard to argue with the opinion that even limited use of a performance-enhancing substance was bound to enhance performance in a substantial way.

David was kicking this around with another lifter, who mentioned that David might want to discuss the problem with a fellow who might have an opinion—a fellow whose thinking didn't always follow the mainstream.  For starters, this fellow often gained a different perspective because he could analyze training issues with a psychological perspective.  Since David had long ago learned the importance of the mental aspect of lifting big weights, he decided to pay the guy a visit.

After describing the situation to the psychologist, David asked what the doctor thought.  Was David deluding himself, thinking he could compete against the part-time dopers?  Was there something from the psychological side of things that might shed some light on his dilemma?

"Let's face it," the psychologist said, "if steroids didn't enhance performance, they wouldn't be banned. So at face value, anyone who uses steroids in just about any quantity will have a significant advantage over anyone who does not." David nodded, as he had heard this story before.

"But," continued the psychologist, "things may not be quite that simple. Weightlifting, as you probably know, was the first sport to use anabolic steroids to enhance performance. Somewhat ironically, and despite public perception, it has also taken the most serious steps to eliminate them—with a testing program and a set of penalties unrivaled by any other sport. What other sport, for example, gives lifetime bans to athletes who test positive for steroids?"

David knew all of this, but he nodded politely again, hoping the psychologist would tell him something he didn't already know.

"Things have changed a lot since the 1976 Olympics, when lifters could stop using anabolic steroids as far as four weeks out but continue using testosterone right up to the day of the contest. By the 1984 Olympics, lifters who wanted to pass the drug test were probably clean in terms of steroids and testosterone for two weeks before they competed, and the performance decrease in those two weeks was so noticeable that it was dubbed 'two weeks weak.' Testing continued to become tighter, and by 1992, athletes who wanted to pass the test were clean for at least 21 days. Experts who might place the overall strength gain attributable to steroids in the range of 10 percent would say that the residual gain at this point was probably in the range of 2 to 3 percent."

David nodded, but before he could say anything, the psychologist continued. "I know what you're thinking—in top-flight athletic competition, performance variations of less than 1 percent can be very significant, often making the difference, for example, between a gold medal and a silver or any medal and none."

David nodded one more time.

"So once again you would think that anything that might give you a 2 to 3 percent strength advantage would translate into a significant performance aid, right?"

Another nod.

"But," said the psychologist, "this analysis can be very misleading because it fails to consider the psychological factors at play."

At last David's ears perked up.

"When it comes to lifting heavy weights, there's a reason why the phrase *mind over matter* has reached the proportions of a cliché—it's undeniable that the mental aspects of lifting are extremely important. Let's walk through how the psychological portion of the equation differs for two lifters on the day of competition. Lifter 1 has been dirty as long as he dared, while lifter 2 has always been clean."

David smiled. The doctor was finally getting to the good stuff.

"Everything else being equal between them, we assume that the first lifter comes into the contest with a 2 to 3 percent strength advantage, but it's a mistake to stop the analysis there. We need to look at the fact that his strength has been on a downward trend for the past three weeks, and consider what this is doing to his head. To understand the impact of this trend, let me tell you about what psychologists call the 'contrast effect.'

"Suppose you have two groups of laboratory animals that are trained to perform some task. The first group gets a much bigger reward for performing the task than does the second group, and as you might guess, the first group substantially outperforms the second. Next, you switch the reward around, giving the first group the small reward and the second group the big reward. What happens? You'd think that they'd just trade performance levels, right?"

The psychologist looked at David, who said, "Sure."

"No," said the psychologist. "What actually happens is that when the first group gets switched from a high-reward to low-reward condition, its performance drops well below that of the group which originally got the low reward. The same process occurs in the other direction—when the group that started in the low-reward condition is switched to a high-reward situation, the rats perform well above the level of the group that originally got the bigger reward."

"So, when you're bumped down to the low reward, it appears to be even lower because you're coming off the high reward, and vice-versa," concluded David.

"Exactly," the psychologist replied, "and that's the psychological process that can work against lifter 1 and in favor of lifter 2. Now, as lifter 1 goes through his warm-ups and gets closer to his opener, the weights don't just feel heavier than the previous set; they feel heavier than the last time he lifted them. And these are weights that were pretty easy just three weeks ago. 'What gives?' the lifter thinks, but we know he's not going to be a happy camper, because everything is going to feel heavier than what he expects. He's being sunk by the negative contrast.

"Lifter 2, on the other hand, is picking up on the adrenalizing effect of performing in front of a crowd, so for him there's a positive contrast because even when he hits his final warm-up weight—a weight that usually feels pretty heavy in training—it feels almost light. Lifter 2 hits the competition platform with positive momentum, while lifter 1 hits it with negative momentum."

"I get it," said David, "but can that difference make up for the strength advantage the first lifter had?"

"Absolutely," the psychologist answered. "If you look at your own lifts and talk to other lifters, you'll see that it's very common to be able to lift at least 5 to 10 percent more in competition than you can in training—this comes back to the social facilitation effect you might have heard about [see *IronMind: Stronger Minds, Stronger Bodies*, p. 100]. Old math, new math or any other math will tell you that this factor, in conjunction with the contrast effect, means that lifter 2 is probably more than equal to the task of overcoming lifter 1 in the contest. Of course, this whole analysis presupposes that the two lifters were basically equal to start off with."

David thanked the psychologist as he headed out the door. He now knew that what he had to do was forget all about what others might be doing and concentrate on making sure that his training was as good as it could be. He wouldn't be coming in two weeks weak—he'd be coming in fifty-two weeks strong.

# 10:  Cults: Collecting the Incapable

| | |
|---:|:---|
| **How to:** | Avoid cult behavior and instead trust in your own experiences |
| **Key ideas:** | ❧ *Cult* – a strong leader exerts undue influence over a group of followers who blindly follow his advice |
| | ❧ *Self-belief* – observing what works well for you and acting on your own experiences |

Mention the word cult and you're likely to conjure up images of a bunch of wackos—maybe from Southern California or Texas.  Maybe they're not the kinds who butcher people, but the members of cults, as we all know, engage in some decidedly antisocial practices.  In all likelihood you wouldn't want to bring one home to meet your mother, right?  It's also true that we live in a world of degrees, and there are a lot of cults around that might never make the cover of your favorite supermarket tabloid yet exhibit many of the same destructive characteristics as the looniest groups.  And yes, folks, there are some cults right here in Muscle City.

Even if they don't inspire their members to commit mayhem, cults, by their very nature, tend to inspire extreme—and often dysfunctional—behavior.  Let's take a look at how they work and how they can exert a negative influence on their members.

Cults begin with a leader.  Think of the cults you've heard of.  The things you're most likely to remember about them are their leaders' names.  Try Charles or David or Jim.  Cult leaders range from the outright psychotic, which is to say they might be certifiably crazy, to the mildly neurotic, which is to say they could live next door to you and barely cause you to raise an eyebrow.  The first group makes the tabloid headlines, while the second group works even muscledom's markets.  This brings us to the second key element in any cult: its members.

Cults could not exist without members; indeed, even if the cult's leader grabs the headlines, the members actually provide the grist for his mill.  Members do the leader's bidding, give him ballast, and become a key tool for recruiting additional members.  Despite the fact that cults put their leaders on pedestals, the members are actually the life blood of the organization.  After all, without members there are no cults.  As you might guess, these people often exist on the fringes of society, and cult membership can give them as much of a happy home as they're likely to find.  In muscledom, the cult members are the ones who buy the leader's ideas and products while spreading his word.

Once a leader has established himself and collected some members, the cult becomes more apparent. For starters, the members immediately define themselves—maybe by using a label for themselves, maybe by dressing in a particular way or, if they're really going for the mystical touch, by using secret signs known only to card-carrying members. It's critical for cults to set themselves apart from others because they not only see the world in us-vs.-them terms, but they also want to sell the idea that they know the true way, even as all others are falling into one abyss after another. To reinforce this notion of having special knowledge, the leader is cast as a demigod who alone knows the true path. Followers can benefit from association with the leader, and all others, of course, are considered pitiful or worse. That's why cults tend to have a certain smugness, as if to say, "I once was a blind fool, following old what's-his-name's routines and using his supplements, but now I am found."

Other than the fact that the members might be a little nutty, what's the real harm in cults? If a cult's followers aren't out hacking people into little pieces, is it really any worse than any other social club?

The problem is that in a cult, a strong leader exerts undue influence over a group of weak follow-ers, and that's when things can go haywire in a big hurry. Cult leaders are dictators after all, whether they're considered to be benign or malevolent. In the muscle world, for example, they're the guys who tell you that you must do this or must not do that. Why or why not? Because they have the insight, knowledge, and experience to know right from wrong.

Don't kid yourself about the world simply being black and white, because other than gravity there are few absolutes in the world, iron or otherwise. When someone tells you never to do something that is either potentially insignificant or has a longstanding history of being done successfully, run from him as fast as you can.

After telling you, sometimes sternly and sometimes sweetly, just what you should do, the cult leader, because he is a control freak, will not take kindly to anything he views as questioning his word. There is a qualifier here, however, because cult leaders often display what psychologists call authoritarian personalities, which, in addition to the above, means that as much as they grind down those they view as underlings, they suck up to those they view as higher than them-selves on some totem pole. This is why cult leaders might do some fast back-pedaling along the way—when they're contradicted by a higher authority, for example, they feel obliged to jump on his bandwagon.

The problem goes beyond having iron-fisted leaders of wishy-washy followers, however. In one study, psychologists who began with the idea of demonstrating that a Hitler could never come to power in the United States were forced to admit that most of us slavishly carry out the orders of just about anyone in authority. This means that a cult leader may be able to induce aberrant behavior among his followers. Adding fuel to this fire is a peculiar set of dynamics that can cre-ate a group that collectively holds more extreme views than any single member does, instead of representing the group average—which means that the group thinking can get out of line in a very big way. These guys can soon have you believing that underwater gravity boot exercises followed by lettuce and grasshopper shakes are the way to 100 percent natural 19-inch arms and 500-pound bench presses.

As with life in general, one of the hardest things you'll ever have to do to make optimal progress with your training is to believe in yourself. Key to this issue of self-belief is the ability to seize what you observe is working for you and strip away what's not working for you. For example, at

IronMind we often remind people that if their experience contradicts our advice, good as our advice might be, they should believe their experience. In other words, even if a certain routine or diet works for 99 out of 100 people, the one person for whom it doesn't work needs to have the good sense and iron will to abandon that approach in favor of one that works for him or her. This sort of independent thinking is the opposite of what cults encourage. Despite what they might say, cults want mindless minions.

In the end, cults are not the province of the strong and the capable. The strong and the capable only became that way by believing in themselves and by acting on their beliefs. Cults have no part in this equation. Cults collect the incapable.

# 11:  Rationalization Revisited

| How to: | Use your mind to take some of the unpleasant edge off hard work so you can reap its benefits |
|---|---|
| Key ideas: | ✤ *Defense mechanisms* – ways we protect ourselves from internal conflicts ✤ *Rationalization* – a defense mechanism and tool our minds use to justify our actions and make us feel better |

Rationalization, as you probably know, usually gets a bad rap.  For starters, it's classified by psychologists as a defense mechanism.  Sparing you a lot of Freudian-based theory, this means that rationalization is a tool our minds use to make us feel good—or at least better—about what we're doing, and that gives it a bad connotation right off the bat.

Let's take a minute to define the process, and then you'll see how you can put a different twist on the beast and turn it into a muscle-building tool.

Let's say that you're basically an ethical person: You rarely rob old ladies, lie to few outside the IRS, and only occasionally beat your dog.  Along comes an opportunity to double your income— the only catch is that to earn the money, you have to work for a patently unethical person. What will you do?  Most people, of course, won't merely accept the offer—they'll leap at it. Because people are also inclined to view themselves as having high moral fiber, however, the act creates some internal conflicts.  On the one hand they prefer to see themselves as good and honest, but on the other hand they know that the party in question is bad and dishonest.  This internal conflict could cause a lot of discomfort if it weren't for psychological processes we employ to reduce the friction.  The processes are called defense mechanisms, and they are so-named for the simple reason that they protect our psychological beings from the discomforts of such conflicts. Rationalization is the defense mechanism that attempts to use seemingly rational arguments to explain and justify the actions in question, with the goal of eliminating the internal conflict.

In the above example you might say something like, "Well, *I'm* not doing anything wrong, just because he is," and go on to develop a detailed argument explaining this position. You might even go so far as to explain why it's good to engage in this activity, however far-fetched the arguments might seem to an outsider. Incidentally, don't sell this possibility short: Hitler once explained that he was doing "the Lord's work," so you can see that the human mind is essentially unlimited in terms of developing justifications for nearly any action.

You can also rest assured that you don't have to be stupid, uneducated, or nearly demonic to engage in this kind of thinking. A renowned research psychologist tells of giving a group of colleagues a block of random data. Rather than immediately rejecting it as meaningless, they busily tried to construct theories to explain it.

In the muscle world there are more than a few opportunities to fall victim to the classic forms of rationalization, and they're not just the painfully obvious ones, like using banned drugs or giving fake endorsements. Here's the kicker: The same basic psychological processes common to rationalization can be used to your decided advantage in the purest of pursuits. Let's see how.

The real hurdle that stops most people short of their lifting or bodybuilding goals isn't lousy genetics, bad information, "drug cheats," or bogus supplements. It's that substantial progress in lifting or bodybuilding involves a lot of very hard work, and most people simply don't have the discipline to meet this challenge.

In line with this idea, it's no accident that by far the single most important exercise for anyone seeking more size and strength—the squat—is also exceedingly unpleasant compared to just about any other. The trick here is to figure out ways to use your mind to take some of the unpleasant edge off squats so that you can reap their benefits. Here's where we can harness a psychological mechanism that works much like our classic friend rationalization.

Now that decades have passed since he was at his prime and because he can no longer simply stand up and issue a challenge to his critics, Paul Anderson is sometimes the target of naysayers who try to take potshots at his lifting feats. The facts, however, are pretty simple.

Paul began training as a teenager, largely specializing on the squat at first, and his gains in size and strength were nothing short of stupendous. Within a few years he had won an Olympic gold medal in weightlifting and was widely regarded as the world's strongest man. In an era when Doug Hepburn was probably the only other man capable of squatting more than 700 pounds, Anderson could do 900, and quite casually at that. Years later, when powerlifting became an official sport and Anderson was long since out of regular training, he would come to meets, and after the lifting was completed, he would pile every plate in the place on the bar and proceed tobang out reps in the squat. Not only were the weights involved far in excess of those anyone in the competition had lifted, but Anderson's reps were commonly described as being "the easiest done all night." Oh, yes, Anderson did his squats without a lick of support gear, not even a belt, and during the first part of his career, Dianabol hadn't even been invented, making the steroid question moot. "Wasn't it lucky," you might comment, "that Paul Anderson loved squatting so much? He really reaped tremendous benefits from it."

The truth is that Paul Anderson, the all-time king of the squatters, used to "dread" squats—to use his exact word. In fact, Paul says he never did a squat that he didn't dread. "What?" you say. "How could that be? How could someone who hated something that much do so many of them and get so good at it?" Because he was smart enough to use his mind to overpower his body. Here's how.

Paul knew that squats were the key that would open the door to the muscular size and strength he wanted—squats were the passport to his goal of developing himself into the world's strongest man. Since he was extremely motivated in his training, he could explain to himself that it was necessary to do squats, that he could put up with the discomfort because by paying that price, he would reap the reward he sought. He could go on and tell himself that, maybe, they weren't too bad, or even that, considering all the reps he had to do, the total amount of discomfort wasn't that much. Underlying it all, too, was the fundamental realization, as Paul says, quoting a country-and-western song, "There ain't no easy way, boy."

Interestingly, the very man who, more than any other, put squats on the map as the real open-sesame to super fast gains in size and strength, the legendary J. C. Hise, once noted that, "Most of us have no love for the DKB [deep knee bend, or squat]. What we want is the big chest, the wide shoulders, the great bodily power that it nourishes."

Whether it's squats or some other inconvenience that stands between you and your goals, use your brain to come to grips with the obstacle and surmount it. Use your brain to convince yourself that what had been standing in your path isn't such a terrible roadblock, certainly not one that will keep you from your goal. Use your brain, if you have to, to turn black and white into shades of gray. In a nutshell, revisit rationalization, and harness its possibilities and continue your progress.

# 12: Get Radical, Get Results

**How to:** | Make radical changes in your training to stimulate further progress

**Key idea:** | ☜ *Radical – revolutionary, rejecting the conventional wisdom*

Once upon a time there was a young man named Tom Stephens. Tom, to all appearances, was a perfectly typical guy who one day decided that he was tired of being perfectly typical. He wanted to be big and strong. The next few chapters are familiar: Tom started to train at home. To his good fortune, he naturally focused on the basic exercises—squats, benches, rows, and the like. Partly because it just made good sense to him, Tom added more weight to the bar at every opportunity. He also ate well and got enough rest, so he had all the ingredients for success firmly in place.

As you might well guess, things went swimmingly for Tom. He got bigger, he got stronger, and while it might not have been in the cards for him to be a world-caliber lifter or bodybuilder, before too long the changes were pretty monumental. Tom gained well over 50 pounds of solid body weight, his thighs were about the size his waist had been when he started training, his chest swelled beyond the four-foot mark, and he now tossed around barbells he would formerly have been barely able to roll across the floor. Tom, whether he realized it or not, was already a success story, but as you might have suspected, he wasn't done yet—he wanted more.

Even though Tom's appetite for continued gains never slowed down, after a while, his progress did. In fact, in time his gains didn't just slow down, they stopped dead in their tracks. Tom reacted logically. First he just tried a little harder, going from being downright religious about hitting all his scheduled workouts to really digging for every single rep possible from every set, to double-checking his diet. Next, Tom tried varying his workouts. He changed the order of his exercises, the exercises themselves, the number of sets, and the number of reps. Try as he might, however, about the most he could squeak out of all these myriad variations was a tiny blip of progress, usually one that had all the permanence of a soap bubble.

Tom hadn't a clue as to what to do next. Kicking it around with a buddy of his, Tom got the name of a fellow who had once helped his friend make progress when all else had failed. The fellow wasn't your typical personal trainer, but Tom figured he wasn't going anywhere anyway, so what could he lose? Since the guy was a psychologist, among other things, maybe he could put a little different spin on things.

Before long, Tom and the psychologist were talking about Tom's training, and even though the psychologist didn't immediately offer some newfangled mental trick, he did seem to have a different way of approaching training.

"You've certainly been very reasonable about your training," the psychologist noted, "and that's taken you pretty far. The problem is that you have now reached the point where merely being reasonable won't work any longer. You need to do something radical to stimulate further progress."

Tom looked blankly at the psychologist and tried to remember whether he might have seen him profiled on *America's Most Wanted*.

"One of the biggest myths we operate under is that things always move forward smoothly if only we know how to tweak them along," continued the psychologist. "The truth, however, is very different: While things can and do progress in an orderly fashion some of the time, the course of history is not marked by a smooth curve but, rather, by a series of jagged steps."

Tom was no dummy, but his eyes were starting to glaze, and the psychologist, who was also not a dummy, noticed this and made a quick adjustment.

"What this boils down to is that even when things are going in the right direction, they don't always move steadily toward their target. The first thing you need to realize, then, is that it's perfectly normal to stall out along the way and even to move backward from time to time. Most people quit at these sticking points, but for the few who persevere, more progress is in store. Remember the cliché, when the going gets tough, the tough get going? That pretty much summarizes the need to dig deeply into yourself when there's no outward sign of progress, and the fact is that there are definite rewards for those who do this."

Tom nodded and said, "I've been trying to do that."

"I know," the psychologist said, "and that's good. But there's a second part to this story."

Tom's ears pricked up.

"Most people don't have the stick-to-it-iveness to get through the times of no progress, and those who do most often try to restart the gaining process by making pretty conservative changes in their training. Maybe they start doing five sets of eight reps in the squat instead of three sets of twelve, or maybe they start doing inclines instead of benches—that kind of thing."

Tom nodded.

"What they're doing is playing it safe, sticking pretty close to the ground they've always traveled, taking the same paths as everyone else. What you need to do instead, however, is to let it all hang out. It's time to get radical. This isn't a modern idea, either, because if you look at the history of strength, for example, the people who really pushed the ante up a notch were willing to turn the iron world upside down. As Zorba the Greek would say, these guys were willing to take off their belts and look for trouble."

Tom was still with him, so the psychologist continued.

"More than half a century ago a fellow named Mark Berry rejected the conventional wisdom and decided that the way to produce top lifters was to build up the large muscle groups first, packing on a lot of productive mass in record time, and the way to do this was to concentrate on but a handful of basic movements—principally the squat. This was a radical notion in its day because the accepted approach called for 1,001 exercises, with no particular emphasis on the big movements. Those who followed Berry's approach quickly made more gains in a month or two than lifters had been typically making in years under the traditional approach. Before long, Berry's training principles were the cornerstone of most top lifters' routines.

"It's no accident that the guys who pushed the standards to new levels in the sport were willing to go out and do things very differently from everyone else—whether it was Paul Anderson pioneering revolutionary training techniques in the 1950s on his way to becoming the world's strongest man, or the members of the mythical Bulgarian weightlifting machine showing the 1970s that they could not only train a dozen times a week, but as a result, they could even upset the Soviet juggernaut as the world leader in weightlifting. To those who braved the frontier, you could say, have gone great rewards."

"So what do I do?" Tom asked.

"Easy," said the psychologist. "Consider what you have done in the past. This is just what you won't do. Forget about making minor changes, such as doing five reps instead of eight or doing alternate dumbbell curls instead of barbell curls. Get radical instead. If you've been training three times a week, try training six times per week. If you've always weighed 220, go to 240. If you've always tried to boost your deadlift by doing deadlifts, forget deadlifts and do power cleans or good mornings instead. That's the kind of thing I'm talking about. Don't limit your thinking too much—be willing to try pretty outrageous tactics as long as they're consistent with where you want to go and how you want to get there."

Being a quick study, Tom caught on to what the fellow was suggesting. He decided that he was going to try a routine he'd once read about. For the next month or so, he was going to do nothing but clean and jerks.

"Hey," he said, "the truth is that I haven't gotten any bigger or stronger for a year, so what can I lose? On the other hand, what if this jolts me back on the road to progress?"

Tom left the psychologist brimming with confidence about his game plan. "Radical," he murmured on his way out the door.

# 13: Eye of the Champion

| How to: | See that making progress requires mental toughness |
|---|---|
| Key idea: | *Mental toughness* – the ability to keep demanding more from yourself |

Time was when there was a nation whose weightlifters were the envy of the world: They dominated international competition, setting world records, winning world and Olympic championships almost at will. These lifters regularly toured the world demonstrating their prowess, yet most of them probably didn't know *borscht* from *banitsa*.

These fearsome lifters, you see, weren't from some Eastern European country nearly hidden on a map—these lifters were from such outbacks as Michigan, Ohio, Pennsylvania, or the really exotic California. Although many of the stars from those glory days are still around, the fortunes of American weightlifters in 1990s could hardly have fallen further. Purely and simply, we not only had vacated the winner's podium and the record book, but our men didn't even qualify to lift in the A-Session at the Olympics or the world championships.

Ask people just how or why things had reached this point, and you'd get some interesting answers. For example, a lot of people mention drugs, saying that our lifters are clean, but the rest of the world is dirtier than sin itself, and if we only played on a level field, we would once again be kings. Money comes up a lot—if we injected big bucks into the sport, everything would fall into place. Then there are those who simply attack the administrators running the sport, whether it's a policy, a particular person, or what they see as a totally misdirected effort that sells too many T-shirts.

For another view, let's turn to one of the best athletes the sport has ever seen, Tommy Kono, who just happens to be an American. Tommy's view should be considered by all iron athletes who are looking for more gains, whether in weightlifting, powerlifting, or bodybuilding. In fact, his view can and should be applied to all walks of your life.

He has been called the greatest weightlifter of all time, and is it any wonder? Tommy won gold medals at two Olympics and a silver at yet another. Not only did he set more than two dozen world records, but for eight consecutive years Tommy was either an Olympic or world champion. He also won Mr. World and Mr. Universe physique titles. Could this guy lift weights or what?

So you think Tommy Kono must have had everything in the world going for him—he must have been genetically blessed, from a rich family, given perfect training conditions? In fact, he got started lifting weights when his family, along with other Japanese–Americans, was locked up in a detention camp at the outbreak of World War II. Ask Tommy, and he'll tell that he never felt he had exceptional talent or made easy gains. Press further, and you'll find out that he prepared for two world championships by training alone in his basement!

What Tommy Kono did have was an extraordinary measure of mental toughness, the ability to keep demanding more and more from himself. If you want an indication of his mental toughness, consider that in contests, his first attempt in the clean and jerk was typically 10 to 15 percent more than he had been able to lift in training. Compare that to all the lifters who fold under the pressure of competition and leave their best lifts in the gym. Champions control their own destinies by looking to themselves for results, and Tommy was a supreme champion.

Ask him what's needed to turn around the fortunes of American weightlifting, and his eye turns inward. Tommy views weightlifting as a mind game, where the unsuccessful lifter puts a cap on what he expects to do. This limits the athlete's lifts—you might say he lifts down to his expectations. Tommy says that "our body is capable of lifting more than we demand of it, but our programmed thoughts restrict our improvement. If our lifting technique is good and we employ leverage at all times [quality training] and follow a sane, progressive training program, there is no reason why we cannot continue to show progress."

Early in his career, his thinking along these lines got a good jolt. He asked Larry Barnholth, the coach of Pete "Boy Wonder" George, when world weightlifting records would stop increasing. "A one-inch-diameter bone can support 10,000 pounds. When the arms are pulled out of their sockets, that's when we've reached the limit," Larry replied. Tommy says he realized that Pete George, who was a world champion at the age of 18, benefited enormously from this positive philosophy. Someone who thinks this way expects to make a lift, expects to make progress, expects success. Not surprisingly, this kind of champion turns inward—he looks for the roots of success in himself, rather than searching for excuses in external factors. Here's what Tommy says:

"How do we approach weightlifting? Are we looking for excuses for lifting poorly? It really doesn't matter what the others are lifting. Think in terms of how you are progressing. If you aren't improving, it doesn't matter whether others are taking steroids or not. If the excuse for your lack of progress is what others are illegally ingesting into their body, even if they stop taking things, it will not improve your progress.

"So let's not look for excuses. Improvement in U.S. lifting starts in your gym, in your team, in you."

# 14: The Quieting Reflex

| How to: | Calm yourself in an unexpected and uncomfortable situation |
|---|---|
| **Key ideas:** | ❧ *Arousal* – three internal and interconnected bodily processes—psychological, autonomic, and motor—that define your state of readiness |
| | ❧ *Over-arousal* – "fight or flight" state of readiness in the face of fear or danger |
| | ❧ *Quieting reflex (QR)* – technique to calm yourself when suddenly over-aroused |
| | ❧ *Competing response hierarchy* – using one internal technique, like QR, to intercept and overcome another internal process, like over-arousal |

Consider your typical nightmare: you suddenly find yourself high on the face of a sheer cliff, your position precarious and your body going into overdrive on the arousal scale—quick, shallow breaths coupled with a racing heart and the ever-present sweaty palms. Who needs a dark and stormy night to make things even worse? You're already gripped with fear, big time.

By comparison, getting ready to walk on stage—whether to pose or lift—seems pretty tame, and merely facing a PR squat weight in the gym should be a cakewalk. All these examples, however, represent situations capable of producing over-arousal, which leads not only to major personal discomfort, but also to impaired performance levels. In previous articles, I've outlined some very effective techniques for managing over-arousal, but they were primarily the type best used in advance of a feared situation; that is, to prepare yourself to deal with those situations. This time I'm going to introduce a very different class of anxiety-management techniques, a tool you'll be glad to have in your pocket when a tiger unexpectedly blocks your path.

The word "arousal" refers to three types of internal processes: 1) psychological, which relates to what you're thinking and doing; 2) autonomic, which relates to such physiological events as heart rate, breathing pattern, and blood vessel size; and 3) motor, which includes such things as coordination, reaction time, and muscle tone. These three sets of processes are interconnected. When you're highly aroused, for example, you think anxious thoughts and have a rapid heart rate, along with a high degree of muscle tension. This is nature's way of preparing you for an epic struggle, and in the days when there were two kinds of people, the quick and the dead, a person's ability to survive was often closely tied to these mechanisms operating at full tilt.

Today we know that too much stress doesn't just make people grind their teeth or give them sweaty palms, it actually kills them. Not so dramatic, perhaps, is the knowledge that while optimal arousal levels in sports vary depending upon the activity, generally speaking, over-arousal is a greater problem for most athletes than is under-arousal. Over-arousal doesn't just give you a queasy feeling in your stomach; it makes you tight, causes you to choke under pressure, and robs you of the performance edge that can make the difference between success and failure. With so much hanging in the balance, it's well worth your time to learn a few arousal–management skills.

The quieting reflex, or QR as it's called, has some key elements in common with other arousal-management techniques. For example, its goal is to establish what psychologists might refer to as "a competing response hierarchy" that, in effect, intercepts the fight-or-flight reaction and puts a lid on arousal levels before they get out of hand. Besides being something that is specifically designed to be used on the spot, QR has the additional advantages of being easy to learn and quick to implement. This is not a technique that will require you to attend a 12-week seminar before you can put it to work.

When do you use QR? Anytime you realize that your arousal level is rising significantly. Obvious clues can include such things as breaking into a sweat, clenching your fists, getting a knot in your stomach, or feeling just plain weak in the knees. More subtle indicators might be tension around your eyes, a sensation of your body getting tight, or perhaps a general sense of heightened awareness. To implement QR effectively, you have to become attuned to your body's signs of heightened arousal and immediately go into motion with a simple three-step action plan:

1) Smile, using both your eyes and mouth. You should begin by actually smiling, but with practice you can learn to do this inwardly, without moving your face.

2) Inhale deeply and slowly, drawing the air into your abdomen with a smooth, measured breath. Be sure to take your time inhaling, taking the deepest breath possible. Some people will find it more effective to inhale through the nose than through the mouth.

3) Exhale through your mouth while letting your face, jaw, neck, and shoulders go limp.

Repeat this cycle as required to keep the lid on your arousal level.

Remember, it's hard to learn new skills under duress, so as straightforward as QR is, be sure to begin applying it in low-stress situations. Continue to practice your technique in increasingly stressful situations, with the goal of making QR an automatic response to stressful situations. It should go without saying that if you hardwire QR, you'll have gone a long way toward not only improving your health but also giving yourself a potent tool for boosting you over many, many rough points in the gym and on the stage.

"It sounds cute," you say, "but is this just another of those mumbo-jumbo things every dime-store pop psychologist will soon be hawking, or is this something that can really work?"

Remember that old nightmare of being stuck on the face of a sheer cliff with nothing but hundreds of feet of air under your heels? Let's bring the nightmare to life, in the form of a voluntary activity called rock climbing. Take comfort in the fact that, according to Dale Goddard and Uno Neumann, authors of *Performance Rock Climbing*, this technique "is used by many top climbers before, during, and after a challenging route."

Hey, if this works for someone who's dangling by his finger tips on the alpine equivalent of an overhanging piece of glass, it just might approach magic the next time you're locked eyeball to eyeball with a bar loaded for a PR clean and jerk or squat.

# 15: Tough Enough

| **How to:** | Fuel your desire to meet the challenge of the hard work required to make progress |
|---|---|
| **Key idea:** | ❧ *Desire* – the key to being tough enough for any workout |

It's no secret that Arnold Schwarzenegger—not to mention a lot of other guys—was originally inspired by Reg Park, and why not?  Park combined a Herculean physique with strength levels that would have embarrassed many a powerlifter.  While it's true that Park had more inherent bodybuilding potential than the average guy walking down the street, one of the real secrets of his success was his ability to work extremely hard.  John McCallum once described watching Reg Park train: when it looked as if Park had ground out his last rep, he did some more—epitomizing the just-one-more-rep philosophy.

Park got an early lesson in dealing with adversity.  When he started training, not only did he have to do it in the family garage, but space was so limited that they had to pull out the car first—remember that the next time you're tempted to whine about your suboptimal training conditions.  Park was the guy who once noted that he could never get his calves to grow—until he got up to about 1,000 pounds on his calf raises.

A real favorite of mine—Louis Abele—was once at the center of a big flap when he talked about how he had little use for people who recommended a take-it-easy-and-grow philosophy.  In his own training, he said, he typically worked to the point of nausea.  Abele, who was an early product of extremely intense concentration on heavy leg and back work, noted that he trained so hard that his teeth ached from the breathing.  Think about that one the next time you feel like dumping the bar midway through a set of heavy 20-rep squats.  Abele, by the way, was richly rewarded for his efforts because he, too, combined world-class strength with a Herculean physique.

It's easy to get fooled into thinking that somehow, somewhere there exists a magical routine and a magical supplement that will allow you to realize all of your bodybuilding and lifting dreams without doing much more than breaking a sweat.  If you believe this idea, we'd like to offer you the Golden Gate Bridge at a great price.

Instead, you need to accept the fact that any way you slice it, lifting weights is hard work. If you want to make progress, lifting weights is *really* hard work. You also need to accept the idea that this requirement for hard work is not reserved for the genetically challenged—hard work is a fact of life for everyone who lifts weights, whether you end up with a 17-inch arm or a 23-inch arm.

"Great," you say, "do you have any other good news? How about at least giving me a suggestion for how to get through all this hard work."

Fair enough.

We got a lot of practical insight into how to deal with the challenge of hard work when we interviewed Alexander Kurlovich for *MILO*, the strength journal.* Kurlovich, you might recall, won the super-heavyweight gold medal in weightlifting at both the 1988 and 1992 Olympics—and he was looking to three-peat in Atlanta. Regardless of the outcome in 1996, however, Kurlovich had already assured himself an elite position in the sport's history. If you're not a weightlifting fan, just think of him as a guy who can hoist more weight from the ground to arm's length overhead than the average bodybuilder or lifter can deadlift, and you'll understand the levels of power we are talking about.

We weren't surprised to learn that one of the prices he's paid for this level of strength is many hours of hard training: Kurlovich has been lifting weights since he was nine, and a typical routine for him involves two-hour workouts twice a day, every day. These workouts are packed with some of the toughest things you can do with a barbell—no isolation movements seated at a machine here.

When we pressed Kurlovich for details, he pointed out that the program follows well-established principles. When we kept pressing, he said to us, "Tell Americans that the main thing is desire. If they have the desire, then they will like to train."

Desire, of course, is what initially sparked your interest in the Iron Game—a desire, perhaps, for bigger arms or the ability to bench press a bar loaded with an impressive pile of 45s. Desire at the level of saying "I'd like to put another inch on my arms" is pretty easy. Having enough desire to get into the gym is a lot tougher. Actually going through the motions required to meet this goal is tougher yet, but those who have enough desire will practically sweat blood in pursuit of their dreams. Desire is the key to being tough enough for any workout.

To help you fuel your desire, we suggest the following approach:

1) Keep your interest fresh by staying immersed in the Iron Game. Read, look at photos, go to contests, and so forth. Involvement is reinforcing, so stay involved.

2) Try to make progress. It sounds obvious, but a lot of people have given up on the idea of making more progress or have sold themselves so short that they have little reason to train hard. On the other hand, when you think you can succeed, you dig a little deeper. There's nothing better than past success to make you believe in future success. And when it comes to training, progress equals success.

*MILO: A Journal for Serious Strength Athletes, July 1994, Vol. 2, No. 2

3) Spend some time consciously using your mind to help yourself build your body. Think of all the time you might spend reading about different routines or boning up on supplements. Now consider how much time you put into the mental side of your training. Do you use mental rehearsal to either sharpen your skills or boost your motivation? Do you develop cognitive pain-tolerance strategies to help handle the killer reps that lead to progress? Do you analyze your training progress to see what has worked for you and what hasn't? Remember, your mind is the gateway to increased progress.

Someone once said that instead of praying for an easy life, you should pray for the strength to deal with the inevitable difficulties. That idea is just as applicable when it comes to lifting weights. Recognize from the outset that training for progress is a tough business, and instead of trying to figure out ways to make it easier, concentrate on whipping up your desire. Enough desire might not allow you to walk through walls, but it will surely march you through the world's toughest workouts.

# 16: Mind-set Makeovers

| How to: | Develop a mind-set that leads to success |
|---|---|
| **Key ideas:** | ✌ *Mind-set* – set of attitudes that affect your behavior |
| | ✌ *Locus of control* – whether you think you are in control of your destiny or just a hapless pawn |
| | ✌ *Internal locus of control* – quality of those who believe they are in charge of their own lives |
| | ✌ *External locus of control* – quality of those who believe that others, outside forces "pull their strings," that success is beyond their control |

The simple truth is that not many simple truths exist: For each rule there are exceptions, and despite our tendency to view the world in black-and-white terms, most things really come in shades of gray. Even so, there are times when it's advantageous to take a fairly extreme perspective. One of those times is when you're trying to understand the personality differences that we all carry into the gym, personality differences that emphasize success or failure.

To illustrate the two extremes in how people mentally approach their training, let's oversimplify things and divide the world into winners and losers. While our immediate goal is to help you use your mind for bigger gains in the world of muscle, our message applies just as much to every other walk of life. Best of all, we'll show you how you can reorient your thinking and become the winner you'd really like to be.

Decades ago research psychologists noticed that one of the ways people differ is in how they approach challenging situations and what they expect as a result. At one end of the spectrum are people who openly seek challenges and expect themselves to succeed. As you would guess, these people are the winners—success is a common experience for them. At the other end of the spectrum are people who try to avoid challenges because they're very fearful of failure. These people are the losers—success is a rare experience for them. People in the first group tend to emphasize the rewards inherent in a challenge and de-emphasize the costs associated with obtaining the reward. People in the second group are the opposite; they tend to de-emphasize the rewards and emphasize the costs associated with obtaining them. Let's see how these attitudes affect you in the gym.

Someone who has the first mind-set comes into the gym expecting to succeed, not only with his general plan to become bigger, stronger, or whatever, but also in terms of having a great work-out that particular day. If his program calls for hitting 12 dips with 150 pounds hanging from his waist, that's what he expects to do. While he knows that he's got to dig deep to squeeze out the last two or three reps, he doesn't let that become an obstacle. Rather, he takes it all in stride, gaining steam from the idea that if he hits the 150x12, he'll have a new personal record and will have taken another step toward his goals by doing so.

Someone who has the second mind-set comes into the gym expecting things not to go very well and reminds himself of all the reasons why he'd be foolish to expect too much from his workout. By the time he gets to his dips, the idea of banging out 5 reps with 25 pounds has taken on overwhelming proportions. You can guess what happens next—he falls short of his goal, which he interprets as showing how correct he was in viewing his potential as nothing but limited.

Understanding the difference between these two mind-sets involves the psychological construct called "locus of control," which boils down to whether you think you're the master of your destiny or you view yourself as a hapless pawn. People who believe that they pull their own strings are said to have an "internal locus of control," and people who feel others are pulling their strings have an "external locus of control." Remember how we noted that winners emphasize the positive and de-emphasize the negative, while losers do the opposite? Psychological research has demonstrated that when you give "internal" and "external" people both positive and negative information about themselves, the externals recall more negative material about themselves than the internals do, illustrating this pattern. This process is the key to developing a successful mind-set.

To succeed, you must first try, but to try hard, you must believe success is possible. Winners blow right through each of these steps: They seek new challenges and because they expect to make good in them, they really put their shoulders to the task. Winners might get themselves psyched by considering other challenging situations they've faced and how they excelled in them. When confronting challenges, they might exhort themselves like The Little Engine That Could ("I think I can, I think I can . . ."). They might use specific psychological techniques to get through the tough steps—whether it's focusing on just one rep at a time rather than the whole set or the whole workout or trying to transform what most people would see as simple pain into what they might call "growth cues"—signs that they're in the process of gaining. They always dangle the carrot of their goal in front of their mind's eye, reminding themselves of how much they want it and how what they're doing right here and right now is taking them closer to their goal.

Losers do the reverse: They rehearse past failures, remind themselves that their bone structure is better suited for the marathon than muscledom and may even think about how badly they might injure themselves trying to lift all those heavy weights. Losers know that failure likely awaits them and that the best way to avoid failure is to avoid challenges, so that's what they do—they forever whittle down the challenges they're willing to accept. Just as winners gravitate toward other winners, losers gravitate toward other losers—so they can reinforce their expectations of failure.

The story could stop here, but the good news is that losers can become winners. If they want to, they can make over their mind-sets. For starters they have to come to believe that they can succeed and that, in fact, their success lies largely within their control. Ironically, lifting weights is one of the best tools in the world for demonstrating this. Consider that just about anyone can make dramatic progress in bodybuilding or lifting—even if not everybody can become a world champion. Even nicer, most people can, for limited periods of time, make extremely fast progress with appropriate, specialized routines. The result of these last two facts is that lifting weights can give you a substantial basis for proving to yourself that you can succeed—and by your own efforts. Consider the skinny guy who has never gained much weight who suddenly sees that in six weeks of over-the-edge intensive training he's put an inch or more on his arms and several on his chest, boosted his squat by nearly 100 pounds, and outgrown two sets of clothes in the process. How can he not believe in himself now? How can he not expect success the next time he faces a challenge?

Or consider the person who's been stuck with a certain PR bench press forever and a day. He thinks he's tried everything and nothing has boosted his bench. He's ready to throw in the towel, but he doesn't. He does more research, develops another training routine, puts his head down and tries yet again, and *voilà*—he has a breakthrough and in four weeks his bench is at a 25-pound all-time high. How can he not believe in himself at this point? How can he not feel like the master of his destiny? How can he not expect success the next time he faces a challenge?

The bottom line is that the next time he'll believe in himself, and because of that, he'll succeed again. Each time the process will gain some momentum. He's doing more than just getting bigger and stronger along the way—he's doing a makeover of his mind-set.

# 17: Perfect Parents

| | |
|---|---|
| **How to:** | Develop a sense of identity for taking risks, succeeding |
| **Key ideas:** | 🐾 *Sense of security* – something that helps offset the fear associated with a risky situation |
| | 🐾 *Modeling* – how parents influence us by what they do |
| | 🐾 *Identity crisis* – when you don't have a solid grasp of who and what you are |

"Psst! Hey, buddy, want to get bigger and stronger? I've got the answer." Building on this basic pitch, manufacturers hock everything from supplements to equipment to secret routines in the interest of boosting your bodybuilding and lifting performance. Some of these things work and some don't, but one thing that is virtually a certain ticket to bigger gains is almost never mentioned: it involves your parents, but not in the way you would probably guess. Let's take a look at this idea and see what it is and how you can use it for developing bigger biceps and a deadlier deadlift.

To set the stage, let's get abstract for a minute and introduce the concept of risk taking. You might think that means anything from bungee jumping to starting a new business, but you're not likely to consider bodybuilding or even lifting. The truth is, however, that to succeed at most things requires substantial risk taking. Along the way in bodybuilding, for example, you have to take risks in the form of everything from facing ridicule to failing to succeed, believe it or not. Parents, in the natural order of things, are our first big influence when it comes to risk taking.

To undertake risk, you must have a sense of security—something that helps offset the fear associated with the risky situation. This concept is embodied in the familiar idea of the security blanket, the faithful companion of any self-respecting young child. The sense of security might be physical, such as a bulletproof vest, or it might be abstract, such as the knowledge that you have a full five minutes to defuse a bomb before it blows, but regardless of the form it takes, it's a psychological phenomenon, and its roots often go back to your earliest childhood.

Nearly half a century ago, psychological research with young monkeys demonstrated the enormous influence of mothers, in particular, by showing that even an artificial mother made out of terry cloth was better than nothing. For example, if you placed a young monkey in a strange environment, one that produced great fear, it would explore the new setting as long as it could touch the terry cloth mother with one hand. No mother, no exploration.

The influence of parents extends beyond just providing the confidence to reach out in new, threatening situations. Parents, for example, influence us by what they do, a process that psychologists call "modeling." While psychological research on modeling initially focused on demonstrating how such things as aggression and prejudice can be transmitted from parent to child, more recent research has shown that our parents' behavior can teach us either to approach risky situations with the expectation of succeeding or to run from them. In the extreme, we can either acquire a sense of helplessness from our parents or a sense of mastery—a sense that we're at the mercy of others or are in control of our lives.

So in a very real sense we learn by watching our parents. Whether they are swashbuckling adventurers or quiet mice will have a bearing on how we interact with the world. Even more directly, parents influence us by either being openly supportive and encouraging ("That's great" or "You can do it") or, at the other extreme, being disapproving and discouraging ("How can you be interested in that?!" or "You'll never succeed"). To be sure, some of us are so stubborn that the more we're told we can't succeed, the harder we try, but most of us need some reinforcement along the way. Tell us that we're off the track and we'll slow our efforts; tell us that we're great and we'll dig a little deeper.

"Great," you say, "but I'm 17 (or 27 or 57). Isn't it a little late for me to influence the way my parents shaped me psychologically?"

Not really, because while it's true that certain early influences might play a significant role in your future, your destiny remains in your own hands to an amazingly large extent. Now that you're armed with the knowledge of parental influence, for instance, you need to structure your life in a way that takes advantage of this process—regardless of how your parents may or may not have initially influenced you. Let's develop a game plan to put parent power to work for you.

For starters, don't try to be the Lone Ranger. Recognize that social forces are enormously powerful and you're better off swimming with the tide than against it. Accordingly, try to create an environment that's supportive and constructive in terms of your goals, just as in a perfect parenting situation.

To do this, hook up with some key people who boost your general sense of security, self-confidence, and ability to master situations. Going back to our natural order of things, these might be your parents, but don't throw in the towel if they're not. It might be your Uncle Lenny; a gruff guy who likes to be called "coach"; someone, maybe older and wiser, whom you met at the gym; or friends who function as your support group. Try to surround yourself with people who are good for you in the ways described above. In the corporate world success is often attributed to having the right mentor(s), and there's no reason to think that success in any other environment is different.

Psychological maturity involves developing a strong sense of identity, a clear feeling of who and what you are. A so-called identity crisis is the opposite because you don't have a solid grasp of that. Strive to develop a clear idea of yourself, learning to trust your instincts and maintaining the confidence to work hard to achieve your goals. Encourage yourself, reminding yourself of both the worthiness of your goals and your ability to reach them. Build on your successes to boost your confidence in the face of fresh challenges, and if you get knocked down en route to your goals, be ready to pick yourself up, brush yourself off, and start banging away again.

Your objective, if you hadn't already guessed, is to become your own perfect parent.

# 18:  Paul's Power

| | |
|---|---|
| **How to:** | Learn some lessons for success from Paul Anderson |
| **Key idea:** | ❧ *Squats* – the world's toughest exercise—and the key to reaching your potential in size and strength |

It read like a fairy tale: Rumors started to circulate that a big fellow from the hills of Tennessee was lifting some extremely heavy weights.  He was said to train alone outdoors, using the most primitive of equipment.  It turned out that this myth was for real because the man in question soon visited the home gym of a world-renowned lifter, who watched him casually do a perfect squat with about as much weight as anyone had ever lifted.  In less than two years, the phenomenon had already exceeded world records on the Olympic lifts in his training and had broken the world record in the squat more times than could be easily counted.  This lifting sensation, of course, was none other than Paul Anderson—the world's strongest man.

Anderson dazzled the strength world as has nobody before or since: he became a world-record holder, a world champion and an Olympic champion in the space of several short years after he began training.  In Moscow people stood in line in the rain for hours for the chance to watch him lift, and after witnessing his performance, they dubbed him "the wonder of nature."  He was featured on talk shows and in magazines and starred in the newsreels of the day.  He traveled the world representing the State Department and, back home in the United States, was the last strongman to be a household name.  To this day, decades after his peak, no one has ever approached his top lifts on the most basic tests of strength.

Paul Anderson passed away in 1994, and while his lifting performances will be talked about for as long as men lift weights, his legacy should include the idea that inner qualities—both mental and spiritual—were underlying keys to his sensational success.

For starters, Paul Anderson was tough enough to do what was necessary to reach his goal of becoming as strong as possible.  Just as it's no secret that to reach your potential in size and strength, you simply have to squat, it's also no secret that squatting is probably the world's toughest exercise.  He reached such prodigious heights in the squat that people naturally assume that he loved the movement.  In fact, several years ago Paul told me, "I have done thousands of deep knee bends, and I've hated every one I've ever done."

He knew, however, that squats were the key to reaching his goals, so he not only did them, he did them with a vengeance. Some people just can't meet this challenge. As Paul told me, "Anyone who can find any reason not to do full squats will find that reason—because they hurt. They hurt when you do them, they hurt when you get through. There's an old country western song about a truck driver who wants a different route, but the dispatcher tells him, 'There ain't no easy run, boy, there ain't no easy run.' Now, that is the way it is in weightlifting: there ain't no easy run. If you don't bend those legs and do those squats, you'll never reach your potential." So Paul gutted out those squats, and you should do likewise.

Paul set no limits upon himself. In an era when 600 pounds was about the most anyone had used for a true deep knee bend, he hit that weight within months after he began to train. Before he was done, he squatted about twice that much—a weight nobody else has even vaguely approximated. Years after he was out of regular training, Paul would show up at powerlifting contests where the top competitor might hit around 700 pounds in the squat, and Paul would casually do a 900-pound squat—typically without a warm-up, often barefoot, never with any support gear and always very easily. He set no limits for himself, and therefore he was free to gain beyond the wildest dreams of most men. You should do likewise and not think small— unless that's how you want to remain.

Paul was a doer. When he set out to become a champion weightlifter, that's what he focused on and accomplished. For example, in his earliest days of training he spent literally hours doing squats: He would do a set, rest and eat, do a set, rest and eat, and so forth throughout the day. When he retired from competition and started a home for troubled youths, he turned his big shoulders to that task with the same zeal he'd put into his lifting career. Acting as the Paul Anderson Youth Home's principal fund-raiser, he typically gave 500 talks a year. So don't sit around and wait for things to happen. Be like Paul Anderson: be a doer, and make things happen.

Paul wasn't held back by what he called the "can't doers." These are the ubiquitous naysayers who mutter, "You can't do that . . . ." Funny as it sounds today, he was often criticized in his early days of training because he focused so heavily on building basic power rather than on just honing his technique. "You can't do that," some weightlifting experts told him. Well, he did— and then some. Time after time, in his weightlifting career and afterward, he ran into the can't doers, but he stuck to his plan and did what he set out to do. You should do likewise.

Finally, Paul's original mark on the world was about as physical as it can get. Here was a 5'-9" man who often weighed about 350 pounds and displayed levels of basic strength that still leave the experts in awe, yet he was a devout Christian, and his spiritual beliefs were the central part of his life. When Paul retired from amateur competition, he focused his life on community service in the form of his youth home, and he worked constantly to spread his Christian message. Paul used to say to people that he was the world's strongest man, yet he couldn't live a day without his spiritual beliefs.

Funny, isn't it, how some of the biggest men are the quickest to realize that they need to look beyond themselves and are among the first to see just how limited all their might and muscle really are.

# 19: Focus Your Firepower

| How to: | Improve your focus and concentration for better results |
|---|---|
| **Key ideas:** | ☙ *Coping behavior* – what a person can do to help him or her manage stressful situations |
| | ☙ *Task-directed* – staying on track with what you're supposed to be doing |

J ack was having one of those days in the gym: even before he started his workout, he felt lethargic, to the point where just about any exertion was going to be overwhelming. After changing, which seemed a fairly monumental effort, he cut his warm-up short and dragged himself through a few sets of behind-the-neck presses. On each set he quit as soon as the reps required a little effort, saying to himself that he was saving himself for an all-out assault on his next set. By now he was resigned to having a lousy workout, and the only remaining question was whether he'd continue like that or just go home.

If this were an unusual occurrence, there would have been no reason for Jack to give this workout a second thought. He could chalk it up as an off day and go merrily on his way. Unfortunately, days like this were a pretty common event. For example, on some days Jack was so distracted by the rest of his life that he deep-sixed his workout on the premise that he was too worn-out by everything that had gone wrong that day. On other days he only did about two-thirds of his planned reps, conveniently skipping the tough ones on each set; and on still other days he chopped out big portions of his workout. While he managed to pump up his pecs and arms on those days—surprise, surprise—he gave the squat rack a wide berth.

In a word, Jack was having trouble focusing, and the results weren't pretty. He stalled, he took shortcuts, he made excuses, he got distracted, he coasted. And he either made no progress or moved at a snail's pace. At that point Jack had two choices: 1) He could accept his lousy progress and derive some comfort from his situation by pointing to inferior genetics or some other external explanation as the reason for his plight, or 2) he could try to accept personal responsibility for his situation and see what he might do to tackle it head-on. Jack, in his heart, was no coward, so he opted for the second choice.

Jack had the smarts to recognize that while his goal was eminently physical, the root of his problem might be mental. He sought out the advice of someone well-grounded in both the world of weights and the workings of the mind—a sports psychologist with great enthusiasm for lifting weights.

After listening to Jack, the psychologist assured him that there was a solution to his dilemma. He also boosted Jack's confidence immediately by saying that Jack seemed to be equal to the challenge.

The psychologist introduced Jack to the concept of "coping behavior," the idea that a person could do certain things to help him or her manage stressful situations. They talked about this for a while, with the psychologist pointing out that working out, especially at the level required to make significant progress, was a stressful situation since it demanded that one do all sorts of uncomfortable things.

"What can you say," the psychologist noted, "when the most effective forms of training for more size and strength require you to lift heavy, heavy objects, always trying to do more than you're easily capable of doing? The very nature of effective training is to exceed your capacity, and that's not a cakewalk. What you need to do is teach yourself coping behaviors that help you manage the stress. Properly applied, coping behaviors will allow you to not only stand and face your tormentors head-on, but to actually vanquish these foes."

At that point the psychologist smiled, rather pleased with what he viewed as a somewhat poetic expression of the situation, but when he saw that he was losing Jack's attention, he quickly came back to earth.

"We're going to teach you how to deal with these distractions by squashing them like so many mosquitoes," he said. "We're going to start by working on your concentration, your ability to focus on the task at hand.

"The type of focus we're talking about will give you two huge benefits. First, it will help you stay what we call 'task-directed.' In other words, it will keep you on track in terms of what you're supposed to be doing. Second, we're going to use this focus to help energize your efforts."

"Sounds good," said Jack.

"To make this concentration thing work, to sharpen your focus," the psychologist continued, "I want you to start turning your attention inward even before your workout. For example, on your way to the gym, I want you to work on forgetting about everything that has gone on that day and everything you have to do tomorrow. Instead, begin thinking about your workout—what you have to do and how you are going to strive for a picture-perfect workout. Think about why you began training in the first place, and the goals that initially attracted you to training and their importance to you.

"Remind yourself that the workout will be tough, but that you'll succeed and that because of your ability to hang in through the tough moments, you'll make the progress you want."

Jack was listening.

"Quit talking, if you can, some time before you actually begin training, and try to not say a word during your whole workout," the psychologist urged, "although talking to yourself can be a good idea. You might also try to train in a quiet environment—even if you're frightened by the idea of training without the adrenalizing effect of mega-decibel Led Zeppelin smashing into your cortex, try training in silence. I want you to turn all of your attention inward.

"You know how the standard advice when squatting is to look up at a spot on the wall to help you maintain good form? Well, that's a good idea, but some people have found that they can work harder on mind-warping sets of 20-rep squats by choosing a small spot on the floor in front of them and keeping their eyes glued to it. This seems to work because, when you look up, it's easier to be distracted by peripheral vision, movement around you, and so forth. Looking down reduces these distractions, so it can help you stay focused on the challenge of knocking off the squats, rather than giving in to the temptation to bag the set part way through it. That's the principle we're using here: Pull all of your attention inward. As far as you're concerned, there's nothing outside of yourself.

"Start off by working on this, and next time we'll take the process a step further."

Jack was thinking about making a wisecrack about shrinks and their 50-minute hours but instead decided to put the guy's ideas to the test—he could wait a little longer to get the rest of the story. Besides, he already had plenty to focus on.

# 20: Dealing With Distractions

| | |
|---:|---|
| **How to:** | Boost your concentration by confronting fear that you can't succeed and fear of injury |
| **Key ideas:** | ❧ *Self-fulfilling prophecy* – mind-set that engineers its own predictions by limiting expectations, effort, and results<br>❧ *Generally accepted principles of safe training (GAPST)* – what you need to know to train safely |

Last time we explained that one way to help yourself achieve peak performances in the gym is to focus completely on your workout, which requires you to do things that boost your concentration. Let's quickly review what we covered and then take things another step.

First, we suggested that you begin this whole process of boosting your concentration by clearing your mind of the day's events before you start training. For example, perhaps you can use the drive to the gym to begin letting go of all the things that have been churning around in your brain throughout the day—all the things that went wrong, all the things that still have to be done, and so forth. If you bring these distracting thoughts into the gym with you, you're almost guaranteed to have a lousy workout, and lousy workouts are the certain road to lousy progress. Don't be surprised to find that putting all the day's problems on hold while you train not only helps you get in a better workout but also helps you solve these problems.

Second, we suggested that after you've dumped all the day-to-day distractions, you do a little psyching up. Begin with good general stuff like reminding yourself why you started training in the first place, work your way through some intermediate goals, like where you want to be in six months, and then end with what you need to accomplish today to reach your overall goals.

Remember to be honest when you're going through this process. For example, if you saw your life pass before your eyes in your last squat workout and your schedule calls for another five pounds on the bar today, don't try to con yourself into thinking the set will be easy. Instead, do yourself a favor and psych up by telling yourself that sure, the set will be tough, but you are tougher.

Be willing to try new things as far as psyching up goes, rather than just getting locked into, for example, deep relaxation and mental rehearsal. We know one hardcore lifter who watches a video of the world's top weightlifters training for the World Championships just before a session. He says it really improves his workouts.

Third, we suggested that you reinforce your focus by managing your physical environment. For example, we pointed out that you can derive great strength, both inner and outer, from quietness, so training in a very quiet environment can be particularly productive. Also, because where your eyes go your mind tends to follow, we warned of the danger of letting your eyes wander—especially in the middle of a desperate set. Find a spot and keep your eyes glued to it. Even go so far as to pick your focal point so that it reduces your peripheral vision. This is why looking down can sometimes be very effective, or why psyching up with a towel draped over the sides of your head can work wonders.

"Okay," you say, "I've got the basics wired. Give me some more advanced stuff."

Most of the time when people talk about focusing, they talk about what they want you to do. For example, they might emphasize drills where you close your eyes and practice counting backward or have you stare at a candlelight without letting your attention waver. We're going to take a different tack and address the two most common causes of lack of focus and then show you how to deal with them.

### I Can't-itis
Nothing can blur your focus and weaken your will like the deep-seated conviction that you just can't succeed. For example, you might be convinced that you fall into a category of people who simply can't gain more than two pounds a year or will never be able to squat more than 400 pounds or really won't find it productive to add more than one pound to the bar at a time or to train more than once every four days. This sort of mind-set is doubly destructive because it becomes a form of self-fulfilling prophecy: it engineers its own predictions by limiting expectations, effort, and therefore results. Maybe there's some consolation in having things turn out the way you bleakly predicted, but most people would find it a lot more satisfying to see that they can wildly exceed their expectations.

Lest you think "I can't-itis" doesn't have the power to rob inches from your arms and pounds from your bench press, consider some examples of how a quitting mind leads to a quitting body. A negative mind-set can actually lead to death. Coroners' reports show that each year people die of what should have been non-lethal injuries because they essentially thought themselves to death. Similarly, Bruno Bettelheim's classic studies of Nazi concentration camp victims pointed out that some prisoners of war lost all hope of ever leaving the camps except as corpses, which could have led to emotionally triggered death. Yes, what you think can literally mean the difference between life and death, so don't underestimate its impact on something as relatively minor as whether or not you crank out a good set of power cleans.

So come on, get positive: Consider what you just might be able to accomplish if you really hit the gas and start to train as if you're as genuinely hungry for progress as you say you are.

## Fear of Injury
Walk into any gym and, along with the people who turn purple with their efforts, you'll see the ones who are always training well within their physical potential. Interestingly, some of these people can be the most vocal, sometimes making noises as if their efforts have brought them to the brink of death, but in actuality, you can see that they're only doing 80 or 90 percent of what they're capable of. Aside from the folks who are just plain lazy or don't know any better, many who always train with the brakes on do so out of fear of being injured. After all, they reason, it doesn't take Einstein to realize that getting crushed under hundreds of pounds of iron would not be a pretty fate. So each time they grab the bar, they hear a little voice saying, "Don't push too hard—you might get hurt."

Some years ago, early in my career as a rock climber, I had some doubts about the sanity of spending every weekend clinging to sheer rock faces by my finger tips and the merest edges of my soles. When I met a fellow who broke his leg literally falling while getting out of bed one morning, my concerns about climbing accidents came into perspective.

Some people really do seem to injure themselves no matter what they do, while others can spend a good deal of time doing genuinely dangerous things with nary a scratch. Why the difference? What can you do to become more like the latter than the former?

For starters, one of the absolutely best ways to get injured is to always think about it. Thinking, here, doesn't mean being prudent about anticipating what might go wrong and planning to forestall such accidents. That's positive and that's what helps keep people alive even when they engage in dangerous activities. If, however, you needlessly dwell on the negative possibilities, you'll unconsciously raise your anxiety level, quite likely to where it will impair both your mental and physical performance. The next step? An accident.

To counter this powerful distraction, be sure to know what you're doing when you train. While there's always the possibility of something going wrong, you'll find that training, even with gut-busting efforts, is one of the safer things you can do. To boost your confidence, take the time to learn your craft and then stick to the generally accepted principles of safe training. That way you'll be able to go flat out, rather than having a pile of destructive psychological baggage slowing you down at each step.

Focusing your firepower and dealing with distractions—learn to do these two things, and you'll have the workouts you need to make the progress you want.

# 21: The Work Weak Principle

| **How to:** | Work your weak areas for significant gains |
|---|---|
| **Key idea:** | ✦ *Weakest link* – your chances of succeeding are only as strong as your weak points |

Once upon a time there was a fellow, call him Jeff, who got interested in bodybuilding. You know the story: he picked up a muscle magazine, saw arms bigger than his legs, and decided he wanted some of that. He trained hard on good basic programs, was often seen sipping a protein drink, and before too long his progress was obvious. Along the way two things happened. First, Jeff decided that he wanted to compete, and he aimed to do his first show the following year. Second, he discovered that, what a pity, his arms seemed to respond with almost no effort on his part, while his calves were pretty much the same slender stalks they'd been before he ever touched a weight.

Even though Jeff might be classified as an intermediate bodybuilder, his arms were already getting a lot of attention—not just from people on the street but in his gym too. In fact, it wasn't long before guys a lot bigger and more experienced than Jeff were coming to him, asking for advice on arm training. Jeff liked that, and he also liked the fact that when he worked his arms, the weights he used attracted more than passing glances.

Calves were a different story. In fact, when Jeff wore shorts, he heard things like, "Hey, Jeff, forget your pants?" And when he trained his lower legs, he remembered the line about picking your parents wisely if you wanted good calves.

As you might guess, pretty soon Jeff had doubled his arm work and all but eliminated his calf training, and when he stepped on stage for his first show, he looked terrific from the knees up, but his calves were so bad that he ended up in fourth place.

Across town from Jeff lived a guy named Pete who'd been bitten by the weightlifting bug. While his long-term goals were to make the 2000 Olympic team and win a medal, right now he was still working to win his state championship. Early on, Pete had gotten the idea that squatting, in weightlifting as in bodybuilding, was the key to his success, so he squatted until his eyes were ready to pop out. At the next workout he squatted even harder and so on, until he got to the point where he could clean and then stand up almost effortlessly with weights he couldn't come close to jerking. Pete got a lot of reinforcement when he squatted ("Are you guys done with those plates? Pete's getting ready to squat") and took a lot of ribbing on his jerks ("Is that a standing incline or what?").

In getting ready for the state meet, Pete followed his usual training routine, working harder than ever to meet his goal of a state title. As the contest developed, Pete seemed to be in a terrific position to achieve his goal: he was in second place, the guy in first place was finished, and Pete still had two attempts left. With things looking that good, it appeared Pete could almost coast to the first-place trophy, but twice he cleaned the weight easily, stood up as if it were a warm-up weight, and then missed the jerk—utterly and completely.

Both Jeff and Pete fell victim to one of the most common errors you'll find in any gym: working their strengths instead of attacking their weaknesses. Take just about any complex activity and it's a virtual certainty that the following will occur:

1) Your success depends on a chain of interconnected events.
2) This chain will only be as strong as the weakest link.

In fact, this idea is so widespread that it has achieved the status of a cliché. Few will argue with it, in principle. In practice, however, most people, perhaps unwittingly, do the opposite—they keep gravitating to their strengths and moving away from their weaknesses.

Strategically, this is a major error because only modest improvement in your weak points will give your overall performance a significant boost. That might seem a little abstract, so let's return to Jeff and Pete and see how this affected their respective performances in bodybuilding and weightlifting.

Having little interest in implants, Jeff decided to get radical in terms of his calves: He heard about a calf routine successfully used years ago by a particularly innovative Mr. America and sometime training partner of Sergio Oliva, one Bob Gajda, and decided to give it a shot.

Gajda, who regarded calves as one of the visual focal points on a bodybuilder, was looking to add some serious size to his already well-shaped calves, so he developed one of the most straightforward and effective calf programs ever seen: every day for two months Gajda did a set of heel raises on the hour, every hour he was awake. In a month he put half an inch on his calves, and in two months he added a full inch. It was easy to see that whatever Gajda's program lacked in convenience, it more than made up for in results, and for Jeff, results was the name of the game.

Jeff knew that even if he could only approximate Gajda's overall results, he would have the winner's trophy the next year. That's exactly what happened.

Pete went through a similar adjustment and realized that as ego-swelling as his squat workouts were, they just weren't helping him advance toward his current goal. He needed to adjust his priorities and do a number of things differently. For example, instead of putting so much time and effort into his squats, he began doing more overhead work—emphasizing jerk supports and a variety of push-presses and push-jerks. The price Pete paid for this reorientation was that he lost some of his dominance in the squat, but a year later he couldn't have been a happier guy: once again he had two tries to win the state championship. This time he not only won the contest with the first of those two tries, but he also went further on his second and set a new state record in the clean and jerk.

Working your strengths is seductive because you get tremendous immediate reinforcement for your efforts, but this is a certain path to limiting your overall progress. The smart move, instead, is to work your weak points because that's what opens the door to big advances.

Just as you expect a paycheck for your efforts on the job, you should expect results from your training. Follow the above advice and see just how rewarding the work weak can be.

# 22: One-Trick Ponies

| | |
|---|---|
| **How to:** | Be creative and flexible in your approach to training problems |
| **Key ideas:** | ♪ *Reflexive behavior* – more primitive: automatically responding in a given way |
| | ♪ *Adaptive behavior* – more intelligent: changing your behavior to accommodate subtle changes in your environment |

Match sprinting is bicycle racing's answer to roller derby and ice hockey—two riders circle a steeply banked track, usually playing cat and mouse, jostling each other or doing whatever else they can think of to win the race. While it's true that sheer speed is the number one asset a match sprinter might choose, sharp elbows come in handy, as do steel nerves.

Using your brain is also important because strategy and tactics play a big part in match sprinting. Sprinters use planned moves and countermoves on the track. No matter how the races begin and unfold, though, they usually end up becoming high-speed sprints in the final 200 meters. Usually. Sometimes, however, one rider immediately takes off like a rocket, hoping to surprise his opponent and hold on to the lead until he crosses the finish line.

Some years ago at the San Jose Velodrome, there was a match sprinter who took this strategy a bit too far, because in virtually every race, that's exactly what he did—he took a flier. One day a sage coach who was watching this guy said, "When you've got one trick, you've got no trick."

This is a vital concept for bodybuilders, and lifters too—this need to be flexible, to have a variety of options at your disposal, to be responsive to a changing situation. Consider the opposite.

Several years ago I got a call from a fellow who, after making polite small talk, said that I had become "disloyal" to the basic concepts of high-repetition squatting. I figured that, as I'd written SUPER SQUATS, reintroduced J. C. Hise and company, revamped a range of classic squatting tools and so forth, it should be clear that I was a big fan of high-repetition squatting. Not to this fellow. What he latched onto was the fact that I also frequently wrote about weightlifting, sports psychology, and other topics that were not specifically squat-related. Evidently, he felt that since I didn't repeat my squat message like a broken record, I was disloyal to squatting. This is an interesting example of the one-trick-pony syndrome we all need to guard against.

Suppose you're fortunate enough to own a pickup truck, a motorcycle, and a GT. Which one do you use to take a load of stuff to the recycling center? Which one gets the nod for a sunny day and that freshly paved winding road to the beach? Which set of keys do you grab when you, your wife, a child or two, and a picnic basket have 100 miles of underpatrolled straightaways and sweepers between yourselves and your favorite lake? Each vehicle has its preferred application, and if you don't try to force the bike to do the truck's job, you'll be much happier with the results. The same thing applies to your training—you need to be ready to exercise some options in order to get the best results.

Consider how lifters train, or are told to train, for maximum progress. Some authorities advise always going for the heaviest possible lifts ("How can you get stronger if you don't lift heavier and heavier weights?"). Others advocate training in the 80-percent-of-maximum range ("You'll just burn out if you go really heavy all the time, so you should train lighter but move the bar faster"). The same sort of divergence comes into play with your workout routine. On the one hand, some top experts would have you do essentially nothing but competition lifts ("A violin player doesn't practice the piano, and the same thing goes for a lifter"). On the other hand, some equally well-credentialed experts advise serious work on assistance exercises (". . . the key to making progress on the competitive lifts").

Even something as seemingly straightforward as training frequency inspires divergent opinions: where some push classic, three-times-a-week workouts, others tell you to train twice a day, every day.

Now let's really stir things up and note that sometimes you can find a single authority pushing one system at one time and another system at another. This can be the result of simply grasping at straws or jumping from one bandwagon to the next. Other times, however, it can be the result of deeper thinking and a clear understanding that, for example, strict exercise form might be best on one occasion and a cheating style might be best on another.

Even if science remains beyond fully understanding the mysteries of creative thinking, research psychologists have demonstrated that effective problem-solvers are flexible. Rather than simply viewing a particular task in a fixed way, they have the ability to view it from a number of different angles. It's this ability to understand different perspectives that provides the solution to what for rigid thinkers is an unsolvable problem.

In a broader sense, reflexive behavior—that is, automatically responding in a given way—is more primitive than adaptive behavior. That's because adaptive behavior specifically requires learning and, it can be argued, is synonymous with intelligent behavior. From a psychological perspective this idea recognizes that humans adapt to subtle changes in their environments rather than automatically responding in an easily predictable way, and this adaptation serves a good, functional purpose.

So use the same sort of strategy in your training: cultivate an arsenal of responses; learn to be flexible and creative. When one routine quits producing results for you, no matter how effective it was in the past, move on to something new. No matter how well all of your friends might gain on program X, if program Y works better for you, stick with program Y. Forever guard against thinking there's just one solution to any problem or that there's one magical way to train that will always work and nothing else will ever work. Don't think this strategy is something to shelve for a rainy day. Instead, to modify the late Mayor Richard Daley of Chicago's advice to voters: "Think early, think often."

Exercise all your options: Don't be a one-trick pony.

# 23: Shaping Success

| | |
|---|---|
| **How to:** | Shape your progress by reinforcing your steps along the way |

| | |
|---|---|
| **Key ideas:** | ☛ *Operant conditioning* – teaching behavior by following the behavior with a specific outcome |
| | ☛ *Reinforcement theory* – when a positive reinforcer follows a specific action, the behavior is more likely to be repeated |
| | ☛ *Shaping* – reinforcing each step, however small, toward your goal, and raising the ante for what gets rewarded along the way |
| | ☛ *Successive approximations* – the small steps toward the overall goal |

When Jack Robinson first picked up a muscle magazine, he was overwhelmed by what he saw. The average pro bodybuilder had muscular girths nearly twice his. Similarly, when Bill Thomas happened upon a lifting magazine, he saw guys playfully tossing overhead weights he couldn't have rolled across the floor. Undaunted by the initial gap, both Jack and Bill began training, and before too long each had done an amazing job of transforming himself along the lines of what had first seemed impossible. What was their secret?

To be sure, both Jack and Bill had followed the principles of sound training—working hard on the right exercises, getting the correct nutrients into their bodies, and so forth—but the real key to their success could not be explained by anything as narrow as the specifics of their training routines or diets. In fact, the real key to the success they enjoyed lay between their ears. Each had learned to use a potent psychological tool for radically improving one's performance. The technique is called "shaping," and this is how it works.

Consider a demonstration of what psychologists call operant conditioning: a rat pushes a lever when he's supposed to and, voilà, a food pellet drops down. The delighted rat thinks he's onto a good thing and keeps pushing the lever, earning more pellets for his efforts. That's simple reinforcement theory: When a so-called positive reinforcer (the food pellet) follows a specific action (pushing the lever), the behavior is more likely to be repeated. This is great for explaining simple behaviors, but how can we explain complex acts—especially those that demand highly refined skills or long-term effort? How, for example, did Jack get to the point where he had boosted his muscle mass by more than 50 percent and could knock off a highly choreographed posing routine at the drop of a hat? How did Bill progress to the point where he could now hoist several hundred pounds in movements he couldn't do with a broomstick when he started?

A key to making this sort of progress is to not only take things one small step at a time but to take them in a very particular way. The essence of shaping is that you reinforce each step, however small, toward your final objective. And you keep raising the ante for what gets rewarded.

For example, if a father were trying to teach his young daughter how to do a somersault, he probably wouldn't have much success waiting for her to execute a perfect 10 before reinforcing her efforts. What he might do instead to shape her behavior is focus on what are called "successive approximations" to the result. These successive approximations are nothing more than the small steps toward the overall goal. The father might, for example, first reward his daughter for getting to her hands and knees, then for doing this plus lowering her head, and so forth. He would keep extending the requirements for reward, in small steps, until his daughter was knocking off a complete somersault and looking, at least to him, like the next Nadia Comaneci.

Using these shaping techniques in their laboratories, research psychologists have been able, for example, to teach pigeons to play Ping-Pong and rats to lift more than double their body weight. The same approach is what turns an initially average person into a muscular force to be reckoned with. Let's see what happened with Jack and Bill.

When Jack's eyes first lit on all the Mr. Everythings and formed a mental picture of himself, the first thing he noticed was the sheer size of the champion bodybuilders. It was no exaggeration to say that they had more muscle on their arms than he had on his legs. Sure, he noticed their shape, symmetry, and cuts, but it was their size that really knocked his socks off. Jack's bodybuilding odyssey began with an emphasis on developing some more mass, rather than trying to accomplish everything at once. "I'll add some size first," he reasoned, "and then I'll turn my attention to the finer points." Working back from there, he began his journey with the classic approach to packing on mass: he specialized on the big muscle groups first. To a naive observer, Jack's methods might have seemed like the long way to his goal, because even though he wanted big arms, among other things, his early training emphasized leg and back work.

Jack had a plan, however, and he knew that if he got his squat up to a decent level, it would make it much easier to reach the rest of his size goals. So he added pounds on the squat bar and on the scale, rewarded himself along the way, kept raising the standard for the next reward, and before too long he was doing a full share of work on the small muscle groups as well as the major ones. By then Jack had already sailed past the guys who hadn't been willing to progress one step at a time and who paid little attention to rewarding themselves for each forward step they took. In fact, most of the guys who'd been training as if they were going for everything at once and who turned a blind eye to their inch-by-inch progress looked pretty much the same way they had when they started.

Jack continued in his style of charting the required steps toward his goal and getting pats on the back as he advanced, and before too long, the guy who once could barely muster an awkward front double-biceps was breezing through a bad-to-the-bone performance at his first show.

Likewise, Bill, who aspired to be a great Olympic lifter, had the wisdom not to wait for his first double-body-weight snatch to get himself some strokes. At each stage he set milestones for himself, and although they might have seemed exceedingly modest, each took him another step toward his overall goal. His early goals didn't even have anything to do with how much he could snatch, for example, but were designed to increase his flexibility and improve his technique. As with Jack, Bill's approach might have seemed pretty lame compared to the guys who just jumped right in with both feet and who did little but curse their own performances, but it didn't take too long to see that Bill must have been onto something good. And while the hard-line PR-at-every-workout and always-demand-more types were surely outlifting Bill early on, it wasn't long before their best lifts were only moderately heavy warm-ups for Bill.

Shaping—the process of rewarding small but ever closer steps toward your goal—is an extremely powerful psychological tool that can be used in a wide variety of circumstances. So whether your long-term goals involve the Olympics or Harvard Medical School, use your head and begin shaping your success.

# 24: Cold Showers

| How to: | Take a bolder approach to your training for progress |
|---|---|
| Key ideas: | ख *Brass-knuckles approach* – jump in whole hog, aim high, and set aggressive milestones |
| | ख *Kid-gloves approach* – begin with modest expectations and take baby steps to your goal |
| | ख *Psychotherapy* – the psychological treatment of some thought, feeling, or behavior |
| | ख *Systematic desensitization* – progress through small but increasingly challenging situations to overcome fear |
| | ख *Implosive therapy* – experience a full-blown anxiety reaction, while experiencing no harm, as way to overcome fear |

There's a gym in northern California that might not look like much: a trained eye might notice that the barbells are world-class, but that's about all there is to brag about. Along with the weights, there are half a dozen lifting platforms, some squat racks, a power rack, and that's it. The floor usually hasn't been swept in a long time, and the last time I was there, the place still didn't have a locker room. What this gym does have is a five-year record of producing some of the most powerful young men in the United States, and at the heart of its program is a 40-something guy who, as you might guess, likes to be called coach.

The coach is missing a couple of teeth, smokes cigars, and plans to move to Montana in a couple of years, and since he's not particularly inclined to be politically correct, he calls them as he sees them. While he can be quite tactful, maybe even empathetic or sympathetic, he's best known for issuing wake-up calls: "Quit being a puke, Louie, and lift this" would be a mild comment from the coach. No namby-pamby, wishy-washy hand-wringing here.

Contrast this with the atmosphere at a gym just a couple of miles away. The second gym looks world-class: it's a mirrored palace of advanced exercise equipment wrapped in such a sparkling package that you'd think the place was a training ground for the custodial sciences. The second gym has an owner who sees it as his mission to stroke the gym's members at every turn. This, quite naturally, leads to rewarding them for mediocrity and helping them make excuses for their failures. In the second gym, healthy young men make sounds as if they're dying when they do inclines with 15-pound dumbbells, and then the owner reinforces them with, "Good set." You half expect him to dab any stray drops of sweat from their foreheads before announcing, "Your towel, sir."

These two gyms reflect the extremes of a spectrum that might be labeled "brass knuckles" at one end and "kid gloves" at the other. The kid gloves approach relies on subtlety and smoothing rough edges—all in the quest to make things as kind and gentle as possible. The brass knuckles approach boils down to recognizing that there's a job to be done, so you might as well do it.

In the kid-gloves approach, you might begin with modest expectations of what you can achieve. Next, you plan out intermediate steps that are also anything but stretches. To round out your program, each day you approach your whole training regimen—from the weights you lift to the food you eat to the thoughts you think—with similar restraint. In effect, you never exceed the midpoint on your internal power band.

In the brass-knuckles approach, you aim high, set aggressive milestones, and are willing to hit redline in your quest for success. If the kid gloves approach is like *aikido*, the brass knuckles approach is like a brawl.

There are times when it really is best to quit dancing around, quit bobbing and weaving—times when it's best to just stand toe-to-toe and go for the knockout. Taking a no-holds-barred approach even has a place in the delicate world of psychotherapy.

Psychotherapy—which is the psychological treatment of some thought, feeling or behavior—usually proceeds by walking on eggshells rather than by taking bold steps. For example, in systematic desensitization, an acrophobic person might begin by imagining himself standing on a chair until he can do that without undue anxiety. He might progress to increasingly challenging situations until he reaches some sort of ultimate goal, such as being able to imagine himself dangling off the face of El Capitan. Each step is small, and he masters it before taking the next one.

This general pattern of making haste slowly is turned on its ear in something called "implosive therapy." Implosive therapy takes the position that many people are so successful at avoiding anxiety-provoking situations that they never have an opportunity to learn not to fear them. Suppose you're claustrophobic, for example, and you manage to avoid riding in elevators, flying in small airplanes, or stuffing yourself in the back of crowded buses. Sure, you cut down your immediate anxiety because you're avoiding claustrophobic situations, but you also continue to fear these things because you never get the chance to learn that they really aren't that awful.

Implosive therapists think that the best way to get someone over an irrational fear is to get him or her to experience a full-blown anxiety reaction while experiencing no harm—this should teach the person not to fear the situation. To produce the full-blown anxiety reaction, implosive therapists pull no punches: they help their clients imagine the very things that terrify them most. So while more traditional therapies would treat a snake-phobic person by helping him or her very gradually approach a snake, implosive therapy would have the person imagine a huge snake crawling over him or her or perhaps being thrown in a pit filled with writhing snakes. Believe it or not, implosive therapy has a significant record of success.

A similar sort of strategy can pay huge dividends in the gym, where you can either walk mincingly along the edges, or you can jump in whole hog. Just as with implosive therapy, the bold approach isn't as crazy as it might sound.

Fans of the kinder, gentler approach to training might make the argument, for example, that sustained progress should be one's overall goal. One should take things slow and easy, never making too big a jump in training poundage, never pushing the envelope in terms of training intensity and volume. The idea is that through the accumulation of countless baby steps, you arrive at your goal.

The logic of this approach appears squeaky clean, and the whole system is so rational, it seems hard to fault. The only problem is that the world isn't always rational, and neither is progress in bodybuilding or lifting. In fact, most people improve in spurts, and the pattern of nearly everyone's progress is actually much more like jagged saw teeth than a smooth curve. Recognizing this fact tells you that going for it—sometimes taking big jumps and expecting to make them—has a definite place in your training routine.

The next time someone screams at you to quit being a baby and to just lift the weight, know that, figuratively speaking, getting slapped in the face from time to time can help bring out your best, and the jolt of an occasional cold shower can kick your training into overdrive.

# 25: Willpower Workout

| | |
|---|---|
| **How to:** | Bolster your willpower for bigger gains |
| **Key idea:** | ⟫ *Willpower* – the motivation that springs from inside yourself and gives you control over your life |

In a perfect world this is how your training goes: you begin with a crystal-clear objective. Then you add a perfect gym, unlimited top-quality nutrition, and plenty of time to train and recover. Because you also have the perfect genetics to reach your goal, your progress is swift and certain—especially as you attack each and every workout like a starving Bengal tiger on its lunch break.

In the real world this is what actually happens:

One day you want to win the Mr. Olympia, the next it's an Olympic gold medal in weightlifting, and on the third day you decide picking up both is the way to go. As your goals vacillate, so does your training plan, going from a straight line to a path that wobbles from the left to the right. Things are also complicated by the fact that your gym's most sophisticated piece of bodybuilding equipment is one poor excuse for a curling bench, and you can't really do snatches or clean and jerks because there's no platform and the owner frowns on people using chalk anyway. In addition, budget limitations confine your supplement program to only the most basic items—

when you're lucky.  Furthermore, between school and a job, it's hard enough to find time to train—let alone to recover.  Of course, those bird bones and high muscle insertions you inherited aren't doing you any good either.  Is it any wonder that your workouts and your progress are lackluster?

When you're in the real world, it's somewhat comforting to think that you are the exception and that most people deal with a much more perfect situation.  In truth, however, most of us have to deal with our mortal limitations day in and day out, so we need to figure out how to make the most of things and get on with the task of reaching our goals.  To help us with this, let's introduce the concept of willpower.

Willpower isn't something you hear a great deal about anymore, and as a concept, it might be a little too slippery or fuzzy to satisfy hard-line research psychologists, but let's kick it around for a minute and see if we can get some useful ideas for boosting the octane rating of your workouts and putting you on track for bigger gains.

The basic notion of willpower is that our motivation springs from inside ourselves and this gives us control over our lives.  Most people probably assume that they would never develop a substance abuse problem, for example, because they have enough willpower to keep things in check.  On the flip side, there's always been a tendency to view alcoholism and other drug dependencies as the problem of weak-willed people.

Without going to the extreme of dividing the world into those with strong wills vs. those with weak wills, what is it that separates the two different types, and how can we add a little might and muscle to our own supplies of willpower?

Strong-willed is how most of us would like to view ourselves.  Strong-willed people, for instance, can establish a goal and make a plan suitable for reaching it.  Even more important, once this plan is established, strong-willed people stick to it—they fight off distractions, are resourceful about dealing with obstacles in their path, and somehow always find a way to get where they want to go.

Weak-willed people are the opposite, and it begins with the all-important task of goal-setting.  One day they want to do this, and the next day it's that; they hop all over the map until they finally admit, for example, that they "want everything: size, shape, symmetry, cuts, explosive power, slow strength, aerobic ability, . . . ."  The problem isn't just that what they want is impossible to obtain but also that some of their stated goals are mutually exclusive, so they often end up training at cross purposes.  It's as if they're always trying to bulk up and cut up at the same time.  When they manage to sort out things so they are going in only one direction at a time, their commitment tends to be so weak that they run at the first sign of trouble; for example, as soon as their bench press stalls out, they're off their powerlifting kick and onto something else.

So what are the weak-willed to do?  Is there a bulk and power routine for willpower?  Here are some suggestions to help you bolster yours.

1) *Set a goal: You have to know where you're going if you want to increase your chances of getting there.*  If the idea of committing to a goal is too frightening, remember that you're not signing up for life.  Try, for example, sticking with a specific program for a six-week cycle.

2) *Put on blinders once you've chosen your goal; otherwise, you might be led astray by all sorts of distractions you meet along the way.* Let's face it, if you ask 10 different people how to approach your training, you'll probably get 10 different answers. Cut down on the distractions once you've charted a course of action.

3) *Believe in yourself and your ability to reach your goals.* No matter what cycle you train on, which mental rehearsal program you choose, or how tiny you make your progressions, you will never improve continuously for long periods of time. In the times of slow gains, no gains, or outright reversals, it's easy to throw in the towel, but if you believe in yourself, you'll stick with it until you start gaining again.

4) *Deal with problems directly, and remember that a partial victory is always far better than a complete surrender.* If, for example, you're having an off day and can't make your planned weights, cut the intensity and boost the volume. You can always salvage some victory from what might have been a dud workout, and that's what you need to do. Don't just head home.

5) *Make haste slowly because, except for special conditions, the matters of gaining size and strength take hard work over a long period of time.* When you get impatient, you only increase your opportunities to get frustrated, and frustration will chip away at your willpower until there's nothing left.

6) *Remind yourself of what is going right, because plenty will be.* Guard against the tendency to chew yourself out when things go south. Did you ever see someone make four weeks of steady progress before missing a lift and then rip himself to shreds? Seek opportunities to reinforce yourself for the things that are still staying on track.

7) *Enjoy getting there or rethink what you're doing because you're probably going to spend a lot more time in the process of arriving than you will as the finished product.* Get to like what you're doing instead of thinking about some light at the end of the tunnel.

These seven little tips about how to think and act will set you on the road to bigger gains in all of your training—think of them as a workout for building your willpower.

# 26: Novel Nitro

| **How to:** | Use novelty to make new gains when you've hit a plateau |
| --- | --- |
| **Key idea:** | ⚬ *Instinctive training* – deciding on the spot how to train on a given day, instead of always following the same routine |

Hang out in any gym or just talk to a handful of lifters or bodybuilders, and you'll soon see that there are at least two very different ways to approach training. In the first you know exactly what you're aiming for. You pick a routine and plan to stick with it for a month or two or three. People who train this way establish tangible milestones for themselves, they persist with dogged determination, and they usually keep the kind of training records that you'd expect from an IRS agent.

The second group of people, however, appears to be on a rudderless ship: its goals and routines change more quickly than the Dow Jones averages. These are the people who might be going for a pro card in bodybuilding one month, a powerlifting title the next month, and most likely will be putting in major couch time shortly thereafter. This second group is clearly going nowhere, but how about the first group? Aren't those people—the steady foot soldiers—the ideal?

On the surface it seems so obvious that success in lifting weights—whether you're a bodybuilder or a lifter—really comes down to doing a little more today than you did yesterday. If you do this while adding adequate nutrition and rest, aren't you virtually assured of gains? So why not keep things simple and pick a good routine and stick with it for a while, adding reps and weight at every turn?

No doubt about it, that approach is the accepted standard for making progress in the gym, and for very good reason—it works. The only catch is that it won't work forever. In fact, the more advanced you become, the harder it is to continue making progress by hammering away at the same old same old. What you need is a way to sidestep your tendency to become complacent and stall out when confronting the same old training routine day in and day out. What you need is a little novel nitro. Here's how it works.

Research psychologists have long documented that unfamiliar things can be very attractive—people like to approach, explore, and manipulate novel objects. Even laboratory rats, given a choice of running down a maze and turning either left or right, tend to choose the opposite turn of what they picked on their previous run. Laboratory monkeys will work very persistently for the chance to manipulate gadgets or take a peek at the experimenter. Humans as young as three months can be trained by using new sounds as the reinforcer. Novelty, scientists have demonstrated, has great pulling power.

"Great," you say, "but what does this have to do with muscles?"

Here's the connection: Mere novelty tends to attract us and hold our attention, so it follows that if you can apply this principle to your training, you're bound to make new gains because you'll approach your training with added gusto. Also, it probably goes without saying that there's a physical parallel to this psychological phenomenon: your body has an amazing ability to adapt to the physical demands placed on it, and once it has adapted, you no longer make progress. That, of course, is why everyone who lifts weights knows that you have to keep boosting your volume and/or intensity, or figure out some other angle, if you're going to keep making progress. If you keep repeating what you did yesterday, you'll keep waking up with yesterday's body.

"Okay," you say, "but how do I put this idea to work in the gym?"

Simple—you keep things hopping as far as your training routine goes, and this applies whether you're a bodybuilder, a powerlifter, or an Olympic lifter. Take a bodybuilder as training-savvy as Larry Scott. Do you think Larry has his routine carved into stone for three months at a crack? No way. He's a big fan of "instinctive training," meaning that he'll say to his training partner, "What are we going to do today?" Then they'll decide which body parts and movements to target that day and develop their workout accordingly. Variety, change, novelty, growth.

If you buy into this basic idea, you might think, "Fine, this stuff may work for bodybuilders, but there's no way it can work for lifters."

Oh, yes, it can—and really big time too.

Consider Louie Simmons and his Westside Barbell Club, a powerhouse in powerlifting, a place where champions are cranked out one after another. Even before you dig too deeply into how they do things at the Westside Barbell Club, it's apparent that they do things differently: lots of assistance exercises, changing movements, using acceleration rather than sheer poundage as a way to make progress, etc. Do these guys hammer away at 12-week cycles built around the three competitive powerlifts? No way. They might not even do the competitive lifts, and they might change their exercises every two or three weeks—they change them as soon as they quit making progress. That's the key right there: the correct use of novelty allows you to sneak around the edges of stagnation and gives you a path to continued progress.

It's no secret that a lot of Olympic lifters and powerlifters sometimes have few kind things to say about what the others do, but get this: Louie Simmons will be the first to say that the training principles he uses with his powerlifters come directly from the classic way the Russian Olympic lifters train. If you ever have a chance to see, for example, the actual training routines used to take a Russian youngster from a raw beginner in the sport to Olympic gold medalist, you might notice a number of interesting things. One will be that the training routine always changes. From day to day, week to week, month to month, and year to year, the athlete is always doing something different. The changes may not be radical, but they are there.

If you can develop this kind of novelty for someone whose entire focus is top performance on just two lifts, imagine what you can do for powerlifters, who focus on three lifts. The opportunities for bodybuilding appear nothing short of infinite.

Returning to our first two groups, the key is to have the purpose and stick-to-it-iveness of the first group but to harness the second group's affinity for change. You want to know where you want to go, but you want to keep things lively enough along the way that you can maintain the pace for the long haul. When you hit a plateau and are looking for your next upward blast, your best bet might be to use a little novel nitro.

# 27: Get What You Expect

| | |
|---|---|
| **How to:** | Boost your expectations for success |
| **Key ideas:** | ❧ *Efficacy expectations* – how well you think you will do on something |
| | ❧ *Self-efficacy* – your sense that you can succeed |

Looking at them, you'd have thought that Ralph and Ted were brothers—maybe even twins. It wasn't that they generally resembled each other; rather, they seemed cast from the same genetic mold. Unfortunately, since both were passionate about bodybuilding, this mold had produced such maladies as seven-inch wrists, lousy muscle insertions, and a general look that ranged from markedly underfed to merely stringy. These guys were not the stuff of Dorian Yates's nightmares.

For all their similarities in appearance, though, Ralph and Ted were strikingly different in how they approached their training. Ralph, for example, fervently hoped that he would one day have an honest 16-1/2-inch arm and the ability to do a legitimate squat with 400 pounds.

Although Ralph would have loved to gain more, when his arm hit that magic mark, he knew he had come about as far as he could go. He was still striving for his target squat, and when he hit it, he would probably have the same sense of closure. Once again, he would have liked to do more, but he was resigned to his fate and knew when he was basically tapped out.

Ted was no dreamer, but he had a hungrier eye: when his arm hit 16-1/2 inches, he didn't run out and have "I succeeded" tattooed on his forehead. Instead, he said to himself, "I wonder if I could get this puppy up to 17?" When he achieved that goal, he asked himself, "What about 17-1/2?" The same thing happened on his squats. After he hit a clean single with 400, he went for a set of five, and then it was a set of 10. No matter what he did, Ted always seemed to have room between his ears for bigger dreams and the heart to go chase them down.

The world is filled with Ralphs and Teds, and if you're more like Ralph, you might wonder just what Ted's secret is. "I know you can't squeeze blood from a rock," you may say to yourself, "but this guy seems to know how to make the most of things. How does he do it?"

About twenty years ago, research psychologist Albert Bandura pioneered work that showed just how powerfully our expectations of success influence our actual success. He called the process "efficacy expectations," and the term more or less refers to how well you think you will do on something. Rather than being just another wishy-washy psychological concept, efficacy expectations turned out to be very important. This factor determines, for example, how hard people try and how long they will keep going when they run into obstacles. Since bodybuilding success requires all the hard work you can muster and because there will always be plenty of obstacles in your path, it's easy to see how high efficacy expectations could pave your way to bigger arms and all the rest.

Your goal is to boost your "self-efficacy," or your sense that you can succeed, and there are four basic sources of information that determine what you expect of yourself. Let's briefly review each of them and outline a program for beefing up your self-efficacy. Follow this program correctly and you are assured of becoming bigger and stronger.

1) Performance accomplishments—what you actually do—tend to be the most powerful and dependable source of your efficacy expectations, so work hard to do things that leave you with a feeling of success. For example, lifters whose entire focus is on boosting their one-rep maximums will spend a lot of time training not on weights around the 100 percent mark, but down in the neighborhood of 80 percent. Sure, part of the reason for this is purely physical limitations, but a major part is psychological: you attack 80 percent weights with the ferocity of 100 percent conviction that you can lift them. As you build this confidence, it will spill over to heavier weights down the road. If your self-confidence is a little shaky, load up on success experiences and avoid failures.

2) Vicarious experiences—what you see others do—have also proven to be extremely powerful influences on what you think and do. Try to surround yourself with models who live and breathe a can-do attitude. Based on research in other applications, it seems that the most powerful vicarious experiences come from seeing a range of people model the success-oriented behavior you want. They should also be people who resemble you or whom you admire, they should really work hard for their success, and good things should follow from their efforts. The worst thing you can do is to surround yourself with naysayers who forever model expectations of limited success.

3) Verbal persuasion—people shouting, "You can do it"—is a favorite technique for boosting performance, but research shows that it is a relatively weak influence on efficacy expectations. Furthermore, the results from verbal persuasion tend to be short-lived. Nonetheless, because verbal persuasion can have a positive influence and because it is so convenient, try to make the most of it by backing up the positive expectations with authentic experience. In other words, match the talking with a little walking: A wise coach or training partner will be a mighty cheerleader when he knows that success is actually within your grasp. Be aware of abusing pep talks. If you develop a history of pep talks that go nowhere, you'll expect failure when faced with more pep talks. Use them wisely.

4) Emotional arousal—how wired you are internally—influences how you approach a situation. For example, if seeing four plates on the bar makes your heart race, your palms sweat, and your knees shake, do you really think you'll hit that squat with the expectation of success? Hardly. You'll be wondering just how big a hole you're about to make in the floor and you'll be whipped before you even get under the bar. Emotional arousal is a tricky thing, though, because being too lackadaisical also works against you—you need to have a little fire to succeed on big efforts.

Ideally, you can learn to control your emotions by influencing your internal arousal levels, learning to jack yourself up or calm yourself down as the situation requires. For starters, try adrenalizing music and verbal persuasion to get cranked up and deep breathing coupled with relaxation suggestions to take the edge off.

Ralph heard about this business, and although he was a little skeptical at first, he decided to give it a try. After all, even though he knew he wasn't Mr. Olympia material, he wondered if he could become more than he was. Two weeks into the program, he noticed that he automatically caught himself saying, "Oh, you could never do that" and replaced it with, "I wonder if I could do that?" Three weeks later he did.

# 28:  Cranking at the Crossroads

| How to: | Avoid trying to go two different directions at once |
| --- | --- |
| Key ideas: | &#9786; *Approach–approach conflict* – facing two competing desirable alternatives <br> &#9786; *Approach gradient* – attraction to a goal increases as you get closer to the goal |

Nick Cramer was a determined young man who knew what he wanted: more muscle. Nick was also pretty sure that he knew how to get it, so he banged away at his training with the conviction of someone who has a clear sense of direction. You know how it goes when you approach each workout with the added zip that comes from knowing where you want to go and being convinced that you're on the right road to getting there. Then one day, one of Nick's pals threw a monkey wrench into his system by declaring, "Hey, Nick, are you still doing that overall size thing? How about specializing on your arms for a while, instead? Big arms, Nick, big arms."

Outwardly, Nick continued to train as he had been doing, but he knew there was a difference. He kept hearing a little voice whispering, "More arm work, Nick. More arm work."

Nick was torn over what to do. Should he continue to train for more overall mass, or should he concentrate on his arms? Being at this crossroads and not knowing which way to go created inner tension that Nick knew was cutting into his gains. He could feel that he was 1) wasting energy as he considered the two alternatives, and 2) losing his edge as he trained because his commitment to his routine had been shaken.

Nick was smart enough to know that you need to have everything going your way to keep making progress. He was also smart enough to know that some people get trapped at crossroads, going around and around but never getting anywhere, and others just plain crash and burn. Nick wanted more gains, so he decided to attack his problem head-on.

How many times has it happened to you? You've trained hard and steadily with an eye on a not-too-distant target, when all of a sudden you have second thoughts about where you're headed. Instead of being able to march straight toward your goal, you're trying to go right and left at the same time, which is a quick route to nowhere.

At IronMind we get a lot of calls and letters from people who are caught in this kind of bind, people who are simultaneously drawn in two directions at once. Because productive training is hard work any way you slice it, you absolutely do not want this type of distraction. You want to have 100 percent commitment to your training, the type of commitment that can only come from being certain of your goals.

Psychologists have a name for the dilemma Nick faced: approach–approach conflicts. As the label suggests, there are two competing responses, and both are desirable. Nick was caught trying to choose between training for overall mass or specifically for bigger arms. Even though both choices represented valued outcomes, because he can't have both options at the same time, Nick's indecision created an inner conflict that he must resolve.

One reason conflicts such as Nick's tend to snowball out of proportion to their actual size is because we often view the competing choices as things that must be grabbed right now or they will disappear. When you were a child and you knew that you could probably ask Santa Claus for either a bike or a sled but not both, picking one option really did rule out the other, at least for the moment.

Now, however, your choices don't necessarily have that sort of rigidity. For example, Nick might have calmly appraised the situation and realized that he was within sight of his short-term overall size goals and that once he reached them, it would be productive to switch to an arm specialization routine for a while. Conversely, Nick might have said to himself, "I actually have been on this bulking-up routine for quite a while and have packed on 30 pounds since I began it. Even though my arms have gone up a lot, I bet a little specialization would bring them up another notch or two. I think I'll hit my arms really heavy for a while and then go back to an all-around size routine."

Once Nick realized that his options would still exist tomorrow and the next day, it took a lot of the heat off his decision. He found it easier to both make a decision and to live with it. Remember, most decisions are reversible, so don't exaggerate the importance of the crossroads you face.

A second thing that will ease the burden of approach–approach conflicts is to remember to take things in their most productive order. A child at Christmas, for example, might realize that if he chooses the bike right now, it's going to be sitting around until the snow melts, whereas he can put a sled to immediate use. When he thinks about it a little more and realizes that his birthday is in April, he can ask Santa for the sled and try for the bike for his birthday. There's no law that says you can't get a bike in the winter or a sled in the spring, but why bother?

Similarly, Nick had the good sense and basic bodybuilding knowledge to understand that because he's 5'-10" tall and weighs 175, the most productive thing for him to do at this point in his career was to keep training for overall size and shape. Sure, he could take a couple of months off and specialize on his arms and maybe add half an inch to them, but if he spent the same amount of time on an overall bulking-up routine, he could put two or three times that much size on his arms. Once he hit around 200 pounds, Nick reasoned, he could specialize on his arms for a while.

Finally, to help manage this sort of conflict, make use of what psychologists call the approach gradient. This concept is based on research indicating that attraction to a goal increases as you get closer to the goal. Lifters might get a kick out of knowing that the original research in this area was done by putting harnesses on rats and measuring how hard they pulled, depending on how close they were to their goal. Isn't pulling and pushing harder what training is all about?

One of the best ways to make use of this principle in your training is to stay close to your goals—take them in small steps. If Nick were going to opt to continue with the overall size routine, he shouldn't look for 25 pounds down the road all at once, because that would reduce his drive and make it easier to question whether he should take his training in an entirely different direction. Instead, Nick should focus on the next five pounds or what he hopes to gain in the next two weeks. By keeping his goals close at hand, he would get a double boost in the motivation department: one from the approach gradient phenomenon and the other from the reinforcement of reaching goals at frequent intervals.

So Nick made his choice, and a few months later, after finishing his overall size routine followed by a cycle of arm specialization, guess who took one look at his guns and asked, "Hey, Nick, what's your secret? How'd you pack so much size on your arms?"

"Don't crash at the crossroads," Nick said with a knowing smile. "Get cranking."

# 29: Z Power

| How to: | Refresh yourself mentally and physically with sleep |
|---|---|
| Key idea: | ☛ *Progressive relaxation* – technique for learning to relax on demand |

It started off slowly. One by one, the guys down at the gym noticed there was something different about Eddie. At first nobody could really put his finger on exactly what it was. If they had Sherlock Holmes's power of observation, they might have immediately come up with some specifics, but the changes were pretty subtle. All they could say was that Eddie was different.

Then one day a few of them started talking about it.

"What's with Eddie?" one of them asked. "We had a bench press contest yesterday, and he smoked me by 25 pounds. Two months ago we were dead even."

"Check out his arms," said another. "If he hasn't packed an inch on them lately, I'm Dorian Yates in disguise."

"It's like he's always in a good mood," said a third, "and he seems to have so much energy."

"It's scary," said a fourth.

Not too long ago, they thought, he had been just like them.

In actuality, Eddie was going through a major transformation. The guys at the gym knew that he was training on the same equipment and using the same type of routines he'd always used, although there certainly was a new level of intensity at work. Maybe he was on a new supplement—or maybe there was something more diabolical underfoot.

The truth is that Eddie had been talking with a sports psychologist one day, and the subject of sleep in general and naps in particular had come up. Eddie had tended to slough off the importance of sleep as being one of those ideas that might have a nice Mr. Rogers-type ring to it but wasn't something real guys in the real world needed to be concerned about. The psychologist gave Eddie a wake-up call when he explained that not getting enough rest did more than make you feel lousy: it eliminated your progress in the gym.

"You've got to remember," the doctor pointed out, "that sleep deprivation has such powerful effects on the mind and body that it has been used extensively as a form of torture in wartime. On the other hand, sleep has such amazing healing powers that even guys who have more than a passing familiarity with, ahem, restoratives, will tell you that nothing speeds recovery like sleep."

The psychologist continued by giving Eddie a quick explanation of how sleep helps refresh you both mentally and physically. He added that while individual requirements vary, most adults seem to need somewhere in the neighborhood of eight hours of sleep a night for top performance. "A real secret to using this whole sleep thing to your advantage is to learn how to take short naps on demand," said the psychologist. "They're an amazingly effective tool for shaping peak performance."

Until then, Eddie had thought of naps as being great for babies and old people but not a training weapon of first choice for serious iron warriors.

"Naps," the psychologist explained, "are an extremely powerful tool that can sharpen you both mentally and physically. You can use them to boost your performance in all aspects of your life and to make you just plain feel better. In addition, they're a portable technique that can be used just about anywhere. They're as natural as can be, won't cost you a cent to use, and have long been a critical success factor for top performers in a wide range of pursuits, from athletes to scientists to statesmen. How can you lose with a system like this?"

"How, indeed?" Eddie thought, nodding his agreement.

"Here's how you use them yourself," continued the psychologist. "One of the keys to successful napping is learning to relax on demand. To do this, we'll use a technique called 'progressive relaxation.' We won't go through the full-blown program originally developed by Edmund Jacobson. We'll just use an abbreviated form that takes advantage of some of Jacobson's key principles."

The doctor explained that Jacobson often suffered from insomnia when he was a student, which he could trace back to tension. "When he taught himself to relax, he was able to sleep. Ideally, you should be able to take a brief midday nap, and when I say 'brief,' I mean a nap lasting about twenty minutes. We're not talking about just conking out on the couch for the whole afternoon every day.

"It would also be ideal if you could take this nap lying down in a quiet place, but don't worry if the best you can manage is to sit in a high-backed chair or to fold your arms on the top of your desk and rest your head on your arms. The idea is to put yourself in the most physically comfortable position that you can.

"Next, start at your feet and work your way up to the top of your head, suggesting relaxation at each step. For example, you might say to yourself, 'My left foot is relaxed; all the tension is draining out of it. My right foot is relaxed; there is no tension in it.' Of course, you must actually physically let go as you give the verbal suggestion, and it's important to give these suggestions in a calm, steady manner. You should work through your feet, calves, thighs, hips, stomach, lower back, chest, shoulders, upper back, neck, face and scalp in this manner. Adjust this pattern to what is most effective for you, but once you have a system that works, stick with it. If you have difficulty recognizing tension in a body part, try flexing it as hard as you can and then gradually letting the tension ease away.

"Remember that I called this relaxation thing a skill, so don't expect to master napping on demand the first time you try it," the psychologist warned, "but you will improve with practice. I recommend that you use this technique every day, and for an added bonus, when you hit a very relaxed state but before you actually start napping, remind yourself verbally and with a clear mental image of something you would like to accomplish—like the PR squat you're going for in two weeks.

"It might not sound like much," said the doctor, "but I can guarantee that if you put this program to work for yourself, it won't be long before your workout buddies will be wondering just what you've been up to."

Eddie followed the psychologist's advice as closely as he could manage and noticed that all sorts of good things began to happen. For starters, he had more energy than ever, his confidence was at an all-time high, and he was making all kinds of new training progress.

Meanwhile, back at the gym, the guys wanted to be cool about Eddie's transformation, but the urge to know finally overcame their hesitation, so they cornered him and asked, "What gives, Eddie? What's your secret?"

Eddie smiled and just said, "I've got Z power."

# 30:  Harry Had-a-Chance

| **How to:** | Keep your motivation high and your gains in perspective |
|---|---|
| **Key ideas:** | ❧ *Loss of motivation* – what happens when you don't feel you have a chance, or if a challenge is too high or too low |
| | ❧ *Comparing apples and oranges* – comparing two things that may seem alike on the surface, but in fact are very different |

You know how this story started: For whatever reason, a fairly typical young man named Harry decided one day that he no longer wanted to be fairly typical physically.  So he benched, rowed, squatted, deadlifted, pressed, and curled, and after a stint of hard work on the basics coupled with far more protein than the RDA might imply was necessary, Harry became something of a physical specimen.  Harry, in fact, added more than a foot to his chest and a full five inches to his arms, and he now curled more than he used to bench press.  If it weren't for what he had read, he would feel pretty good about himself.

What Harry read wasn't just one thing—it was a combination of stories about Mr.-this and Lifting Champion-that, all of whom were so far beyond Harry that he couldn't even claim to be sucking their exhaust fumes.  These guys were just plain out of sight.  You might think that Harry would have simply shrugged at this point and continued pounding away at his training, resolving to keep doing what he was doing, especially because it had been working so well for him.  That would have been the rational thing to do, but Harry, like most of us, really wasn't an extraordinarily rational creature.

At first Harry pretended that he didn't mind being so far in arrears, but deep down he knew that wasn't true, and a little voice kept whispering in his ear, "These guys are blowing your doors off, Harry, so what's the point of continuing?"  Before too long, all this self-doubt had a predictable result: Harry's motivation started taking such serious hits that he was missing workouts.  When he did make it to the gym, his training was lackadaisical at best.

Fortunately for Harry, his buddy Steve was not only a good friend but also someone who could see that Harry was starting to come unglued.  Steve suggested that Harry talk to a guy who trained at their gym, a psychologist with a keen interest in muscles and strength.  Harry figured he had nothing to lose, so he cornered the guy one day after they were both done training and laid out his dilemma.

The psychologist listened attentively to Harry's description of what he was going through and then asked a simple question: "It's as if you don't really have a chance, isn't it?"

Harry had never put it in those terms before, but that was the exact problem. He nodded, thinking maybe talking to this guy would do him some good after all.

The psychologist continued. "Harry, I could give you a lot of theory at this point, or I could cut to the quick. The point is, simply, that when we feel we don't have a chance, we just lie down and die, so to speak. Actually, some people literally do lie down and die, but that's another story. To keep you working, striving to do your best, you have to have a sense that you can achieve your goals—a sense that you really are in the hunt."

Harry couldn't see anything wrong with this, and he certainly knew that he didn't feel he was in the hunt right now, so he nodded again.

"People tend to lose motivation if the level of challenge is either too high or too low for them," the psychologist went on. "Make something a certainty or make it an impossibility and most players will head for the sidelines. Make the chances of succeeding somewhere in between 0 and 100 percent and you'll get more people trying harder.

"You've gotten spooked by all these stories of guys with 22-inch arms and 750-pound squats. Given these numbers and where you are right now, it's no wonder that your motivation to train is getting shaky—the gap between those numbers and yours is so big, you think you can't close it."

Nobody had to convince Harry of the truth here. This was exactly what he felt.

"What we need to do," said the psychologist, "is to trim this difference, to make you feel as if it's worth it to keep fighting. Otherwise, you'll quit training altogether or you'll have to become one of those guys who sit around and whine about being genetically disadvantaged, and end up settling for less than you can become. You can make more progress, Harry, but to boost your motivation for your next round of gains, we need to close the perceived gap between yourself and the guys you're chasing.

"To do this, we're going to work from both ends simultaneously: We're going to bring these other guys down to earth a little and at the same time puff you up a bit."

Harry was already starting to feel a little better, so he cracked half a smile.

"You know the guy with the big arms who had you psyched out? Did you ever consider that, for starters, the measurement attributed to him had a good chunk of imagination thrown in? Did you remember that he weighs about 75 pounds more than you? Did you think about the fact that the picture you saw of him was taken when he was getting ready for a contest and that there are times during the year when he looks as if someone let all the air out of him?"

The psychologist had Harry's attention now, so he went on.

"And that powerlifter who has you psyched out because he's squatting 750 would probably get buried with 500 if he did it the way I've seen you do 405. You see, Harry, you've been comparing apples and oranges, and in this analysis you're making yourself look a lot worse than you really are."

Harry, like just about anyone, enjoyed hearing that he was doing better than he thought, so his morale was definitely climbing by now.

"Considering the fact that some of the bodybuilders you read about have wrist bones nearly an inch bigger than yours, you should automatically knock about 2-1/2 inches off their true arm measurements to put their development on a par with yours. And before you get too glassy-eyed reading about some of their competition squat numbers, see what those guys can do Olympic-style, without their support gear. See what I mean?"

Yes, Harry did see exactly what the guy meant. It was as if Harry had been beating himself up for nothing—thinking that his case was hopeless—when he actually was doing pretty well. In fact, Harry felt his motivation returning big time. Suddenly he was all fired up, ready to make his next round of gains. The difference? Harry had a chance after all.

# 31: Hardcore Hybrids

| | |
|---|---|
| **How to:** | Apply techniques and lessons from outside your field to your training |
| **Key idea:** | ❧ *Cross-over training* – learn from examples outside your immediate circle and adapt them to your own situation |

Walk into any reasonably good-sized gym and you'll see the bodybuilders in one zone, the powerlifters in other, and the Olympic lifters in yet another. Sure, the bodybuilders need mirrors, the powerlifters need power racks, and the Olympic lifters need platforms, but since there's rarely any mingling between the three groups, you might think they had absolutely nothing in common and were separated by walls.

Not too long ago, you could almost expect someone who lifted weights pretty seriously to compete in at least two of these three branches of the Iron Game, and some guys were triple threats—dangerous in bodybuilding, powerlifting, and Olympic lifting. Today, however, with the ever-increasing levels of competition, specialization has become essential for maximum success. The line "Jack-of-all-trades, master of none" seems to apply here.

Generally, all this emphasis on specialization is well and good, but there are times when it pays to stray from your own group and see what the other guys are doing. In fact, sometimes the smartest thing you can do for your own training is to take a lesson or two from the other corners of your gym.

Someone who has done exactly this and has become one of the hottest powerlifting coaches around is Louie Simmons, of the highly successful Westside Barbell Club. From the specialization perspective, you'd probably guess that the secret to the club's success is a careful concentration on traditional powerlifting training. In actuality, the secret is that Louie has read all the classic ex-Soviet Olympic lifting training books he could get his hands on and then used these principles for his powerlifters. Imagine this: his world-class powerlifters do most of their training using 65 to 80 percent of their top weights, but they explode on every rep and go heavy on their assistance exercises. Does it work? With an average size of only 22 members, the Westside Barbell Club has produced 16 world champions and 23 national champions, with top lifts of a 1010 squat, a 712 bench press, and an 821 deadlift. Is there any question that they know a thing or two about effective training for powerlifting? Is there any question that the application of information about Olympic lifting to powerlifting was extremely rewarding?

Then there's the case of all the bodybuilders who said, "Well, I might not want to look exactly like a lifter, but they sure are thick and they have a lot of size in the large muscle groups. What's their secret?" Thus, bodybuilders learned the value of emphasizing the so-called basic movements, multi-joint movements using the body's largest muscle groups, and going for ever-heavier training weights. Ask even some of the top competitors on the professional strongman circuit and they'll tell you Dorian Yates is one strong guy. Did you think he built his mass doing isolation moves with aerobics-room size dumbbells? So if you want more mass and thickness, shouldn't you be thinking about how lifters train? In case you think this is a passing fancy, remember that Arnold Schwarzenegger was inspired by Reg Park, who was not only at the top of the bodybuilding world in his day but also could have embarrassed some of the world's leading powerlifters with his strength.

Case studies of effective cross-over training include Paul Anderson, the last American super heavyweight to win an Olympic gold medal in weightlifting. Even though Olympic weightlifting is an extremely technical sport, Paul used to train primarily on power movements. His routines looked much more like a contemporary powerlifter's training than like an Olympic lifter's training. Why? Paul said that he decided a successful weightlifter should be strong, so that's what he set out to do, first and foremost. Once his base strength had been established, it was easy for Paul to dominate the world on the Olympic lifts. Considering his world records, as well as gold medals from the world championships and the Olympics, it's hard to fault Paul's logic.

The whole idea here is to develop sometimes radical new ways to train by looking around yourself, trying to learn from examples outside your immediate circle and then adapting what you've learned to your own situation. The examples above should certainly demonstrate how effective this approach can be at the individual level. It's not uncommon to find that the people who reached the top of their game did so with the help of principles taken from another, but related, area, but this idea works on a larger level as well.

For a while, the relatively small country of Bulgaria had the fiercest Olympic weightlifting program on the face of the earth, a program that could slam even the giant Soviet Union sports machine in international competition. Among other distinguishing characteristics, the ultra-effective Bulgarian training program was (in)famous for taking training intensity and volume to unheard-of new levels. The traditional idea of merely training heavy three days a week gave way to six days per week, then seven, with most days having multiple workouts. The inspiration for this revolutionary approach, supposedly, was the observation that manual laborers work hard day in and day out, so why shouldn't weightlifters be capable of similar workloads? Not only did the basic logic prove sound, but the coaches found that the harder the athletes trained, the stronger they got—not a surprising statement, in general, except when you get down to the specifics of just how hard these guys ended up training.

When looking for ideas about the best age to begin training their lifters, the Bulgarians are said to have noticed that two Americans—John Davis and Pete George—had become world champions as mere teenagers. Youth and strength mix well, they reasoned, so they began screening potential weightlifters in their early school years. By the time they would be getting driver's licenses in the U.S., the elite from this program were already well on their way to becoming world and Olympic champions—proving the wisdom of not only learning from others but also surpassing the original source of inspiration.

The moral of this story is that there can be great value in checking out what's going on in the far corners of your gym and beyond. Take a risk, venture out of your familiar zone, and see what you can pick up from the other guys—see if you can't learn some tricks that just might boost your own performance another notch or two. Go ahead, take a walk on the wild side.

# 32: Racing for Results

| | |
|---|---|
| **How to:** | Know whether or not your progress is too fast |
| **Key idea:** | ❧ *Negative momentum* – occurs when you crawl along through a routine |
| | ❧ *Positive momentum* – builds up when you go fast and things are really clicking |

Fred Grabler had a funny problem: he was making progress so fast that he wondered if it was *too* fast. Just so you understand how bad things had gotten for Fred, in the past month, he had gained about twenty pounds of muscular mass, resulting in more than an added inch on his arms and several on his chest. That these gains weren't some imaginary bloat was clear since Fred's squat had increased over fifty pounds in this same period, and his other big lifts were gaining at a similar pace. Fred, as you can understand, was pretty ecstatic about his progress and would have had no reason to question his gains, but a few of the guys at the gym kept telling him that he should take things slower. They said, for example, that he should increase his training weights in smaller steps, that what he was adding each week should be spread out over a month, and so on.

Fred was confused. "Don't we train to make progress?" he asked himself. "Shouldn't I be trying to gain as quickly as possible?" "Is there something wrong with making as much progress in a month or two as most people would be happy to make in a year or two?" To get to the bottom of this mystery, Fred sought the advice of a fellow who not only had decades of experience lifting weights, but also had a unique handle on the mind–body link since he was a psychologist as well as a lifter.

When he arrived at the psychologist's house, the good doctor had his head under the hood of an exotic car whose electrical system had him at least as mystified as Fred was concerning his rate of training progress, but like any good counselor, he immediately put aside his own concerns and interests so that he could listen attentively to Fred's problems.

Fred explained how lately he was making such great progress that it was causing problems: some people were telling him to slow down, but what's wrong with making progress as quickly as possible, anyway?

"Nothing, actually," said the psychologist, "nothing at all, as long as you really are making progress, and aren't doing something harmful in the process."

"What do you mean?" asked Fred.

"Well, for example," said the psychologist, "how often have you seen someone put on a pile of lard just so he could look bigger? Or there are any number of outright dangerous things people have done in the name of making progress. But as long as you're not making any of these mistakes, the faster you can make progress, the better.

"This isn't a modern problem," the psychologist continued. "The original quick gainer was J. C. Hise, who set the Iron Game on its ear when he packed on about thirty pounds of mass in a month, back in the early 1930s. Some of the traditionalists were appalled and did whatever they could to discredit this approach. Hise, for his part, thought it was just fine to make progress as quickly as possible and used to wonder why anyone saw merit in gaining at an artificially slow rate."

Fred nodded.

"Usually," continued the psychologist, "to make fast progress, you have to work hard, in the correct way, and a lot of things—some of which you can't control—have to click for you. Nobody can make extremely fast progress forever, or we would all be world champions in a year, but most of us can make fast progress at least some of the time. And during those times, why crawl when you can run?"

"So it's O.K. to make fast gains when everything is going right?" asked Fred.

"It's not just O.K., sometimes it's the smartest thing to do," said the psychologist. "Let me explain what I mean.

"On paper, you can make a very convincing case that if you take small enough steps, you can make progress indefinitely, right?" asked the psychologist.

Fred nodded.

"But we know this isn't true, because most people still stall out and what usually ends up happening is that when you get too focused on taking baby-sized steps, you make baby-sized progress. Besides, it doesn't always make sense to move forward as cautiously as possible.

"Mountaineers, ice climbers in particular, can take the time to put in tons of protection along their route, to help safeguard themselves if they fall. On the other hand, the clock is ticking while they are doing this, which increases chances that they might get nailed by a storm, get swept away in an avalanche, or just get brained by a falling rock or a chunk of ice. They have to figure that each minute they spend on the mountain adds an element of risk, so moving as quickly as possible is sometimes the safest thing to do. The same thing with guys who drive logging trucks on remote roads—they can go extra slowly to try to avoid accidents, but there is an element of danger simply by being on the road, so some reason that faster is safer.

"It might not seem so dramatic, but the same process is taking place in the gym," continued the psychologist. "Once you start on a routine, you have to figure that it's something like a lit fuse—as much as possible, you should almost think of yourself as racing for results, because the clock is ticking. Staleness, boredom, and all those other things that cause a routine to quit producing results will happen even if you move along at a snail's pace. Plus, it's not unusual to find that you build up negative momentum when you crawl along. On the other hand, when things are really clicking, why not let 'em rip? You'll also probably find that you build up a lot of positive momentum when you go fast."

Fred was getting the picture, and he was also starting to feel pretty good about his recent gains. "Sure," he said, "I won't be able to make fast progress forever, but when there's the opportunity, I'd be pretty dumb to ignore it." You could tell by the way Fred walked out the door that his problems were history.

Having helped Fred, the psychologist once again turned his attention to his car. As he prepared for what he expected to be a tedious series of tests throughout his car's electrical system, he routinely started with his battery. He hadn't expected any problem there, so he was startled to hear the telltale crackling sound of electric current, and he was stunned when presto! the lights flipped up and on, and he knew his electrical problems, at least for now, were a thing of the past. He knew that he didn't know exactly why everything suddenly fell into place so quickly and easily but he also knew that it's wise to accept good fortune graciously. "Thank you, thank you, thank you," the happy man said under his breath.

# 33:  Jack and the JND

| How to: | Figure out how much weight to add each workout to make the best gains |
|---|---|
| Key ideas: | ❧ *Absolute threshold* – amount of stimulation required to notice something in the first place |
| | ❧ *Just noticeable difference (JND)* – amount of difference between two stimuli before one can be distinguished from the other |
| | ❧ *Weber's Law* – pattern that JNDs are constant fractions of the original stimulus |

J ack Griffith was nobody's fool—he understood that unless his workouts got progressively tougher, he wouldn't make progress. But what confused him was just *how much* tougher he should make each workout in order to make the best gains.

Jack knew from talking to a buddy of his down at the gym that there were times when things just clicked and you really could expect to make very fast progress—even faster progress than some people would think was possible. He also knew that there would be times when you could bank on making virtually no gains. But how about all the time in between these two extremes? What should he be doing then?

Jack was smart enough to realize that even though his goal was bigger and stronger muscles, psychological considerations were of major importance, so he took the advice of one of his workout buddies and sought the opinion of a guy who had solid roots in both research psychology and lifting weights.

"So, most of the time, how much weight should I be adding to the bar?" asked Jack, wrapping up his description of what confused him. "I know one guy who swears by these little quarter-pound washers that he adds to the bar, and I know another guy who swears at them. The first guy says these washers are the key to continued gains, and the second guy says they are for lightweights. What do you think?"

"It's usually a bad idea to make sweeping generalizations," said the psychologist, "so let me start by explaining a very important psychological principle called the 'just noticeable difference'—known as a JND for short. Let's get abstract for a minute, but if you can hang in there, we'll quickly return to earth and you'll see how this principle can help you make such good training progress that you would think someone would be trying to sell it.

"There was a time when experimental psychologists concentrated on studying the sensory processes and how changes in sensory stimuli affected responses. In part, this research was very popular because it allowed research psychologists to conduct precise laboratory investigations. Originally, most of this research was basic science, but later the results came to be applied, first in World War II and still later, in the field of human engineering—just so you know that what we're talking about isn't only for crazy scientists running around in white lab coats.

"One of the first characteristics studied by these researchers was the amount of stimulation required for perception. For example, how much light does it take before you notice it? How loud does the music have to be before you hear it? That type of thing. This is called an 'absolute threshold.'"

The psychologist noticed that Jack was starting to get a glazed look, so he said, "Hang in there for another minute or two, Jack, we're almost back to the gym. It will be worth it."

Jack was a little dubious, but he decided to hang on for the rest of the ride.

The psychologist continued. "Just as it takes a certain amount of stimulation to notice something in the first place, these researchers thought there must also be a certain amount of *difference* between two stimuli before one can be distinguished from the other. So they studied the question, 'How much of a difference is required before it's noticeable?' The amount that was noticeable was defined in statistical terms and was called a just noticeable difference and was abbreviated JND."

"This might not sound like much and you're probably wondering what any of this has to do with lifting weights," said the psychologist, looking at Jack.

He was right, but Jack, being a polite young man, only said, "Well, sort of."

"The amazing thing is that these JNDs turn out to be constant fractions of the original stimulus. You might not care that this pattern is called Weber's Law, but the implications for your training are nothing less than monumental."

Jack's eyes narrowed a little because he was starting to see the point of all this. Maybe this research had something scientific to say about how much more weight he was supposed to be throwing on the bar for optimum progress. That would be worth waiting for.

The psychologist could see that Jack was already catching on, but he didn't want to rush to a conclusion.

"If I played some music for you, it turns out that it would take around a 10% boost in volume before you would notice it—this ratio would be constant across the whole range of decibel levels. And when it comes to weights, the same thing happens.

"Namely, it turns out that it takes about a 2% increase in weight to notice any difference— that's both hard science straight from the research laboratory and what anyone who's lifted for a while can also tell you, based on in-the-gym experience. You just can't feel any difference when you add 2-1/2 pounds to your 300-pound squat, but add the same 2-1/2 pounds to your 8-pound Weaver stick maximum and the difference will hit you between the eyes.

"So when you consider that you're always trying to boost your training load, you can see that this 2% figure has pretty profound implications—anything less probably won't even be noticed. This means that while you can certainly add quarter-pound washers to the 300 pounds you squatted in your last workout, this increase is actually less than what you can probably handle, which means you'll be making progress slower than you're able. Ideally, you should be using this 2% figure to gauge the rate at which you increase your training weights."

"I get it," said Jack. "So if I add any less than something around the 2% range, I'm not really doing myself any favors because all I'm doing is taking baby steps toward my goals when I could be moving a lot faster. On the other hand, if I try to take increases way beyond the 2% range, I'll probably fall on my face. This is great stuff—thanks much."

The psychologist wished he always talked to people as bright and appreciative as Jack, but he smiled. "Here's a guy who's about to make some great gains," he thought to himself, as Jack headed for the gym.

# 34: Unconscious Assistance

| | |
|---|---|
| **How to:** | Let your unconscious mind boost your motivation and improve your performance |
| **Key ideas:** | ❧ *Priming* – getting your unconscious mind to influence what you do |
| | ❧ *Implementation intentions* – specific type of plans for reaching goals, including how, when, and where certain things will be done |

Why do some people make progress, while others get stuck in the same place forever? Is there some secret? What's the story?

After all, there are a lot more people who want to make progress in their training than there are people who actually do make progress. At first glance, it might be tempting to sort out this difference by using any number of exotic explanations, but in the end, there is a direct link between motivation and progress: highly motivated people move forward and those with little motivation tend to tread water or just sink. When you consider that lifting weights is hard work, and lifting weights to make maximum progress is very hard work, it's easy to understand why motivation is such a powerful determinant of your success. "So," you say, "I'll buy your theory, but that's the easy part. Tell me something I don't know that will help me boost my motivation!"

Standard approaches to boosting motivation rely on such time-honored techniques as the classic pep talk: "Come on, you can do it . . . ." This is the classic win-it-for-the-Gipper strategy. Sometimes a little added edge is sought by including an element of threat or fear ("If you don't do this . . ."), or an element of embarrassment or ridicule ("Even my grandmother could . . ."). Despite their outward differences, all of these approaches to boosting motivation depend on conscious mental processes—they are designed to work with your full awareness of what's going on. There's certainly nothing wrong with this strategy, but what if we could manage to bring unconscious processes into the mix? Is it possible to use our unconscious mind to boost motivation and trigger more progress?

For a long time, unconscious mental processes had fallen into relative disfavor with research psychologists, but for the last decade or so, they have been making a comeback. One of the lessons learned from this research is that our minds react automatically to things around us, before we are even conscious of them. These automatic reactions can influence both our thinking and our behavior. Let's introduce two tools for boosting your motivation and improving your performance by putting your unconscious mind to work.

The first technique is called "priming," and it works by getting your unconscious mind to influence what you think and do. For example, in one study, research psychologists primed subjects with stereotypes of old people, and then timed how fast they walked down the hall when they thought the experiment was over, compared to subjects who hadn't been primed this way. The primed subjects walked slower! Highlighting the power of the unconscious mind, the primes used in this research were words like "Florida," "bingo," and "forgetful"—words that were associated with stereotypes of the elderly, but were not related to physical attributes. Once primed, the unconscious mind went to work.

You can prime yourself for the type of training that leads to progress by using cues that encourage your unconscious mind to spur you on. For example, bodybuilders have a long tradition of using inspiring photographs to help trigger high-octane workouts: keep your motivation high by fueling your unconscious mind with visual images of the body you want and also of the effort required to get it. Talking about effort, we know an Olympic lifter who watches a video tape of world champions training right before he works out. That's because he noticed that the top guys are the ones who train the hardest, so he primes his brain with imagery of them in gut-busting workouts. He swears it does the trick. Whatever your specific approach, the important thing is that you find cues that stimulate the type of drive needed to reach your goal. For example, when you're getting ready to back out for a heavy, heavy set of squats, it's no time to think about tiptoeing through the tulips. Instead, you want to get primal, reaching back to the automatic fight-or-flight systems that kept your predecessors away from saber-toothed tigers. And speaking of tigers, we know a powerlifter who swears just thinking "tiger" gets his juices flowing.

Another successful strategy for harnessing your unconscious involves creating a very specific type of plans for reaching goals. Called "implementation intentions" by research psychologists, these plans contain such details as how, when, and where certain things will be done to reach a goal. The idea here is that once you define specific tasks and then tie them to environmental cues, the unconscious mind can help to automatically trigger the appropriate behavior.

"Sounds cute," you say, "but does it work?" One study found that when people set goals to complete a task (something difficult that they had avoided doing), under one-quarter met their goal. When they had to form the specific sort of plan that spelled out how, when, and where, the completion rate nearly tripled! How many people do you know who keep repeating the same bodybuilding and lifting goals, month after month, year after year, but never really do what's necessary to reach them? This is exactly the sort of situation that can benefit from using this detailed-planning technique to bring the unconscious mind into the battle.

For example, one reason why those highly-detailed cycling programs can be very productive isn't just the fact that the weights are cycled, but that on every workout, you know exactly what you are expected to lift: "It's Wednesday, so this must be 390 in the bench press." And so forth. The environmental cue, the workout day, is associated with a specific performance, which should help you take each critical step along the path to your overall goal. This type of approach gets added zip because you know what is expected beforehand, and your unconscious can begin working ahead of time, preparing you for meeting your objective.

By the way, these cues can also be internal. For example, a technique that can bring great results involves always demanding a certain number of additional reps after a certain effort or pain threshold is hit. Thus, you can train yourself to always strive for three more reps after you hit a certain threshold in curls. Or, a certain level of breathing—hard enough to normally make you want to quit—can be used as the cue to, for instance, stop thinking, or take two extra breaths, or use some other strategy specifically designed to get you through the whole set on the way to your overall goal. After you have used any of your techniques a few times, the correct response will become automatic, thanks to the power of your unconscious mind.

Thinking, no doubt, plays a tremendous role in your progress, but there are times when the smartest people—very consciously—let their unconscious minds do some of the work.

# 35: Training Tablets

| How to: | Make wise use of a training tablet or training log |
|---|---|
| **Key ideas:** | &#9753; *Training log* – records and notes of details of training workouts |
| | &#9753; *Goal setting* – important, because if you have a goal, you can stay directed toward it |
| | &#9753; *Self-efficacy* – your belief that you can do something, that you can succeed |

"Chest - 29", Expanded - 30", Waist - 26", Arms - 8", Flexed - 9", Height - 4'-8-1/2", Bodyweight - 74-1/2 lb. March 27, 1942." Not exactly in the mold of a strongman, right? Who would have guessed that from these modest beginnings would emerge the sensational career of Tommy Kono: more than two dozen world records, gold medals in two Olympics (plus a silver in another), six world championship victories, and a string of physique titles, including Mr. World and Mr. Universe. The list of Tommy's accomplishments goes on and on, but you get the picture.

Marking each step along the way, as Tommy gained over 100 pounds of muscle, were a series of 10 training logs—these books recorded "every set, rep and weight lifted in training and in competition" during the fifteen-year period, as Tommy built himself from a skinny boy into one of the greatest stars ever seen in the sport of weightlifting. Lest you think these training books were mere busy work, a series of milestones standing more as a curiosity than as a training tool, consider that Tommy would later say: "The more I became involved in weightlifting, the more training notes I started keeping. It was at this point that I noticed that the amount of improvement made in my lifts was in direct proportion to the amount of notes I kept."

Tommy's training logs tracked not only what he actually lifted, but they also contained notes about new ideas, technique, goals, training methods, and so forth. Tommy explains that his training book became "a diary of everything concerned with weightlifting. I referred to it often in checking the progress I was making and to correct any weak points of my lifts by reviewing the technique notes I kept."

Contrast this systematic approach with the more common one of maybe scratching down a routine on the back of an envelope, maybe bringing it to the gym, and maybe consulting it—with mediocre results usually following this haphazard approach. On the other hand, making good use of a training log allows you to put some powerful psychological tools to work for yourself, and that's why training logs can be so productive. Let's briefly touch on a few of the ways a training log can give you a big psychological edge, an edge that translates into bigger gains.

One of the most exploited topics in popular psychology, from self-help to performance enhancement, is goal setting. And for good reason: if you don't know where you are trying to go, you're unlikely to get there by the shortest path. On the other hand, if you have a goal, you can do everything within your power to stay directed toward it. IronMind receives a steady stream of calls and letters from people asking for training advice. Some of these people know exactly what they want ("I'm trying to increase my crushing grip" or "I'm trying to add 25 pounds to my bench press"), and others don't ("Well, you know, I want to make progress and I was thinking that maybe . . ." or "I just want everything"). You can guess how much easier it is to be helpful when someone knows exactly where he is trying to go. When you use a training log, you can set goals—by the workout, the week, the month, the cycle, or whatever else might work for you. Your goals are set in black and white, and there will be no question about whether or not you reached them.

Once a workout is completed, you can't go back and change it—any of those additional growth-exploding reps you could have done but didn't are now gone forever. And all those gut-busting reps you did do, the ones that will give you the gains you want, can never be taken away. A training log helps you understand this sense of finality, because each time you write a set in your diary, you can think of it as being carved in stone. Your training log will take on the significance and permanence of stone tablets, and this will serve as a tremendous incentive to make each workout the best it can be.

Giving people feedback has proven to be an incredibly powerful tool in everything from learning new skills to boosting productivity: this is one of the key benefits a coach should be providing. Otherwise, it's like target shooting in the dark. When you have a training log, you have a feedback trail: for example, you can see what happened when you went to 36 sets per body part versus what happened when you tried an abbreviated, so-called high intensity program. You can see the results of explosive training with 75% of your one rep max versus the constant search for new PRs. It's all right there in your training log: a written record giving you feedback on everything you tried, from training to supplements to how the phases of the moon might have affected your power clean.

Having this type of feedback is a powerful reinforcement, in that knowing how you did can actually help motivate you in the future. Let's say that you start a new program and that even within two weeks, you can see that something is happening, something good. That's reinforcing, meaning that you are more likely to continue doing what you were doing. What could be better: it's as if your training log can create training momentum for you because each workout you record can help fuel your next one.

Self-efficacy is a term psychologists use to refer to something like our beliefs that we can do something, that we can succeed. While this might sound like just another fuzzy concept which has little bearing on real world behavior, it isn't. In fact, self-efficacy is a powerful predictor of all sorts of behavior. As you might guess, our past experience has a strong influence on our sense of self-efficacy: this is why success breeds success and why failure breeds failure. Now think of what happens when you buckle down and commit to a training program that has well-defined goals that are aggressive, but realistic. You practically bleed to do it, but you make each workout as planned and record your progress at each step in your training log. There it is: definitive proof of how you mastered the situation, which is pure rocket fuel for your sense of self-efficacy, and this, in turn, will help trigger your next round of progress.

One of the nicest things about training logs is that you can gain all of their advantages at almost no cost, in terms of time or money. Once you get in the habit, you will automatically record each set as soon as you've finished it, and at your leisure you can study your results. As far as the training log itself goes, there are a number on the market you can choose from, but you can also just use a simple pad, notebook, or calendar—anything that allows you to record what you've done will work. The great Tommy Kono recorded all of his workouts on stenographer's pads, which you can buy for a dollar or two.

Most of us could never begin to approach Tommy Kono's success as a weightlifter, but if we train hard and smart, we can make what still amounts to sensational progress. And the first step in this direction is to make wise and generous use of a training log.

# 36: Active Recovery

| How to: | Improve the stress–recovery cycle of your training |
| --- | --- |
| Key ideas: | ❧ *Active recovery/active rest* – idea that certain types of low intensity activities do more to accelerate recovery than merely lying around |
| | ❧ *General physical preparation* – activities that build basic flexibility, endurance, and speed–strength |

Whether you're a bodybuilder or a lifter, making progress in the gym largely boils down to properly managing the stress–recovery cycle. Generally speaking, the stress portion of the equation comes from what you do in the gym—this is where you lay the foundation for future growth. This is what your carefully designed training program is all about. The recovery portion of the equation takes place largely outside the gym, and it primarily involves such things as nutrition and rest. This is the phase of your training that allows your body to capitalize on all the hard work you did in the gym. Given the opportunity to recover properly, your body has the amazing ability to adapt to the stress of training, and the result is a bigger and stronger you. We want to make this process as efficient as possible, for maximum progress.

Let's take a closer look at the recovery side of this equation and, in particular, review a concept called "active recovery," with the idea that this principle just might help add the next half-inch to your arms and 25 pounds to your best bench press. The best part of all is that active recovery, unlike training, is inherently relaxing.

What do you do if you're really tired? Sleep, right? And even in today's world, nothing outdoes sleep for its deep-down ability to help your body recover. Recognizing this fact, the history of lifting weights is filled with examples of people who, for a brief period of time, went on extreme programs where all they did was train, eat and sleep. And at least for short periods, this type of routine can do shocking things to your body. The problem is that it also does shocking things to your social life, not to mention your economic well-being. Even without going to these extremes, there are practical limits to how much you can sleep before it becomes unworkable and starts to have a negative effect on your overall life. Thus, simply loading up on sleep is not a long-term solution to your body's need to recover from hard training.

A whole different approach to boosting your recovery falls in the arena of so-called active recovery techniques, borrowing from a concept first pushed by the renowned weightlifting coaches of the former Soviet Union. At the time, athletes from the Soviet Union stood at the pinnacle of the weightlifting world, and their training techniques received worldwide attention as they pushed new ideas related to tonnage, cycling, training frequency, etc. While much was written about the training side of the equation, the recovery side got much less press, even if it, too, had its unique features. To fully appreciate them, let's first pause and see how they differed from what had preceded them.

Back in the 1930s, the first radically effective muscle-building programs were developed by such American lifting pioneers as Mark Berry and J. C. Hise. This was the crew that brought us the fabled 20-repetition squat programs that remain some of the most effective bulk-building strategies on the face of the earth. The rest side of the equation pushed by this school boiled down to getting as much sleep and relaxation as possible, and the general advice given was that any extra running around would only decrease the benefits of one's training. Peary Rader later summarized this philosophy with the recommendation not to run if you could walk, not to walk if you could sit, and not to sit if you could lie down.

People have taken this idea to heart, and I once knew a guy who was trying to teach himself to brush his teeth and open doors, etc., with his left hand because he was convinced that by doing all this extra work with his right hand, he was holding back his arm development!

Contrasted with this philosophy, the former Soviets developed an approach that was nothing less than revolutionary: called active rest, this school of thought advised that certain types of activities actually did more to accelerate recovery than merely lying around. In fact, in addition to using such tools as saunas and massage, this approach to active recovery recommended the very same elements that were used for what they called "general physical preparation." In other words, the very same activities that were used to build basic flexibility, endurance, and speed–strength were also recommended as active recovery tools: running, skating, rowing, cycling, a variety of games, etc. So now instead of just vegging out in between heavy workouts, the athlete might be playing a little volleyball or going out for a cross-country run or taking a hike—all to accelerate his recovery. To emphasize how this sort of approach went hand-in-glove with the heavy weight workouts, this group recommended that the athlete's general physical preparation work actually increase as his training load increased—the exact opposite of what the conventional wisdom would recommend.

The theory was nice and a staggering pile of Olympic gold medals backed it up, but perhaps the most convincing thing of all was that this stuff seemed to work for everyone—you didn't have to be a Byelorussian world champion to benefit from it. Now even the guy who was struggling to build a 17-1/2" arm or hit a 300-pound power clean had a good reason to pick up his running shoes instead of the remote control. It wasn't just that both his physical and mental health would be better for it; it would prove to be the fastest way to get bigger, stronger muscles.

And lest the couch potatoes of the world be too ruffled by these recommendations, remember that to derive the active rest benefits from these activities, they need to be performed at relatively low intensity levels. This is the time to jog, not run 100% intervals. This is the time for a casual bicycle ride, not the time to pretend you are dropping Lance Armstrong. This type of training should be fun, not grueling.

Fun workouts, improved mental and physical well-being, bigger and stronger muscles—what more could you want!

# 37: Angles and Edges

| How to: | Use creativity to unstall your progress |
| --- | --- |
| Key ideas: | ❧ *Guerrilla approach* – sneaking up on your training from the perimeter instead of an all-out frontal assault<br>❧ *Creativity* – putting a new twist on an old concept |

Most people who fail to make progress in their training do so because they don't try hard enough or long enough—they just plain throw in the towel before they ever really get going. It might be that they shy away from the tough exercises that make you gain. Or when they do them, they slack off and have all sorts of excuses for why they just can't lift any more than they have been for the last three years. Or maybe they just sing a song of general genetic woe, putting the burden for their stagnation on the scrawny shoulders of their forebears.

Given the fatal results of quitting too easily, it's always good to keep in mind the image of pounding, pounding, pounding—coming on strong right up the middle. That's why we all like to make heroes of the one-more-reppers, the guys who look like dead meat on the third rep, but actually grind out a full ten. Such bull-headed determination pays big dividends when it comes to size and strength, but there comes a time when you just can't make any more gains by crashing up the center, a time when you have to start to find some new angles, a time when you need to work the edges. In fact, learning to work the angles is a certain way to give your training an ongoing edge.

The basic principle behind training for increased size and strength is that by coaxing yourself to do more than you have in the past, and then providing the elements needed for recovery, your body will adapt by getting bigger and stronger. Nice theory, and it really does work. The problem is that you blow up if you stay with the same basic program too long. For example, many people have found that they really can add five pounds to the squat bar every workout for a few weeks or so while they are on a specialized 20-rep squat program, or when they start with a moderate weight and are cycling toward a one-rep maximum lift. Good as these programs are, however, it would be the kiss of death to try to stick with them forever. So instead of trying to milk a certain routine too long, or just focusing directly on a certain lift, thinking that you can force progress on it month after month, you need to develop some horse sense about when it's time to switch to another approach.

To help get the right mind set for this next step, try to think of yourself as being a guerrilla: instead of going for a massive frontal assault, you are looking for opportunities on the perimeter. You're going to look for these opportunities for advancement by checking different angles and by scouting around the edges. Pure and simple, you're going to sneak up on the lift or the body part that has stopped gaining. And this calls for a little creativity.

Creativity means different things to different people, but what we're concerned with can be nothing more or less than putting a new twist on an old concept. For example, there was a great strongman who always switched to one-arm dumbbell presses whenever he stalled out on presses behind the neck. Not a radical departure, but enough of a new angle that both body and mind responded according to plan: this allowed him to sneak up on his press behind the neck, and he started gaining size and strength again. You can also take things a bit further. For example, today it's well accepted that banging away on a few basic exercises is the key to big gains in bulk and power, but that was once a revolutionary idea, and Mark Berry, who developed this notion, was considered a heretic by the proponents of the thousand-and-one exercises approach. And, believe it not, there was a time when one set was the standard fare, but when J. C. Hise and others started doing multiple sets, their progress was astonishing, so others followed suit.

When you consider that even a guy who's been going to a gym for only a few months has probably seen around a dozen different types of curls, you would think that bodybuilders would never get stuck in training ruts, but because we're all creatures of habit, they do, even when their routine is no longer working. If you're caught in this bind, instead of repeating the same thing over and over, continuing to go nowhere, try hitting things from a different angle. It can be as simple as changing your sets and reps, but a better approach would be to change the exercises, as well. You can also change the order of exercises, the days you train, the time you change your clothes, or where you train. Even a new T-shirt has been known to produce enough novelty to spark a gain or two. The important thing is to change what you do. How much? Enough to attack your workout with some gusto and to get somewhere for your efforts.

Lifters seem to be more constrained when it comes to training variety, which might result from powerlifters focusing on but three lifts, and worse you would think, Olympic lifters focusing on just two. But don't let that be an excuse for you. Consider snatches. You could do snatches from the floor, from boxes (of different heights), or from the hang (below the knee, at the knee, or above the knee). You could also do power snatches in each of these lifts. And all those options are without even beginning to talk about the many applicable assistance exercises.

Remember, it doesn't always take a radical change to get the fresh results you want—just going from the floor to the hang might be all you need to hit a PR snatch.  Remember, you want to sneak up on the lift that has been defying progress—hit it from an unguarded angle and it will fold like a tent.

As you go about making these changes, always keep your goal in mind: you might be hunting around the edges, but don't confuse the means and the end.  For example, let's say you're dying to get your bench press moving again, and you reach the point where more benching just isn't doing a thing for you.  So you make some changes, such as concentrating on some partials and doing a tremendous amount of triceps work.  This is perfect, but you don't want to fall into the trap of trying to become the next partial bench press king or the grandmaster of the French press.  You're doing these things to boost your bench press and as soon as they quit becoming productive for that purpose, it's time to move along again.

It's nice to be stubborn, but when coming straight at your training quits yielding results, it's time to change.  It's time to play the angles and work the edges.

# 38:  Pick Your Personality

| How to: | Build a winning personality |
| --- | --- |
| **Key ideas:** | ❧ *Winner* – person who makes progress, expects to succeed, and does |
| | ❧ *Personality* – your personal characteristics are often influenced by the social situation you are in—and are malleable and can be changed |
| | ❧ *Loser* – person for whom failure seems to be a required result |

Go in any gym and you'll see some people who you just know are going to make great progress: they attack their workouts; they don't coast through the tough exercises; they make each set count.  And they have an air about themselves—it's as if they expect to succeed and you can almost feel it.  It's the same for them outside the gym, too, and others can't help but notice it.  They talk about how these people are winners, attributing all manner of good things to them and summing it up by saying they have terrific personalities.

You know the other half of this story: the people who seem destined to lose at everything they try; the people for whom failure seems to be a required result no matter what they are doing.  Building biceps, taking a test, handling a job: it's always the same and it isn't good.  Once again, others take notice of these people and write them off as chronic losers, people whose personalities mark them as perennial bottom feeders.

The truth is that what we often take for permanent personality characteristics are extremely malleable; these are usually things that can change with the social situation we're in, things that we can help control. This means that what you are isn't what you have to be. You can change who you are and become what you want. Before we touch on how to make the sort of changes you would like, let's take a minute to explore just how flexible our "personalities" are. Let's begin by considering the importance of the social situation in determining how we think and act.

Twenty-some years ago, Stanford research psychologist Phil Zimbardo and his colleagues conducted a daring experiment: they recruited "normal" students for a prison study, randomly assigning them to be either prisoners or guards in the study. Conditions were as realistic as could be managed, from the time the students were "arrested" by the local police to their incarceration in barred cells. Very quickly, the stereotyped relationships and behaviors of prisoners versus guards developed: the prisoners became passive and depressed, while the guards became aggressive and abusive. The first prisoner had to be released in less than a day and a half, due to uncontrollable crying, disorganized thinking, fits of rage, and so forth. It wasn't pretty. The pattern continued and things become so strained that what originally had been planned as a two-week experiment had to be terminated after a mere six days. Remember, only random assignment determined who had been a prisoner and who had been a guard.

Not so overtly startling, but just as telling, was a body of psychological research demonstrating that, lo and behold, people weren't as consistent as you might think from one situation to another—they might be honest here, dishonest there, and somewhere in the middle in a third situation. This posed a big problem for classic personality theories that would have made us expect people to behave very predictably, according to their personalities, across a variety of settings. Now it was clear that particular situations influenced a person's behavior in a very particular way.

The moral of this story is that you might think you are destined to waste away as a wannabe or a wallflower, but you really don't have to. You can recreate yourself in whatever image you want, Viking warrior, Amazon queen, or anything in between. Less dramatic, but more to the point, you also don't have to be the person who tends to miss workouts, makes a half-hearted effort when in the gym, and always finds the best reasons for not sticking to his program. You can be a winner. Here's an outline of how to do it.

The first step in your transformation is to pick the type of personality you want to have. In our example, you would want to be someone who isn't just enthusiastic about training when he's lying on a couch watching his favorite muscle video. You would want to be the type of person whose deep-rooted enthusiasm motivates and sustains each workout. You look forward to training and can't wait to get started when it's time to do your first set. You can't wait to get to your heavy sets and you welcome the chance to set a new PR, no matter how hard the required effort or how small the step forward. After training, it's an automatic, natural reaction to get the nutrition and rest required for optimum recovery and progress. You're brimming with energy and it seems as if the harder you train, the harder still you want to train. It's great—you've become a self-sustaining automatic training machine.

To reach this state, you need to cultivate the right thoughts and behaviors. Gone are the people who liked to tell you that lifting weights was a waste of time. Gone are the people who tell you that you're genetically suited to be a wimp. Gone are the people who say that they never built more than a 16" arm so why should you expect any more. Gone are the people who always say "no," "can't," and "never." Gone are the thoughts of everything that could possibly go wrong along the way. Gone are the late night binges that cripple the next day's training. Gone are the junk food diets that can undo the best efforts in the gym.

In the place of all these downers are the elements you need to build the successful you. What are some the pieces you'll find helpful? Here are the people who have always believed that you can do what you dream about. Here are the people who are in charge of their own lives. Here are the people who like to challenge themselves and never settle for yesterday's best. Here are the people who do the things that others said were impossible. Here are the thoughts of how to make the next step forward, to make the next round of progress. Here is the discipline to eat, sleep, and think in a way that almost guarantees progress.

As you can see, building a winning personality isn't just a bunch of emotional cheerleading or fanciful visualization—it's serious work. Along the way, you have to keep your eyes and ears open, trying to learn things that will help you reach your goal, many of them hard facts, and you have to keep your sleeves rolled up to do the work that will get you there. It's a challenge, but look at what you stand to gain.

It's your choice, winner or loser: pick your personality.

# 39: Grow With the Flow

| | |
|---|---|
| **How to:** | Turn out your best possible performances in training |
| **Key ideas:** | ❧ *Flow* – mental state in which you may not be aware of what you are doing when you are engaged in activities that you like for their own sake |
| | ❧ *Flow channel* – good balance between your skill levels and performance expectations |

Consider the typical person in the middle of a typical set, and what is going through his head as he completes his reps: "Wonder what's for dinner tonight?" "I think I forgot to mail the car payment." "Who's that doing curls over there?" Not exactly focused on the task at hand, this person's mind is everywhere but on what he's supposed to be doing: knocking off a set with full concentration. Even if it's the typical pattern, this is not the way to train for best results.

Next, consider the ideal situation, and just to make it more appealing, let's make you the hero. You're in the gym, but not even really aware of your surroundings. Each rep is done with your mind fixed on the business at hand, but it's all being done without thinking about it, and while you're training like a madman, it's as if you're not even really there. It's as if you're impervious to pain and it's someone else banging out all of those reps. It's the perfect way to train.

The first person is caught up in all the random thoughts and worries that run through his brain. He's preoccupied with all sorts of things, and ironically, even if one of his preoccupations is doing well on this set, all of these thoughts amount to distractions from his training. The second person is enjoying what psychologists call "flow," a mental state in which you might not even be aware of what you are doing, but one that allows you to turn out the best possible performance.

"So," you ask, "just what is this flow and how do I get more of it?"

Flow has been studied extensively by University of Chicago psychologist Mihaly Csikszentmihalyi for about twenty years, and it characterizes peak performances in everything from skiing to surgery, with plenty of applications to bodybuilding and lifting in between. Typically, Csikszentmihalyi found, people in flow were engaged in activities they enjoyed for their own sake, not for some external reward. In other words, they liked what they were doing and weren't just doing it for fame or riches. Also, the usual activities presented a constant challenge and presented immediate feedback about one's performance. Sounds as if lifting weights is a perfect fit—the challenge for improvement is always present, you always know exactly how well you are doing, and most of us lift for love, not money.

Daniel Goleman, a Harvard Ph.D. who covers the behavioral and brain sciences for *The New York Times*, explains that when we're in flow, we're making the best possible use of our emotions for maximum performance. When we're in flow, he says, we're bound by neither the "ennui of depression [n]or the agitation of anxiety." What happens when you're depressed? Nothing, because when you're really bummed out, you pull in, batten the hatches, and freeze in place. When you're really anxious, you also don't get anywhere, even though your guts might be churning and you might be making all kinds of nervous, half-hearted movements. Somewhere in between these emotional extremes, Goleman points out, characterizes the experience of flow, and it provides the emotional basis for optimal performance: "In flow, the emotions are not just contained and channeled, but positive, energized, and aligned with the task at hand." Translate that into meaning that you're having an amazing workout or a fantastic competition.

In terms of how to achieve flow, Goleman suggests beginning by paying extremely close attention to what you are doing, because concentration is the essence of flow. Goleman notes that it might take a little effort to get focused at the beginning of your task, but once started, your ability to focus will take on a life of its own. Let's see how this might work for bodybuilders and for lifters.

One of the most effective ways for bodybuilders to capitalize on this is to begin a workout with a favorite body part or a favorite exercise. Maybe you don't feel 100% like training, but you're willing to at least do a little forearm work, for example. So you start off easy, working through some of your favorite moves, and build up a little steam, and before you know it, you're blasting through your whole workout—and doing a terrific job on it, too.

And for lifters, this might be why you see world champions who can clean and jerk 250 kilos be deadly earnest about their first warm-up set, even if it's only 60 or 70 kilos. If things work right, their concentration increases in sync with the weight on the bar, so if things go perfectly, they hit the right gear mentally when there's the need for a big physical effort. The best part is that if everything really goes right, even a PR weight will end up feeling light, and the workout, even though it should have killed a horse, will leave you feeling exhilarated.

In addition to your concentration, entering flow depends on how tough your task is. Actually, what matters is how tough your task is compared to your skill level. Csikszentmihalyi represents what he calls the "flow channel" as being a good balance between your skill levels and the performance expectations. Conversely, when skill levels are well below performance expectations, anxiety will result—which will block flow. Similarly, when skill levels are well above performance expectations, boredom will result—which will also block flow. Maybe this is why so much effective training involves weights that are in the range of 80–90% of one's absolute maximum. The idea here is that you're most likely to enjoy flow when you have to stretch a little so you don't get bored, but not too much so you don't get anxious.

Interestingly, even though flow involves high degrees of concentration and performance, the brain is actually in a cool, quiet state. Remember how we noted that the experience of flow makes top-level performance seem easy? It's as if brain activity mirrors this ease. Once again, when you're stressed out, fatigued, bored, or subject to any number of other negative emotional states, your brain is working much less efficiently, and therefore, much harder.

Training is the key to gaining, so anything that helps you train harder while making it seem easier sounds like a fictitious magic wand. Yet, research has shown that there is a psychological state that can do just that. So be wise and grow with the flow.

# 40: Progress: It's Your Responsibility

| | |
|---|---|
| **How to:** | Take responsibility for your training performance—and succeed |
| **Key ideas:** | ❧ *Personal responsibility* – a sense of personal control over and responsibility for your outcomes |
| | ❧ *External forces* – things outside yourself and your control |

At a certain moment in time, two guys in two different gyms are about to do a set of squats. Both guys have 315 on the bar, and for both of them, it's a heavy weight. The kicker is that the two even look pretty similar: they're about the same age, have similar physiques, and so forth. What's funny is how differently they approach the set.

The first guy remembers all the bad stuff he's ever heard about squatting: how squats will ruin your knees and break your back, and if they don't kill you, they'll at least leave you with a big rear end. He even tells himself that it's okay not to squat because there are other exercises that are supposed to be just about as good. He builds on this foundation, reminding himself that his last set, 275, felt heavy, heavy, heavy and it's really not very likely that he'll make the 315. "Oh, well," he sighs, "I guess I can try, but I don't think I'll make it." And he doesn't.

The second guy thinks about all the good stuff he's ever heard about squatting: how they're a magic wand for gaining size and strength even if they're a lot of work. He reminds himself that the greatest squatter of all time, Paul Anderson, said he always hated doing squats but that he put up with them because he knew they'd help him reach his goal of being the world's strongest man. The second guy remembers that more than 50 years ago, heavy squat programs gave body-builders and lifters a whole new idea of what "fast gains" and "big gains" meant. Using this as a warm-up, the second guy thinks to himself, "I can do this weight." And he does.

This is only the tip of the iceberg. If you really want to see how differently these two guys approach their training, listen to what they say to themselves after this set.

The first guy says, "See, I knew it. I knew that weight was too heavy. I knew I couldn't do it. I'm not built for squats, and they're dangerous anyway. If I had better genetics, I could do it."

The second guys says, "See, I knew it. I knew that even though it was heavy, I could do it. I knew it wasn't much more than I did last week, and if I tried hard, I could do that weight."

Psychologically speaking, the key difference between these two guys has to do with the idea of personal responsibility. That's not the type of responsibility that keeps people from driving when they're drunk or letting children play with loaded guns. It has to do with your deep-down beliefs about who's in charge: you or someone else. Notice that the first lifter in our example looks outside himself for reasons to explain why he can't squat 315: it's a dangerous exercise, he's not built for the movement, he's genetically disadvantaged. He attributes control of his fate to what psychologists would call external forces, things outside himself. The bad part about his approach is that if something is external, you can't control it. That reduces your motivation in a very big way. Why try to do something that's beyond your control? This lifter admitted defeat even before he got under the bar.

The second lifter has a very different way of looking at things: he feels that through his own efforts he can make the weight. This is a crucial difference because this lifter sees himself as being responsible for outcomes. It's this very sense of personal responsibility and personal control that motivates him to try harder.

The eminent research psychologist Martin Seligman has demonstrated that when people, or animals, have no sense of controlling their fate, they quit trying and accept whatever happens, no matter how shocking. On the other hand, if you teach them that they have control over what happens to them, they take charge of their situation, which gives them tremendous advantages. For anyone who's lifting weights, the implications are striking.

Consider the person who feels he's buffeted by external forces that he can't control. He's forever blaming his lack of progress on everything from genetics to his gym to "those drug fiends." Because he sees himself having little responsibility for or control over these elements, his training gets less than a 100 percent effort.

On the other hand, the person who feels that what he does directly influences what he gets always digs a little deeper. This is the guy who makes the last three reps that the other guy never even tried. This is the guy who takes the time to pick a good training routine and stick with it. This is the guy who takes his nutrition and his recovery very seriously because he feels they matter.

Generally, when you're aiming for a star, it's hard to go overboard in terms of taking personal responsibility for your fate, but there are exceptions. Suppose you're sitting a red light, and out of the blue a car slams into you. Do you take responsibility? "Of course not," you say, but some people blame themselves for everything that goes wrong in their lives, whether or not it was something they could have controlled. When they do this in a big way, they can become seriously depressed. Be sure to keep an eye open to the real possibility that there are some negative things that happen in your life that you may not be able to control. There really have been crooked judging decisions, fraudulent food supplements, and worthless routines. Don't make yourself responsible for things that are clearly beyond your control.

Also, as Seligman points out, it's wise to consider bad events as temporary. When you do miss a weight, don't think that means your progress is over forever—you just missed the weight today. Next workout or the one after that you'll probably make it. It might be that you were tired today, a little overtrained, or any number of other things, none of which are permanent.

Seeing yourself as being in charge and putting setbacks into the proper perspective are two of the keys to making progress: it's your responsibility.

# 41:  Atlases in Atlanta

| | |
|---|---|
| **How to:** | Learn from the champions |
| **Key idea:** | ⮞ *Champions* – have the pride to perform and always find a way to succeed |

A lot of people would say that Olympic lifting has become the wallflower of the Iron Game, left on the sidelines while bodybuilding and even powerlifting burn up the dance floor. Tell that to the thousands of screaming fans who jammed into the Georgia World Congress Center for 10 days of weightlifting competition at the Atlanta Olympics. Many were probably seeing their first Olympic lifting contest, but that did nothing to dampen their enthusiasm. And as good fortune would have it, what they saw was one of the greatest weightlifting competitions in Olympic history. The lifters came in many sizes, from less than 5 feet to more than 6 feet in height, and weighed anywhere from less than 120 pounds to more than 400. Despite their differences in appearance, the weightlifters competing in the Centennial Olympic Games demonstrated that the champions always find a way to succeed. Champions have the pride to perform, and it's a lesson with universal value.

Here's a 60-second refresher course in Olympic-style weightlifting. Lifters are divided into 10 body weight classes, in which they compete in two lifts: the snatch and the clean and jerk. In the snatch the lifter rips the bar from the platform to arm's length overhead in one movement.

Even though the top super heavyweights lift around 450 pounds this way, the bar moves too fast to follow with the naked eye. Each lifter gets three attempts in the snatch. The second lift is the clean and jerk, a two-part lift that involves getting the bar to one's shoulders and then ramming it to arm's length overhead. The top super heavyweights lift close to 575 pounds this way. Once again, each lifter gets three attempts. Each lifter's best snatch is added to his best clean and jerk, and the lifter with the highest total in each body weight class wins the gold medal.

The 64-kilogram (141-pound) class captured the eyes of the world because it featured the "Pocket Hercules," Naim Suleymanoglu, going for his third Olympic gold medal, something that had never before been done. Standing in his way was Valerios Leonidis, who for the past three years had been putting big-time pressure on Naim, to the point of setting world records even when Naim got the titles. People had been talking about this confrontation all year, and the audience included no less a luminary than Juan Antonio Samaranch, then-president of the International Olympic Committee.

Before the lifting began, Suleymanoglu, usually unshakable, was visibly concerned. In fact, there was a report that he had been seen smashing his head against a bathroom wall. Leonidis opened things up by snatching 309 pounds, and Suleymanoglu followed with 320, which Leonidis also made. Next, Suleymanoglu tried 325, which he missed. Leonidis also missed 325, but Suleymanoglu made it on his third try—giving him the lead going into the clean and jerk.

Suleymanoglu started the clean and jerk with a first lift of 397 pounds, just under the world record, and made it. Leonidis took the same weight for his opener and also made it. The tension was mounting as Suleymanoglu took 408 for his second attempt and in making it, not only got a world record but appeared to have locked up the gold medal as well. Then Leonidis called for 413, for yet another world record and the lead. When he made the lift, it proved that the big guys, whatever their size, come to play hardball. Suleymanoglu called for the same 413 for his last lift. If he made it, it would put him back in gold medal position, although Leonidis would still have one lift left. Suleymanoglu is one tough cookie, and he proved it yet again by sticking the weight. For the last lift of the contest, Leonidis took 419 pounds—a huge weight but what was necessary for the gold medal. Unbelievably, he actually got the bar to his shoulders and almost stood with it.

Champions know they're in for a dogfight. Where losers quit at the first sign of trouble, champions rise to face each new challenge. So it went, with the heroes proving their mettle whether or not they ended up winning gold medals. Marc Huster was expected to be in a two-horse race with Pyrros Dimas for the 183-pound title, but when Huster made only one snatch and virtually eliminated himself from the running for the gold, even the silver medal was looking distant. Huster rallied, nailed all three clean and jerks and ended up, on the final lift of his class, with a world record clean and jerk—the heaviest lift not only of his class but of all time, plus an Olympic silver medal. Not bad for a guy who had been against the ropes, bleeding badly just half an hour earlier. Win, lose, or draw, champions pick themselves up and rally. Where losers throw in the towel, champions redouble their efforts.

American lifters not only haven't been scaring the weightlifting world lately but have had a recent history of leaving their best lifts behind in big international competitions. Not so with 238-pound Wes Barnett in Atlanta. Cooking with gas, Wes snatched 364, 375, and 386, demolishing his personal record and the American record and showing everyone just what kind of lifting he's capable of. Why stop there? Wes cleaned and jerked 474 and 485 for another pile of records before actually racking 496. The mass media might have missed the significance of Wes ending up in sixth place, but the weightlifting world knew that he had just made history by proving that he, and other American lifters, could truly be in the hunt for Olympic medals. Champions exceed expectations.

The super heavyweights, the glamour class of weightlifting, provided a fitting finale for such a superb contest. While many would have bet anything that Stefan Botev had the gold medal after he snatched 441 pounds, it was not to be. Ronny Weller bumped him into second place with a huge 562-pound clean and jerk; then Andrei Chemerkin, who had one lift remaining, asked for 573 pounds. If he made it, it would be good for a world record in the clean and jerk, an Olympic record in the total, and oh, yes, the Olympic gold medal. He smoked the weight.

Another lifter who proved that you don't have to win to be a champion was Alexander Kurlovich, a pre-contest favorite for this class. Kurlovich won gold medals at two Olympics and had the opportunity to join Suleymanoglu in the exclusive ranks of three-time Olympic gold medalist in weightlifting. Kurlovich has the killer instinct and the string of international victories and records that you would expect. He was also old by the standards of his sport and had been hampered by a groin injury. He called for 430 pounds for his first snatch, a big weight anywhere, anytime, and he missed it—badly. He took it again and missed it again. The place was buzzing-because Kurlovich, the legend, looked for all the world to see as if he were going to bomb out—and in the Olympics, no less. Kurlovich is a warrior, however, and rather than running from adversity, he turned it to his advantage. And so, with gray hair at his temples and his back against the wall, Kurlovich showed just why he's the champion he is as he made the 430 on his third and last try. Champions know that when the going gets tough, it's time to turn up the heat. Losers quit early on, but winners know that it's never over until it's over.

# 42: Training: It's Good-Mood Food

| | |
|---|---|
| **How to:** | Relieve anxiety, irritability, and depression through training |
| **Key ideas:** | • *Acute stress* – can be triggered by just about anything that has gone wrong in your life that may manifest itself in headaches, high blood pressure, upset stomach, and the like |
| | • *Episodic acute stress* – ongoing form of acute stress, when you feel as if you are constantly under pressure |
| | • *Chronic stress* – ongoing, day-to-day stress that gives rise to feelings of helplessness |
| | • *Irritability* – reaction to a specific event, as when someone cuts in front of you in traffic |
| | • *Anxiety* – general feeling of intense fear or worry, gnawing feeling of great apprehension |
| | • *Depression* – when everything seems too hard and hopeless |
| | • *Runner's high* – feeling of well-being from exercise from release of endorphins |
| | • *Norepinephrine* – chemical in the brain that increases with exercise and is stress-response related |

Feeling a little stressed out, as if your nerves are frayed? Maybe a little general anxiety is keeping your day off balance? Or is a touch of depression keeping you glued to your couch and feeling as if doing just about anything is too big an effort? Don't worry, it's perfectly normal to feel a little bad from time to time. And as long as it's not an ongoing situation, one of the most effective ways to counter feelings of stress, anxiety, and depression is a little training. Let's take a closer look at what might be making you feel bad, and how a little exercise can help.

Acute stress can be triggered by just about anything that has gone wrong in your life: maybe you were in a fender bender, or you just got dumped by your significant other, or maybe you're way behind on an important project. You might have anything from a tension headache to a back ache to jaw pain, or any of a range of stomach-related ailments. You might also have high blood pressure, dizziness, or chest pains. Not a pretty picture, and it can get worse.

What psychologists call "episodic acute stress" is an ongoing form of the above, and it describes the life of all the people who are always in a rush, constantly feeling they have too much to do, and all the "awfulizers" who think the world is a terribly dangerous place where anything that can go wrong will. Worse still is chronic stress, which is the type that grinds you down day after day. Maybe you're stuck in a job you hate or a relationship that isn't working, or are literally caught in a war. This type of stress is what gives rise to feelings of helplessness, and makes people quit trying to find solutions to their problems.

Irritability, anxiety, and depression are considered the three stress emotions, and they will probably be present to some degree regardless of the exact form of stress you are under. Irritability is what makes you go berserk when someone cuts in front of you in traffic. Anxiety is a general feeling of intense fear or worry—it's not specific, like being afraid of falling off a cliff, but it's a gnawing feeling of great apprehension. Something's not right, in a big way, even if you don't know exactly what it is. Depression is characterized by decreased activity and effort—everything seems too hard, so you do nothing. Severely depressed people literally don't get out of bed; everything seems just that hopeless.

As you can guess, any of these negative emotional–behavioral states will cut into your training big time. Unnecessary stress will cut into your ability to recover, which will put the brakes on your progress. Anxiety will keep you from being able to fully concentrate on your training, and all your workouts will become a matter of mechanically going through the motions, and you'll get about the same results as if you were just watching someone else train. Depression will just plain keep you out of the gym, so you know what that will do to your gains—wipe them out.

If you told your grandmother that one of the things you just learned in college was that exercise makes you feel better, she might wonder just why your parents had to spend so much money to make you so smart. What even your wise grandmother might not know, however, is that the positive emotional effects of exercise appear to be rooted in your brain chemistry, and they can actually prove to be a potent therapeutic tool. Here goes.

We've all heard about endorphins—the source of the so-called "runner's high." It's another brain chemical, however, that's been getting a lot of attention lately. It's called norepinephrine and it might help the brain manage stress. For the last five or ten years, animal research has shown that exercise increases concentrations of norepinephrine in the portions of the brain that are stress-response related. Interestingly, some antidepressant medicines are also known to increase brain concentrations of norepinephrine.

One theory that researchers have come up with is that exercise gives our bodies a way to practice dealing with stress, and just as with everything else, this practice makes you good at it. On the other hand, if you're sedentary, you lose this edge, and your body becomes less efficient in dealing with stress.

Whatever its exact mechanism(s), the positive mental health benefits of exercise are becoming so well accepted that they have become an integral part of some therapeutic practices. In fact, clinicians and researchers who study the benefits of exercise consider it useful for relieving the symptoms of not just anxiety and depression, but also of more serious disorders. "Exercise is about as close to a panacea as you can get. . . . It's a health inducer, a stress reducer and a self-confidence booster," says Jerry May, Ph.D., psychiatry professor at the University of Nevada–Reno School of Medicine.

What's also nice to know is that you don't have to launch into a workout suitable for Mr. Olympia or an Olympic gold medalist to reap the benefits of exercise. In fact, research conducted by a variety of scientists studying the issue has supported the idea that even a moderate amount of exercise can yield significant improvement in things like anxiety. This is particularly encouraging because when you're feeling down, the thought of facing a three-hour workout isn't just what the doctor ordered.

If feeling down has become a way of life for you, seek competent professional help. If feeling down is something that crops up from time to time, accept it as a normal part of life, but don't just let these feelings keep you pinned on the ropes. Fight back with a little training, and remember that a little might be all it takes. This is not the time to try squatting 400 pounds for 20 reps. Instead, begin by just pumping up your favorite body part, or do technique drills to improve your clean, or go jogging at a nice, comfortable pace. The first thing that will happen is that you'll feel better—you'll know because you will feel like stepping up the intensity. This renewed drive will help you train a little harder, which will give you your next round of gains, which will make you feel even better. Funny how when things start going well, they just keep getting better.

When things are going great, we think of training in terms of adding another inch to our arms or another fifty pounds to our deadlift. When things aren't going so great, we have a chance to learn that exercise does even more for us: it makes us feel good. And when you feel good, there's nothing you can't do.

# 43: Repeat for Defeat

| | |
|---|---|
| **How to:** | Avoid repeating mistakes over and over |
| **Key idea:** | *Reinforcement* – when your efforts are rewarded along the way, making it difficult to break the pattern |

You know the line about those who are ignorant of history are doomed to repeat its mistakes. The funny thing is that even though we all know our personal histories in exquisite detail, we're remarkably prone to keep repeating the same mistakes over and over again. Let's take a look at this process, see how it robs you of the training results you want, and most important of all, lay out a program that will break this cycle and put you back on the road to big gains.

One of the easiest ways to understand how this behavioral pattern sabotages our best efforts is to take a look at how it works in personal relationships. Ever known someone with whom you just couldn't get along, someone whom you liked at some levels, but who always ended up ticking you off? It might have been in a personal or a professional relationship, but the pattern is the same. What often happens is that even after repeated blow-ups, usually over the same type of thing, instead of realizing that the relationship just isn't working and that you should withdraw from it, you keep going back to it. "Maybe it will be different this time," you say, but after 23 eruptions, you'd think you'd be a little smarter about what was coming down the road, but you're not, so you repeat for defeat, again.

The same thing happens in training. Take an exercise that has a lot going for it: the bench press. Who doesn't love to bench? You can move big weights in the movement, it hits some of the most impressive muscles in the upper body, and you do them lying down. What could be better? The problem is that maybe you've found in the past that in addition to all those benefits, benching also has a big personal cost to you—you always end up with shoulder problems. If you learned from past experience, you'd know by now that benching and your shoulders just don't get along, but it's a lesson you seem to have forgotten because you keep coming back to bench presses—each time hoping that things will be different now, but each time they turn out the same. You start your cycle with light weights, and everything seems fine. You're enjoying all the benefits of the movement so, naturally, you not only stick with it but boost your efforts: greater intensity, higher volume.

One morning you wake up and there's a twinge of pain in your shoulder, and even though you know, or at least should know, just what's going on, you play a familiar game. "It will go away," you say to yourself, so you keep benching. The pain keeps getting worse, but you tell yourself, "I'll work through it," and you keep plugging away at your bench press routine. Being a determined sort of person, even though your shoulder is getting pretty bad by now, you keep pushing up your training weights and you're sporting some impressive new muscle for your efforts. When you can no longer rotate your arm enough to put on a shirt without excruciating pain or when you notice subcutaneous streaks of blood on your shoulder, the light finally goes on and you quit benching—until the next time.

You could keep banging your head against this wall forever, and there are solid, if not good, reasons why we tend to do this. For starters, whether it's a person or an exercise, the problem situation always has some good in it. This is what entices us in the first place and keeps us coming back for more. Second, even though we're talking about situations that always end with an explosion, this result isn't instantaneous, and you can't always predict exactly when it will occur. This adds to the seductiveness of the situation because it builds our hopes that this time things will be different, which they never are, and since our efforts are getting reinforced along the way, it becomes extremely hard to break the pattern. Don't underestimate the power of this type of learning: classical psychological research has demonstrated time and again how brutally difficult it is to break response patterns that are reinforced in unpredictable ways.

"O.K.," you say, "so what do I do to get out of this jam?"

First, you have to recognize and accept the problem. This means nothing more than understanding, for example, that you just can't get along with so-and-so, or that benches trash your shoulders. Second, you need to come to grips with what's attracting you to the problem situation in the first place, and what the danger signs are if its not working. In the bench press example, the appeal is in the big weights, the muscle you build, and being able to do the movement while flat on your back. The downside is the shoulder pain you invariably develop. The third step is to figure out a way to hang onto the pluses, while avoiding the minuses.

Continuing with the bench press example, you might find that you can do dumbbell bench presses and hold onto all the good things associated with benching while avoiding the bad things. This is a pretty perfect situation because the substitution requires hardly any adjustment on your part—it would be like ending a difficult personal relationship and immediately having someone fall into your lap who had all the qualities you liked in your ex, but none of the ones you disliked. It's nice if that happens, but don't count on it.

More than likely, there will be tradeoffs involved, and this is where it might take a little more initiative and resolve to deal with the problem situation. Continuing with the bench press example, you might find that if you switch to parallel bar dips, you can hold onto the first two benefits (big weights and nice muscle), but have to give up the third (being able to lie down while doing the movement). While this wouldn't seem to be such a remarkable adjustment to make, especially considering all of the benefits it will provide, even this level of adjustment seems to overwhelm some people, and they will fall back on their old ways. "Maybe this time my shoulder will hold up under the benches." But, of course, it never does.

The next time you're frustrated by a problem situation in your training or your life in general, ask yourself whether it's something that has happened before. If the answer is "yes," maybe it's time to do something else: to beat defeat, you have to know when not to repeat.

# 44: More Motivation: The Training or the Titles?

| How to: | Reach championship-level motivation to guarantee making progress |
|---|---|
| **Key ideas:** | ֍ *Ego-oriented goal* – a type of primary goal that involves things like winning or beating another person |
| | ֍ *Task-oriented goal* – a type of primary goal that relates to how you are performing the activity itself, like your form, technique, or level of progress |
| | ֍ *Motivation* – at its maximum, requires several parts task-oriented goals to each part ego-oriented goals |

It's no secret that motivation is what fuels your workouts—when your motivation is running at high levels, you have the type of workouts that virtually guarantee progress, and when your motivation is low, your training takes the type of turn that will cause you to slide backwards. Everyone probably buys this basic idea, but how do you go the next step? Just what is this motivation stuff after all, and what kinds of things can you do to help boost yours? Being a smart guy, you know that even though motivation might sound like a mushy concept, there's nothing mushy about adding another inch to your arms or 50 pounds to your best power clean— and you also know motivation is a key ingredient in making this kind of progress.

We all know the familiar Hollywood approach to motivation: our hero, usually a big-time underdog, trains his heart out, always spurred on by the image of defeating Mr. Big . . . if you listen carefully, you might be able to hear the music from *Rocky* in the background. And taking their cues from this type of approach, a lot of people focus their motivational efforts on things like trying to win a certain contest or beating a certain person. In fact, this kind of tactic can work, but as we'll see, it's only part of the story, and for most people, most of the time, it's not the best route to take. Let's back up, spend a couple of minutes talking about a couple of key principles involved in understanding motivation, and then apply what we've learned to your training. If this sounds fuzzy, remember that our goal is to produce results that can be measured in pounds and inches—which is about as concrete as you can get.

Some years ago, research psychologists developed a theory of motivation that looked at the two primary types of goals people try to achieve. One type is ego-oriented, which means things like winning, or beating a specific person. This is the familiar Hollywood approach to motivation. The second type of goal is task-oriented, which means things related to actually going through the motions. For example, a task-oriented approach to your training would mean focusing on your form, your level of progress, and so forth—it puts the spotlight on what you are doing, without measuring it in comparison to another person.

Researchers have found that as children, we generally all start off leaning toward task-oriented goals, but as we get older, we shift toward ego-oriented goals, although our exact orientation is the result of what our parents, teachers, and coaches emphasize. For example, if a coach is tough on mistakes, pits athletes against each other, and dotes on the stars, you'll have an ego-oriented environment. On the other hand, if a coach emphasizes effort over results, values all athletes, and urges everyone to improve technically, you're likely to find a task-oriented environment. You can extend these patterns to a wide variety of situations, but the general patterns will always remain the same.

"So," you ask, "how do these two types of goals affect my motivation, and what in the world do they have to do with my lifting?"

An ego-oriented approach can, in fact, be very effective for an elite athlete—winning an Olympic gold medal or beating a certain guy might require just the sort of added stretch that can be prompted by this approach. But there's also a downside to this approach, and it's a big one. Researchers have found that people who over-emphasize ego goals can have a tough time dealing with defeat, so it can leave them in a fragile position when they're not at the top of the heap. As you would guess, people who are strongly motivated by ego goals tend to just plain quit when they're not doing well, and in general, seem to derive less long-term satisfaction from what they're doing compared to people with more balanced goals.

On the other hand, a task-oriented approach gives the athlete a stable base for continuing to hammer away, day after day. That's because the task-oriented athlete focuses on such things as his technique and how much progress he has made, without comparing the results to others. This perspective appears to be much better for sustaining consistent long-term effort and is better suited to weathering the inevitable slumps. Even the superstars need to put in plenty of training time, and maintaining task-oriented goals is the best way to sustain your motivation all along the way.

The recipe for maximum motivation consists of something like several parts of task-oriented goals to each part of ego-oriented goals—this will keep you going day after day, through the valleys and over the plains of your training. Try to reserve the ego-oriented goals for the added surge required to break over the summits, when you're digging deep to make the final, gut-busting push. On a day-to-day basis, take the perspective of enjoying your training, trying to do the movements correctly, and trying to coax progress by doing a little more today than you did yesterday. Take satisfaction in this type of progress, regardless of the guy next to you who might have ten plates on the bar, and at the same time, remember that progress isn't in a straight line, so there's no need to think your world has fallen apart when you have an off-day or lose some ground you had fought hard to gain.

Odd as it sounds, the real key to sustaining championship-level motivation over the long haul is to focus on the training, not the titles.

# 45: Good Workouts Guaranteed

| | |
|---|---|
| **How to:** | Stick with your training and make every workout productive |
| **Key ideas:** | ✎ *Progressive resistance* – principle at the heart of every training program: do more today than you did yesterday |
| | ✎ *Double progression system* - you keep trying to add reps until you hit a certain goal, and then you add weight to the bar, starting again to build up the reps |

It'd be nice if you could decide one day that you wanted to look like Dorian Yates or be as strong as Ed Coan and—pop!—three months after hitting the weights, you'd emerge as the finished product. Unfortunately for everyone in a hurry, building serious levels of muscle and strength takes years. Sure, you can make amazing progress in amazingly short periods of time, but to hit peak levels, you have to be in it for the long haul. To make matters worse, there's no union contract here that says if you punch in, you get paid: in this game, there is a strict relationship between the quality of the input (training, diet, psychology) and the quality of output (gains in size and strength).

It doesn't take a rocket scientist to figure out that where most people break down is in their training: they either have half-hearted workouts or, the ultimate in undoing progress, they just plain skip workouts. Let's take a look at one of the primary reasons why most people lose it in their training, and see how we can turn things around. We'll see how you can not only make your training something you'll stick with, but we'll even see how you can make every single workout productive. "Now that's a trick worth learning," you say.

Whether you've read a pile of books and magazines about training or gotten everything you know from your buddy who does curls and bench presses (nothing more, nothing less) three times a week, you know that the essence of lifting weights is progressive resistance. For the history buffs, you know that it all goes back to a character in ancient Greece, one Milo of Crotona, who started carrying a calf on his shoulders every day. Nature having its way, the calf got heavier day by day, so Milo's training load automatically went up each workout. Milo went on to become a ferocious wrestler and a legendary strongman, and unbeknownst to him at the time, his basic training principle—progressive resistance—would later be at the heart of a vast industry, including everything from basic barbells to complex machines.

The importance of this principle—do more today than you did yesterday—is crucial to your long-term success, but it also leads to the undoing of many a training program. Here's how.

Armed with the knowledge that you're supposed to keep your training load going north, you use the classic double-progression system in your training: it sounds like a mouthful, but all it means is that you keep trying to add reps until you hit a certain goal, 12 reps for example, and then you add weight to the bar. This will probably reduce the number of reps you can do, so you start building up the reps again. You might not have even known this is what it's called, but that's how you've been training, and your military presses are a good example of how the system works. You started off doing 100 pounds for 10 reps. The next workout, you did 100 x 12 so you added five pounds to the bar and squeezed out eight reps. You kept at it until you could do 12 reps, and then you added another five pounds to the bar. Sticking with this approach, you've now got 150 pounds on the bar—nothing to scare off the big boys, but certainly not a mere whisper of a weight.

Last workout, you got 10 reps with the 150, so you were hoping to hit the full 12 today. Instead, you got 7 reps. This is where things can break down, and it starts inside your head. If you're like most people, you chew yourself out. If you're really hard on yourself, you view this as a failure, which by extension makes you a failure. Pushing things a little farther down this path, because you're smart enough not to want to fail or to think of yourself as a failure, the ultimate reaction to this pattern is to just quit training altogether. And that's exactly what happens to a lot of people: they bail out at the first sign of things getting sticky.

The obvious problem with this approach is that if you quit training, you'll never achieve all that you're capable of, and you'll certainly never achieve the Yates–Coan level. The more subtle but more serious problem with this pattern is that you can be absolutely certain that no matter what anyone tells you, no matter how you cycle or even if you get yourself a set of microscopic plates, progress is not a straightforward thing, which means you're guaranteed to not be able to go forward without interruption. And while you might agree with that idea in principle, you might miss the implication that in some workouts, you will have to accept going sideways or backwards, instead of forward.

To deal with this situation, you need to understand that sometimes going sideways or backwards is the way to go forward. This might sound Zen-like, but it's a secret that will help you gain and gain. Here's how it works.

Progress isn't forever, without interruption, or we'd all be world champions. Still, to hit what we're capable of means that we have to stick with our training for years and years. This might sound like an impossible situation, because what sort of an idiot is going to keep banging his head against the wall, having crummy workouts year after year? The key is to quit having crummy workouts, and the way to do that is to realize that even though your long-term goals always involve bigger weights and more reps, today's workout just needs to be the best you're capable of performing. It's really that simple: make this workout the best you're capable of performing and your long-term progress is guaranteed. Forget about beating yourself up about what you did yesterday and what you think you're supposed to be doing today. To reach what you want for tomorrow, what you really need is just to do your best today.

So you're back in the gym, and you only hit seven reps with the 150. You don't chew yourself out, because you know you put everything you had into that set—which is great. If you're more interested in keeping your reps at the high end of your target range, you might drop the weight a little and finish off your training with the full 12 reps per set. If you're more interested in keeping the weight up, you might stick with the 150, even if it means getting 5 reps on the next set. Either way, you pat yourself on the back, because you're training as hard as you can and you know that's the way to make progress—and sooner or later, this technique will take you to 150 x 12 and beyond.

You know that to reach your overall goals, you have to have good workouts year in and year out, and because you now realize that having a good workout means doing all you're capable of doing—no more, no less—that's exactly what you're having: a good workout. It's guaranteed.

# 46: Plunge in for Progress

| How to: | Move ahead in your progress by jumping in with both feet |
| --- | --- |
| **Key ideas:** | ❧ *Systematic desensitization* – cognitive therapy technique for overcoming fear by staying relaxed while imagining progressively more threatening situations |
| | ❧ *Mental rehearsal* – training technique in which you mentally practice whatever skill or situation you're trying to master |
| | ❧ *Plunge therapy* – jumping into an activity without mental preparation |

Progress is an amazing thing—a little today plus a little more tomorrow and the next day, and all of a sudden you've taken a big step forward. When you look at all the ways there are to make progress, you'd think it was only a matter of time before everyone reached the moon. Unfortunately, most people end up parked in a rest stop, far from their original destination. Going forward must not be as easy as it seems.

Let's take a closer look at this thing called progress, analyze a common approach to sustaining gains that sometimes stall, and then lay out a program that deals with the problem. The result of following this program should be progress. If this approach works for you the way it's worked for a lot of other people, it will help you reach the next level of strength and development, again and again.

Consider some of the most common techniques recommended for making continued progress: cycling, using tiny plates, double progression, etc. Many of those approaches apply the time-honored principles of taking baby steps and relying on the sneak attack. The idea is that you can get to the heart of things by working around the edges, which can often be safer, easier, and remarkably effective. Some people might argue that the full range of mental training techniques relies on similar principles.

For example, rather than dealing with a deadly fear of snakes by jumping into a pit of writhing vipers, you might use a technique like "systematic desensitization" to imagine yourself success- fully and calmly dealing with progressively more threatening situations with snakes. You might, for instance, first learn to stay calm while imagining that you're looking at a harmless little garter snake in an aquarium at the other side of a pet shop. You might keep working your way through ever more threatening situations until you can calmly imagine yourself letting a large boa constrictor curl around your shoulders. This technique works along the perimeter by having you imagine the scary situations (rather than face them physically), by keeping the situations progressive (the easy ones come before the hard ones), and by allowing you to go back anytime you need to (an escape route is available at every turn).

Similarly, the various mental rehearsal techniques have you mentally practice whatever skill or situation you're trying to master, with the idea that this then transfers to real-world perfor- mance. For example, you might improve a skill, such as learning how to do a squat snatch by using mental rehearsal along with actual practice to speed up your learning. Once again, mental rehearsal relies on an indirect attack and has proven extremely useful in an amazingly wide range of situations.

If these approaches are so good, you wonder, what's the problem? The problem is that as suc- cessful as the techniques are, they don't work for everyone all the time, so you need an alterna- tive. What better way to go than to reverse the field and just take a plunge? Here's how it works.

As a child you might have used this basic strategy the first time you tried a high dive: you might have gone to the end of the diving board, lingered, backed off, gone to the end again, and sooner or later you just closed your eyes and went for it. That's the idea here: there comes a point when it's time to put up or shut up, and what often proves to be the best way is to quit thinking and just plunge right in. Let's put the technique to work for you.

Start off by thinking about where your training is breaking down, and consider the following three types of situations.

1) You've been trying to use a variety of psyching techniques to boost your motivation for training, and what you've noticed is that while you can be very successful at getting psyched for a specific situation (for example, squeezing through a tough set of squats), the technique doesn't work as well for your overall workout, so you still tend to skip a lot of your training.

2) Try as you might to knock down the fear you have about lifting a certain weight, all that happens when you confront it mentally is that your knees shake. In fact, your reaction is so strong that you're starting to dread the mental training as much as the real thing.

3) It seems that what you really need to do is stop the little voice in your head that's whispering things like, "You can't do this" and "This weight will probably kill you," rather than getting the voice to go in the opposite direction and whisper things like, "You can do this" and "You can lift this weight."

If you're running into any one of these, you're a good candidate for plunge therapy. Quit think- ing about it, and just jump right in. Because this approach requires no mental preparation, you'd think it would be easy to do, but it's a skill that has to be acquired. You'll have to practice shutting down your brain and learn to simply execute the task at hand. Here are some pointers.

Try to train alone and don't talk—even to yourself. Establish your precise lifting pattern on your warm-up sets and keep doing exactly the same thing(s) on your heavy sets. Try to build momentum by starting small and working your way up, squaring off with your challenges at each step. Don't rest long in between sets. It's better to walk around with purpose than to wilt on a bench as you're resting. Keep your workouts short and intense—this isn't the time for training sessions built around eight sets each of 25 different movements. Review your successes after each workout and give yourself a pat on the back.

Lifting weights is about as physical as things can get, so it should be no surprise that to make progress you have to actually move some iron. Quit thinking, quit talking, quit avoiding—and plunge in for progress.

# 47: Fine Lines

| | |
|---|---|
| **How to:** | Make tough training decisions involving complex information |
| **Key ideas:** | ❧ *Detraining* – what happens when you are undertraining and your progress slides backwards |
| | ❧ *Social pressure to conform* – most people follow the herd, no matter what they say to the contrary |

Chances are good that when you first started training, life was simple: your workouts were based on three-days-a-week whole-body routines, your diet consisted of a lot of nutritious food with some basic supplements, and best of all, your gains were pretty consistent. It was a nice setup because not only were you moving forward, but also you were armed with the reassuring sense of knowing exactly what you were supposed to do. For example, about the only type of training decision you had to make was whether you'd add 5 or 10 pounds to the bar when you made all your reps—or you might work out on Tuesday, Thursday, and Saturday instead of Monday, Wednesday, and Friday. On the diet side, you might have had to decide whether it would be steak or chicken for dinner. Your world was nice and simple.

It would have been very comfortable if things had remained that way, but they didn't. For starters, your zeal for progress inspired you to read everything you could find about training and to talk to everyone who might have an opinion. At worst, this created a sense of confusion that paralyzed your training or sent you backward. At best, it created a sense of complexity that forced you to actively make decisions about what to do next, and some of those decisions were just plain tough. We're going to take a look at the toughest class of decisions—the ones that involve fine lines.

This is territory you have to cross to go beyond the intermediate class in terms of strength and development, so the quicker you learn to manage those decisions, the quicker you can move along to your next round of gains. To illustrate what we're talking about, let's use two examples: training frequency and drugs.

One of the most common questions we get at IronMind Enterprises involves training frequency: people are constantly asking whether we think, for example, they can really squat heavy twice a week. We usually tell them that most people can actually squat heavy at least three times a week, and this typically produces a thunderous silence on the other end of the phone. The issue, we explain, is that while the dangers of overtraining are real, there's also a very real downside associated with undertraining. Sure, we explain, you can make progress if you only train once per week, but by doing that, you're probably going to move forward at an artificially slow pace—for each two steps your training might have taken you forward, you will slide backward one because your body started "detraining" during the long rest in between workouts. Then we add that some of the world's top Olympic lifters squat every single day, and sometimes they have more than one squat workout per day. Any way you slice it, there's a lot of room between those two extreme points, and chances are good that your optimum training frequency is going to be someplace in between. But where?

Our advice in these situations is to aim high and come to grips with the need to walk the fine line between undertraining and overtraining. If you go too far to either side, the results will be the same: you'll slow down your progress. What that forces you to do is to become somewhat flexible in your thinking about how often to train and to understand that anyone who tells you that you must do this or that is probably an armchair expert at best.

How about drugs? It used to be simple. "Drugs" in the bodybuilding and lifting world pretty much meant anabolic steroids and amphetamines—everyone knew that Dianabol was a drug, but Blair's protein wasn't. Today the range of hard drugs available is staggering, but what's also happened is that the simple question of what constitutes true drug use isn't as simple as we might like. I know a powerlifter who gets really irked because so many competitors in one of the major "drug-free" organizations head for cigarettes and beer right after the contest. "Aren't nicotine and alcohol drugs?" he asks. The bigger issue for many will involve the new class of supplements—supplements that edge ever closer to what the world once considered the province of drugs.

Once upon a time food supplements were concentrated food: wheat-germ oil contained "the essence of wheat," protein supplements were built around milk, egg, meat, or soy protein sources, and so forth. Now you can buy, for example, melatonin or DHEA—outright hormones— not from a shadowy figure in a furtive drug deal but from a mainstream supplement company in a chain drugstore in Anytown. Just to make things really slippery, some of those high-tech supplements are on IOC banned-substance lists, even though they're not only readily available but also touted to the general public as being good for your health. Figure out that one.

That's the whole point: you have to figure out a lot of things for yourself. If you're beyond the beginner stage in your training, you have to start to make a series of decisions about what to do next, and many of them will involve confusing choices. Tougher still, if you decide that you're not a lemming and you're not content to blindly follow the dictates of some authority, you will often find that you're either standing alone or you're not one hundred percent sure you're doing the right thing. You will find that there's tremendous social pressure to conform, and you need to know that most people are inclined to follow the herd, no matter what they say to the contrary.

Some of the most shocking research in the history of experimental social psychology delivered convincing evidence that most people blindly obey authority figures, to the point of inflicting pain and injury on innocent people. Not a comforting thought, but one that should alert you to the level of challenge you face.

To make maximum progress, it will help to be a little crazy—but not at the risk of being a fanatic. You'll have to flirt with overtraining, knowing that undertraining is like racing with your parking brake on; you'll have to make your own decisions about what is a drug and what is a food supplement. You'll have to walk a fine line, knowing that the rewards of accepting the challenge are continued progress and a clear conscience.

# 48: Gene Genie

| How to: | Control your environment for world-class gains |
| --- | --- |
| Key ideas: | *Serotonin* – neurotransmitter; low-levels are linked to alcoholism, suicide, depression, etc. |
| | *Expectations* – powerful forces in your life, affecting everything from everyday performance to life and death |

With all the talk about genetic this and genetic that in bodybuilding, you might get the feeling that your future depends almost solely on your gene pool: if you chose your parents wisely, there are big titles in your future, and if not, you might as well crawl into a corner and cry. In fact, this tendency to reduce the world to a series of gene maps isn't limited to a ten-foot radius of the dumbbell rack; genetic explanations are popping up for an ever-increasing range of behaviors and characteristics. Once born, what's a poor body to do?

There's something enticing about genetic explanations: they're very tidy; they relieve the person in question of direct responsibility; they offer the promise of solutions in the form of pills. What could be easier? For example, the neurotransmitter serotonin has been getting a lot of ink lately, and for good reason. Low levels of serotonin appear to be linked to everything from alcoholism to aggression, from overeating to depression to suicide. Powerful stuff, this serotonin. It seems reasonable that people could correct their genetic deficiencies by taking medication to boost their serotonin levels, and that's just what some would suggest.

Things aren't always as simple as they might first appear, because researchers have found that serotonin levels are not just the result of what's inherited—they are also the result of environment. Research has shown that monkeys raised by their peers had low levels of serotonin compared to those raised by their mothers, and the differences began to appear in monkeys as young as two weeks old. Similar patterns have been found in a variety of research programs, all indicating that serotonin levels are most likely the result of environment as well as genetic inheritance.

"So what's that got to do with adding an inch to my arms or 25 pounds to my squat?" you ask. The point is that you might be tempted to attribute all manner of good and ill to genes and just collapse on the couch, letting those genes do their stuff. Far more productive is an approach that says something like, "Genes certainly are powerful, but so is my environment. I can't alter my genes, but my environment is almost completely under my control. If I have some ideas about how I'd like to change myself, I'd better develop a top-notch environmental attack plan."

To control your environment for world-class gains, here are some tips.

First, you need to establish a good working knowledge of bodybuilding and lifting, learning what works and why. If you're just starting off, you probably don't know a Zottman curl from a bent press, and it's easy to believe whoever tells you something first, often, or loudest. If you stick with your training for a while, though, you'll start to understand what works—not just what supports a particular person's pet ideas or commercial interest, but what works for most people most of the time. Read, watch, ask, listen—use everything at your disposal to increase your base of knowledge. And don't think this educational process is just another dull study session with little real payoff, because learning what works will produce dramatic results. There are countless guys walking around who gained 20 pounds of muscle in their first two years of training, but once they learned how to train productively for size, they packed on their next 30 pounds of muscle in six weeks.

Once you've established a sound base of training knowledge, make sure you put it to good use. There are plenty of people who, for example, know that they should be sucking in protein to the tune of at least a gram per pound of body weight a day, but they continue to peck at meals that would leave their 85-pound octogenarian grandmother ravenous. On the other hand, the people who actually eat the way they should produce eye-popping transformations. Similarly, you might know that it's time to quit pounding away at 100 percent maximum efforts in your attempt to boost your bench press, but you keep making the same mistake, week after week, month after month. When you get caught in a bind like that, it's good to step back and pretend that someone else with your exact profile has come to you for training advice. What would you tell this person to do? Be sure to follow your own advice.

Always remember that even though they dwell between your ears, your expectations are a potent force in your environment, and they're under your control. The field of psychology is filled with dramatic examples of how expectations are powerful forces in our lives, affecting everything from classroom performance to whether we live or die. Always remember that you don't leave your expectations in the locker room when you train: if you expect to fail with 300 pounds today, you almost certainly will, and if you expect to succeed, you probably will. What's more, because your expectations are influenced by the people around you, be careful in picking your associates—that applies not only to people you train with, but also to everyone in your life. It's especially important to beware people who sell you short, limiting your expectations and thereby ensuring that you'll do less than you're capable of doing. Remember, if you expect limits on your performance, you usually get what you expect. On the other hand, if you expect big results, that's exactly what you'll net.

While the idea that properly designed training cycles or small enough increases can guarantee steady progress forever belongs in a fairy tale, always remember that your target is above you. That means, in a general sense, no matter what you did today, if you want to improve, you have to do more tomorrow. Most people grasp this principle at a gut level but make the mistake of thinking in terms of dramatic steps forward and seeing progress as a smooth, ascending spiral.

In actuality, huge gains are made one small step at a time, and the road upward has plenty of dips and bends. The point is to keep your motivation for forward progress at high levels. That both sustains your efforts in a down period and gives you the confidence to make dramatic breakthroughs when the opportunity arises. Your motivation is largely under your control, unlike the biochemical pattern you inherited from your parents.

Looking in the mirror might make you wish you had a magic wand for adjusting your genetic inheritance. Instead, take charge of your environment, let it help you work some real magic, and you'll never wish for a gene genie again.

# 49: World-Class Confidence

| How to: | Beef up your confidence in competition |
|---|---|
| **Key ideas:** | ⮚ *Self-confidence* – belief in yourself that you can master the challenges that face you |
| | ⮚ *Optimists* – those who remain hopeful, even if things are looking grim |
| | ⮚ *Pessimists* – those who think something is going to go wrong—and it does |

At the extremes, there are two very different types of people when it comes to competition: for some, competition brings out the best; for others, it's an added pressure that crushes them. For example, there are athletes who set all their personal records in lifting contests and often advance in the final placings because they come through with a clutch lift, frequently one that's heavier than they have ever even attempted before. Then there are lifters who seem to fold in the face of competition and perform well below their capabilities. Let's take a closer look at what separates the two groups and see how you can become a better competitor. You can also apply this same process to all aspects of your life.

One of the key attributes of great competitors is a burning sense of self-confidence. They are "I think I can do this" people, people who, when presented a challenge, assess it and conclude that they can master it. As you would guess, the poor competitors tend to be less well-developed in this area: they're the ones who always hear a little voice whispering, "I'm not sure you can do this," or even worse, "You're going to fail."

If it sounds as if the great competitors are more likely to be optimists and the poor competitors are more likely to be pessimists, that's because it's true, and this difference in psychological orientation leads to profoundly different perceptions and results. Successful competitors remain hopeful that they can master the situation even if things look grim at the moment; they're the guys who might start in the last row of an auto race, but their unswerving belief in their abilities sustains them as they knock off car after car. Unsuccessful competitors, on the other hand, might start from the pole, but somehow they just know that something is going to go wrong, and it does. Great competitors know they will find a way to succeed, and poor competitors know they will find a way to fail. Both turn out to be right.

In case you're trying to sort out where you stand in terms of self-confidence, consider the following questions: Do you tend to be sad, depressed, or lonely? Do you tend to doubt yourself? Do you feel uncomfortable in social situations and find it difficult to meet new people? Do you frequently feel misunderstood? If you would generally answer "yes" to these questions, you're probably pretty low in self-confidence; and if you generally answer "no" to these questions, you're probably pretty high in self-confidence.

Low levels of self-confidence often keep you out of competitive situations in the first place. "Why should I enter?" you say to yourself. "I'll only get beaten." In fact, if you're low in self-confidence, you'll tend to try to avoid all manner of risks—which will be a sure ticket to a boring, unfulfilling life. If you're low on self-confidence and you do get into a competitive situation, you'll probably throw in the towel early on. Objectively speaking, you'll quit way before you really have to, and why not? You "know" that you're incapable of succeeding, so why struggle in vain?

If you have high levels of self-confidence, you will seek out challenges; after all, you expect to succeed. If things go wrong, as they almost certainly will some of the time, you not only don't fold your tent, but you also gird your loins and mount a rally of great intensity. To help you in your battle, there are a number of psychological techniques you can use to your advantage.

Be aware of your thoughts, watching out for negative ones and eliminating them as they pop up. To eliminate the negative thoughts, you might only have to think about them rationally, and they will disappear. For example, if you need a 525-pound deadlift to win the contest and the weight scares you, remind yourself that you've already done 520 and another five pounds won't even be noticeable. If you need a little more power in dealing with negative thoughts, use positive affirmations to build up a positive outlook. Get yourself psyched to the eyeballs by reminding yourself of your past accomplishments, that you achieve your goals, and continue in that manner until you absolutely know you can handle the situation. It will help if, prior to your competition, you spend some time relaxing and visualizing yourself succeeding. As you use this type of mental rehearsal before competition, it will become easier to tap into it just before the heat of battle.

Do you think this is all so much psychobabble, with little relationship to the world of heavy weights? Consider Germany's Marc Huster, a world champion weightlifter, and how he performed at the Atlanta Olympics.

Coming into the competition, Huster was expected to have a ferocious battle for the gold medal with Greece's Pyrros Dimas. Huster missed his opening snatch, a devastating start, managed to make it on his second attempt, and then missed his third attempt. In the meantime, Dimas had not only made three perfect lifts, but he also broke Olympic and world records in the process. Barring a catastrophic mistake by or injury to Dimas, Huster's chances of winning the competition were effectively zero, and in a world that divides the universe into the gold medalists vs. all others, Huster could reasonably have been crushed.

Before coming out for the clean and jerk, however, Huster had a little chat with himself. He told himself that he hadn't done well in the snatch, but that was over and things were going to start anew with the clean and jerk. He reminded himself that this had happened to him at the 1993 World Championships and that he'd rallied for a world record in the clean and jerk. He told himself that his training had been going well. He formed mental images of himself succeeding. And when Huster came out for his first clean and jerk, he was ready for a big fight.

Once again, Dimas was picture perfect and pocketed his second Olympic gold medal, not to mention a million-dollar payday, for his performance. Among other things, Dimas's last lift set a new world record in the clean and jerk. Nothing could top his performance—or could it? Huster, who had made his first two attempts, still had one attempt remaining after Dimas was finished, and when he called for a world record, he rocked the hall in Atlanta. When he made the lift, in grand fashion, it stood as one of the most tremendous comeback efforts you'll ever see in strength sports, because where most others would have crashed and burned, Huster rose to the occasion and soared to new heights.

Not every self-confident person can become a world champion, but every world champion is a self-confident person.

# 50: Private Parts

| **How to:** | Look inward for your training satisfaction and enjoyment |
|---|---|
| **Key idea:** | ❧ *Intuitive–instinctive* – your own sense telling you how to tweak your training for continued progress |

With results like bulging muscles and the strength to move mountains, it's easy to fall into the trap of thinking that lifting weights is an extremely public activity. It is to a point, but to get the most from your training, you have to understand that lifting weights is an intensely personal activity. Let's see how this process works and what the implications are for you in the gym. We'll use the information to develop a game plan to help you stride toward your goals.

Consider Dave Duped, a nice guy who, being smarter than average, decides that it's a good thing to be big and strong. Dave immerses himself in the activity—reading this, eating that, training this way, dressing that way. Things seem to be going pretty well. Dave is definitely making progress, but because he's hitched his wagon to the way other people have told him to act, he goes into a tailspin when he runs into two authorities who disagree, and when his social support system flags, Dave's training slides into neutral. Thus, when he reads one article that tells him he should avoid power cleans like the plague and another that says the power clean is one of the greatest lifts going, Dave is paralyzed, without a clue about what to do next. And when the guys at the gym skip a workout to catch a ball game, Dave heads home to the couch. The problem is that he's made his training too much of a public activity, and by tying his training to things outside himself, he ensures that his progress will suffer.

What's called for here is a little independence from the outside world, a shift in perspective to one that views training as an intensely personal activity.

Taking this approach are all those people who, whether in a crowded gym or alone in their garage, seem lost in their training. It's not as if they don't know a Zottman curl from a Zercher lift, but they're so immersed in what they're doing, they're unaware of what's going on around them. For these people, going to the gym is like going to church. They're in a special place dedicated to a higher purpose, and the experience doesn't just change them, it leaves them better. These people might have their lucky sweats, but they're not worried about dressing to please everyone waiting in line for the pec deck.

Similarly, they are immune to the social pressure that drives their compadres from this week's wonder routine to next week's. In fact, the people who really get plugged into the private approach to training seem to have some type of pipeline to training wisdom because they're the authentic intuitive–instinctive trainees—they develop a sense that tells them how to tweak their training for continued progress. They aren't blindly tied to a rigid training cycle, for example, but know how to bob and weave along the way, holding back when they have to and bursting over the top when the opportunity arises. They're also great innovators when it comes to training; they come up with new exercises, new programs, and new concepts, and as a result, they also end up defining new standards—whether for themselves or the rest of the world.

Instead of looking outward for the reasons they train in the first place, they look inward. Thus, instead of just training to win this contest or to receive that reward, they train because they enjoy the process itself. They train because they enjoy training. Why shouldn't they? For all they put themselves through in lifting weights, they make the process enjoyable. For these people, training represents a series of personal challenges that they meet, which gives them a tremendous opportunity to create a history of success. When they reflect on their training, they know they've been somewhere, and their progress gives them a sense of self-satisfaction they couldn't buy anywhere, at any price. In fact, their training doesn't just make them feel good; it makes them feel terrific.

Ask any reasonably alert person if you can boost performance by rewarding it—with money, for example—and he or she will waste no time in answering, "Of course." The truth, however, is that research psychologists have amply demonstrated that what is generally taken as the iron-clad ability of rewards to boost performance doesn't always describe the way things work. In fact, paying someone to do something he or she previously did for free can lead to decreased performance. Conversely, our best efforts, particularly if creativity is valued, seem to arise in situations where we're intrinsically motivated—the process is internal, and we're fueled by a passion for the activity in and of itself. When the process, not the result, is what's dear, we're not only likely to hit our peak, but we're also likely to enjoy ourselves the most. Maybe there's something to the starving artist concept after all.

The above means that as much as you want to, for example, squat 400 for 10 reps, you should focus on enjoying each workout, taking satisfaction in setting a goal for that day and reaching it. Learn to revel in not just each workout but, ideally, each set you do. Instead of thinking of your workouts as something you have to endure to reach some goal, think of them as something that makes you feel good, something you like doing.

If your training isn't going according to plan, whether you're stuck at a plateau or using any excuse imaginable to miss a workout, analyze whether you've fallen into the trap of giving your private parts a little too much public exposure.

# 51: In Charge of Champions

| How to: | Know if you have what it takes to be a champion |
|---|---|
| Key idea: | *Champion* – one who has the right stuff to produce gold medals: strength, technique, and psychological make-up |

Imagine this: your mission is to produce a stunning array of world champions in the highly competitive arena of Olympic-style weightlifting, and you have at your disposal just about whatever you might want to help reach your goal. For starters, there's no need to limit your athlete pool to a scanty group of scrawny walk-ins who might be better suited to watching slow-pitch softball than trying to lift several times their body weight from the ground to arm's length overhead. You have highly refined scouting tools, and you're not kidding about this evaluation business. You might test 100,000 prospects and identify perhaps 70 as having enough potential to give your program a try. What you end up with is a group of athletes who have the ability to lift weights most of us can barely roll across the floor—think of relatively slender 150-pound guys who can lift more than 350 pounds from the floor to overhead and you'll get the picture.

Make no mistake about it, Xiong Han Yang, the head coach of the Chinese national men's weightlifting team, one of the most fearsome lifting machines on the planet, thinks the first key to producing the champions he wants is to select the right athletes—the ones who have the potential to develop the right stuff to produce gold medals. As he sees it, the right stuff takes the form of three elements: 1) strength—no surprise, since we're talking about the ability to lift big, big weights; 2) technique—the Olympic lifts are highly complex athletic moves that require speed, flexibility, and coordination; and 3) psychological makeup.

Coach Yang says there are three principal psychological qualities necessary to be a champion. First, you have to want to be a champion. "I want to be a champion," you say. Yeah, and you'd also like to drive a Lamborghini. How much do you really want to become a champion—are you willing to walk over hot coals to meet your goal or do you wimp out at the first sign of distress? Becoming a champion requires a level of commitment that most people simply can't muster. Ask yourself some hard questions about how many workouts you've missed in the past year, whether you tend to overtrain or undertrain, what kind of limits you put on your performance, and so forth. Remember, nobody but you will see the answers to these questions, so you might as well be honest and get the benefit of knowing where you stand.

The second important key, Coach Yang says, is to develop the confidence that comes from having a high success rate in training. For example, there are a lot of stories about how few lifts three-time Olympic champion Naim Suleymanoglu missed in a year's training. Even if some of that's exaggeration, you get the point—champions don't practice missing lifts, they practice making lifts. How do you do? If you're missing half a dozen lifts per workout, you need to rethink your training philosophy because all you're doing is undermining your confidence. If you're missing a lot of lifts, it really is reasonable to expect that you'll miss a lot of future lifts. Not exactly the way a champion should think, is it? Once again, there's no use in kidding yourself—if a little self-reflection, coupled with a review of your trusty training diary, reveals too many misses, it's time to do yourself a favor and come back down to weights you can lift. Oddly enough, if you've been missing too many lifts, reducing your training weights might be the single best way to get stronger. Fast.

Finally, Coach Yang looks for lifters who can apply tremendous focus in competition. Think of athletes who, under the pressure of a big contest, can walk up to a weight they've never even tried before and smoke the lift. Think of lifters who succeed when they have their backs against the wall, when they have one do-or-die attempt at a weight, and you'll understand not just what this kind of focus means but also why it's so critical to championship levels of performance. Interestingly enough, in my years of watching the top lifters in the world, one of the most striking characteristics they display is the ability to come through in a clutch—where lesser men fold, the champions charge forward. That's why they're champions. The principle is just as applicable if you've been squatting with 220 pounds and looking forward to the day when you'll be able to handle two 45s on each end of the bar. "That would really be something," you say to yourself. When the time comes, if you've got the right stuff, you'll blow it up like nobody's business.

Most of us wouldn't rate as the janitor in a highly selective lifting program, but that should never deter us from reaping all the riches good, heavy training produces.

It should be very reassuring to know that no matter what your structure, fast-twitch muscle supply, or pattern of muscle insertions, you can think like a champion and become better today than you were yesterday. That's not such a bad deal, is it?

# 52: Grinders

**How to:** Get dramatic gains with big efforts on the basic movements

**Key idea:** ❧ *Grinders* – basic free-weight movements with big poundage on which you grind out more reps than you comfortably can

The Iron Game has a dirty little secret—and it's the real key to most people's progress. It alone will transform a bag of bones or a tub of lard into something approaching an authentic husky. The secret isn't anything illegal, and it isn't linked in some obvious way to your DNA patterns. For all its wondrous benefits, there's no place you can buy more of it. It is, however, equally available to all, and it's just as useful whether you're a lifter or a bodybuilder. In fact, it transfers extremely well to all parts of your life. If you could put it in a bottle, you might think of it as something that enhances good fortune because the results that follow are nearly always positive and often so stunning that you would think the stuff should be banned.

We call the secret "grinders."

To back up a little, it's no secret that the movements that produce the most dramatic gains are the time-honored basic lifts. They're done with free weights, the poundage is substantial, and they're the type of exercises that make your eyeballs pop out with another rep or two or ten. And that's the essence—you grind out more than you comfortably can; you stretch beyond what's easy; you stick doggedly with it way beyond what most people would consider reasonable. Grinders call for having a quit switch that's set somewhere around the red line.

Grinders aren't flashy, they're never fashionable, and most people avoid them like the plague. Sure, they work like nothing else on earth but at a price: you pay for grinders in the currency of hard work. If you want to succeed, you might as well learn about grinders as soon as possible, so you can reap the benefits.

Consider the average person who lifts weights. For starters, he or she probably chooses a gym for all the wrong reasons. Maybe the aerobics class looks good, or all the machines are strictly the latest generation; maybe the color scheme makes it easier to coordinate his or her training clothes. Once in the gym the person picks a training routine that represents the course of least resistance: lots of machine work; most movements done sitting down; training frequency and intensity reduced; multi-joint, basic movements avoided. That's not a good attitude for grinders.

Grinders tend to fit in places that lean toward the primitive. It might be that primitive surroundings inspire brutal efforts, but at the least, your focus is locked on the rep you're struggling to complete, not the color or condition of the vinyl. One of the most famous lifting gyms in the U.S. had holes in the floor and a locker room that was so disgusting, the municipal health department told the owner to redo the whole thing or be shut down. The lifters barely noticed the surroundings, and nothing they saw deterred them from training there. Down the street was a slick gym with a nice this and an even nicer that; the lifters there were strictly local and regional level. The lifters from the first gym frequented the Olympics and the World Championships.

One of the best setups I've ever seen for grinders was in China. World-record holders, world champions, and Olympic champions were more common there than 300-pound bench pressers in any chain gym. How could athletes of that caliber be expected to produce their world-class results in anything less than a world-class environment, right? Consider the facts: for starters, the squat racks were the old-fashioned design that looks something like a pair of barstools. Many were made from wood, none was adjustable, and they were the wrong height for almost everyone. Short lifters had to pile up plates on the platform under the bar so they could reach it. Tall lifters had to stack plates on top of the rack and then balance the barbell on the stack to raise the bar enough to get under it. Some put plates under the legs of the racks to prop up the whole affair. Things were shaky at best, and more than once the bar fell off the racks or lifters nearly ate it going up and down from their improvised step under the bar. Even though the local lifters kept the lifting area neat and tidy, more than once a rat greeted me in the bathroom— not exactly an advertiser's dream. Nonetheless, there was nary a whimper from the lifters.

It's tempting to write that despite all those suboptimal conditions, 700-pound high bar, rock-bottom squats with no belt, no wraps, no spotters were ordinary fare. In truth, because the lifters were unfazed by their surroundings, grinding through their training regardless of what went on around them, they produced elite performances. That gym witnessed some of the hardest training on the face of the earth, and the next year many of those lifters were competing in the Atlanta Olympics.

A grinder is any set that has at least one rep you could easily have failed to make, and a world-class performer consistently gets rep after rep, lift after lift, workout after workout—each step marked by reps that surely might never have been born. Grinders might take the form of a world champion missing a huge weight a few times before making it or a beginner gritting his teeth to make his full set of squats with 200 pounds.

Some movements are better suited to grinders than others. For example, quick lifts, such as snatches or power cleans, are executed with great speed, so you can't really grind through a dubious rep, although you might have to grind through a series of misses before finally hitting a successful snatch with a heavy weight. Isolation movements and just about anything on a machine can be attacked in grinder fashion, and the results will be good—although the leg extension machine is not well suited to grinders because of possible knee injury. Best of all, however, is grinding through the big free-weight movements. None rivals the cornerstone of them all: the squat. In fact, the squat is so well suited to grinders that in classic 20-rep squat programs, the tough guys end up grinding out 20 reps with their usual 10-rep weights—and as anyone who's been lifting weights for a while can tell you, the results of such programs are mind-boggling.

Some people fail on grinders because they try to go too fast too soon, meaning they try to attack a weight that's too big for them. Because you have to be able to lift the weight in order to grind out reps, it's important to start with something within your ability. Always remember that when it comes to grinding, it's the size of the effort, not the size of the weight, that's important. If you do them properly, grinders will reveal their magical properties: little grinders today lead to big grinders tomorrow, and that's the path to progress.

# 53: Take the Blame If You Want to Gain

**How to:** | Take the blame for your failures so you can generate outstanding results
---|---

**Key ideas:** | ⋅ *External focus* – blaming others or outside events for your failures or lack of progress
---|---
| ⋅ *Internal focus* – taking direct responsibility for your own failures and progress

What makes one person succeed, no matter what? Why do some people fold in the face of the slightest opposition? Why do some people make excuses for everything that goes wrong, while others simply go about trying to make things right? What can you do to develop the ability to forge forward, through any and all obstacles that appear in your path?

More times than I can remember, I've watched a world-class lifter, with his back to the wall, pull off a lift that nobody would have believed possible. Maybe the lifter missed his first two attempts and, down to his last shot at staying in the contest, he makes the lift. I've even seen people in this situation ask for an increase and then make a good lift. We're talking big-time contests here: World Championships, the Olympics, and the like. These people know how to dig deep, how to not only keep going in the face of adversity but also go a little harder when things get tough. Consider, for example, Olympic gold medalist in weightlifting Naim Suleymanoglu, who was doing snatches in the training hall at the Atlanta Olympics and before too long had the bar loaded to more than the world record. He missed it. He tried it again and missed it again. He took it a third time and missed it yet again. He took it an unbelievable fourth time and made the weight. A few days later, in one of the highlights of the 1996 Olympics, Naim went lift-for-lift with arch-rival Valerios Leonidas, held him off, and won a historic third gold medal.

Or there was the time in China when a guy named Marin Shikov, at the end of his second tough workout that day of heavy snatches and clean and jerks, worked up to a heavy single in the squat. The single was so heavy that he missed it, and since he wasn't surrounded by an army of spotters or the security of a power rack, he dumped the bar on the lifting platform. Obviously, when you've gone through a tough leg and back workout and miss a limit squat, you call it a day. But nobody told Marin this. He stripped the bar down, power cleaned it, put it back on the racks, reloaded it, tried the squat again, and just as in his first attempt, when he couldn't stand up with the weight, he dumped it. Surely anyone with any sense would know that it was time to call it quits, but once again Marin must have been clueless because he stripped the bar down yet again, power cleaned it, put it in the racks, reloaded it, and *voilá*, ground out a very tough, successful lift.

You might not know Naim Suleymanoglu or Marin Shikov from Salvatore Ferragamo or care a hoot about picking up an Olympic gold medal in weightlifting, but if you're serious about making progress in your training and your life as a whole, developing a bit of their drive can open the door to a lot of really good things. Let's take a look at one aspect of how the way you think and act controls your ability to generate outstanding results.

Once upon a time, if you were walking down a sidewalk, tripped and fell, you would quickly get up, brush yourself off and hope that you were spared the embarrassment of anybody's noticing what had happened. Now, when the same thing happens, a lot of people look around for some-body to sue, someone to blame for their accident. They might try to claim that the sidewalk was poorly maintained, with anthills sprouting up here and there, or that there should have been signs warning pedestrians that walking is a potentially hazardous activity or that, perhaps, the sidewalk contractor was insufficiently schooled in the chemistry of sidewalk composition and the physics of sidewalk design. We've come so far in our attempts to avoid personal responsibility that even if a dead-drunk driver goes several times the speed limit and has an accident that kills everyone in his car who wasn't wearing a seatbelt, there's a massive movement to blame the whole thing on a bunch of guys waving cameras in the distance. Examples in bodybuilding and lifting are no less ludicrous and, more important, no less likely to obscure the path to progress.

For instance, it's amazing how many people blame others for misleading them about everything from training routines to diet—with straight faces they describe in exquisite detail how they were led astray, often for years at a crack, before they saw the light. Or they excuse their lack of progress by noting that they have this or that genetic deficiency that keeps them from becoming world champions—ignoring the fact that five years into training they're still squatting with no more than a couple of plates. And let's not forget the drug line, either—that everyone who out-performs them is on some drug, even though they themselves have not made one iota of progress in the past year, and their own accomplishments would have been insignificant decades before anabolic steroids were ever invented. Excuses like these shift responsibility to external sources, psychologists explain. Let's see how this works, putting the whole thing in the context of helping your lifting move forward.

When we look to external sources for explanations of our failures, it bolsters our self-esteem. This, of course, is a good thing a lot of the time, but it can also lead to some very unproductive behavior. Consider, for example, the lifter who has made virtually no gains since starting to train. If the lifter lays the whole affair at the feet of an unproductive routine he was duped into following, he feels good about himself: After all, he was the innocent victim who was defrauded by a villain. Consider the challenge to his self-esteem if he says instead: 1) "Maybe I didn't do such a good job evaluating the training program in the first place," and 2) "Maybe I didn't really train as hard as I should or could have." This second approach, which gives what psychologists call an internal focus to your failures, is a little rough on your self-esteem, but it also carries a tremendous advantage: it provides the opportunity to do better in the future by taking direct responsibility for your progress. I know a general contractor who has little sympathy for anyone who is swindled on a building project: "It's their fault for not checking references before they started the project." It's a tough one to swallow if you prefer to play the victim's role, but it's hard to fault the logic of his stance: take some responsibility for how things turn out.

The same thing applies in the world of weights. What sort of idiot follows lame advice for week after week, month after month, year after year, and then tries to pin the blame on anyone but himself? When you've been squatting with the same weight for so long that the plates are prac-tically rusted in place on your bar, how can you blame anyone but yourself for your lack of gains?  If you've missed more workouts than you can count in the last year, do you really have to look outside yourself for the causes of your failure?

Foster the belief that your future, for better or worse, lies largely within your control, and cultivate a belief that your ability to mold your destiny comes from your control of what you do right here and now.  And remember that sometimes when things go wrong, if you take the blame, it will only help you gain.

# 54:  Dealing With Disappointments

| How to: | Turn devastating disappointments into shining successes |
|---|---|
| **Key ideas:** | &#10148; *External temporary setbacks* – time to regroup and charge forward again |
| | &#10148; *Permanent internal factors* – time to change course and go with your strengths |

Unless you lead a charmed life, you can be certain that somewhere along the line things are not going to go the way you planned.  It might be in your personal life, your training, your competition, your career—or all four.  Let's take a look at a couple of examples that illustrate two basic strategies for managing events that go sour.

Life in the old Soviet Union wasn't adorned with MTV, malls, and Mercedes—in fact, compared to what we have in the West, life would have seemed harsh.  In the United States a kid might grow up dreaming about going to Stanford law school or starting the next software giant or being a movie star or any of the other endless possibilities.  Dreams in the Soviet Union weren't so varied, but one of the most prevalent, one that was open to just a privileged few, was that of becoming an Olympic gold medalist.

Alty Orazdurdiev was a product of the fabled Soviet sports system.  His talent was identified early in his life, and at an age when an American kid might have been glued to a computer game or lazing in front of a video, Alty was already engaged in the serious business of turning the dream into reality.  The full force of the great Soviet athletic machine was at the disposal of his coaches, and day by day, year by year, it appeared that he was coming closer and closer to realizing the dream.

Things changed one day in a way that nobody could predict, and the mighty Soviet juggernaut was no more.  To ease the transition, the 1992 Olympics saw the appearance of the so-called Unified Team, an amalgamation of team members from all the former Soviet republics competing together one last time.  The name sounded good, but at least in the sport of weightlifting, it was anything but accurate. Rancor and dissension were everywhere, primarily because the athletes felt they were the victims or beneficiaries of the personal and political prejudices of the head coach, Vasily Alexeev. Remember, what we're talking about here was a battle-hardened group of athletes who, by their late teens, had more training and more international experience than many of the world's other top athletes will see in their entire careers. Those guys were used to intense competition because in the old Soviet Union there was so much talent, so much depth in weightlifting, for example, the lifters used to tell us that winning the World Championships was easy—the tough part was getting selected for the team!

The 1992 Olympic team selection process spared the athletes none of that but with the additional twist of an imperial puppeteer who turned the worlds of more than one weightlifter upside down.

Coming into the 1992 Olympic Games, Orazdurdiev was considered a red-hot property in the international weightlifting world: his results at the 1990 World Championships were extremely impressive and, coupled with the lifts he was making shortly before the Games, most experts considered him nearly a shoo-in for a gold medal.

For Orazdurdiev, however, what was to be the dream of his life turned into a nightmare, the horror of which was played out before the weightlifting world in Barcelona. As he prepared to weigh in, head coach Alexeev pulled Orazdurdiev out of the competition on the spot. Instead of Orazdurdiev, a lifter named Ibragim Samadov would be representing the Unified Team. Orazdurdiev burst into tears, absolutely devastated by the move, which was doubly cruel given its timing—the last possible moment for making the change. As it turned out, this was just the beginning of the drama in that weight class: when Samadov ended up in third place, he refused to accept his medal and was disqualified and summarily banned for life.

With the gutsiness you would expect from him, Orazdurdiev bounced back at the 1993 World Weightlifting Championships—he equaled the gold medal total from his class at Barcelona, even though he lifted in the class below!

Change continents now, and let's make up an imaginary guy living in Chicago. The guy's big, really big, and he lifts weights, but he's really attracted to the strongman competitions. What he'd like to do is win the World's Strongest Man competition.

The 6'-3", 340-pound guy can lift all sorts of things the average guy couldn't dream of budging, and his sheer size makes most people believe just about anything he says about his strength. One thing leads to another, and the big guy gets invited to an international strongman contest. The idea is that the contest is a bit of a proving ground, a place where the athletes and those who run the contests can see how everyone stacks up. It's easy to talk about how strong you are, how hard you train, and how you plan to win this contest or that, but the beauty of competition is that it exposes the pretenders—it's the time for walking, not just talking.

When you're the size of our fictional character, it's easy to fall into the trap of overrating your strength because you're almost always the biggest guy in any crowd. That might lull the unwary into a false sense of accomplishment when it comes to their physical power.

When our imaginary Big Guy arrives at the contest, though, he finds out that size-wise, he's just one of the gang. This shakes his confidence momentarily, but taking a deep breath, he continues.

The first event involves lifting a crude barbell overhead, and when the Big Guy can't do the starting weight, the seasoned eyes in the crowd and on the field notice the chink in his armor. The second event brings virtually the same result. As the weekend wears on, this fellow doesn't just finish last in each event, he tends to fail at the earliest possible opportunity. To any who watch him, it's apparent that this just isn't his thing—for all his size, he just doesn't have the strength and other qualities required for success in this arena.

Coming back from Europe, the Big Guy realizes that, hey, he really isn't much better at this strongman stuff than a lot of tougher-than-average 200-pound guys—which is to say, he realizes that he's out of his league. He isn't about to wash his dreams down the drain, however, so he thinks about things. He knows that he really is a lot stronger than most people. He comes to understand that what he really likes is performing, not competing, and that kids in particular seem to like him. He knows from past experience that it's relatively easy for him to get publicity, and most people will believe absolutely anything he says about his strength levels. One year later the Big Guy is a big success doing community strength demonstrations. He even hits the smaller TV talk shows—they love him as he bends bars, pulls cars, and tells kids to listen to their parents and stay off drugs.

Cutting to the chase, both Alty and the Big Guy illustrate two fundamental ways to deal successfully with disappointment. When things don't go your way, stay calm and consider whether the disappointment is the result of temporary external circumstances, as in Alty's case. Once the circumstances change, it's time to regroup and charge forward again, hell bent on success. On the other hand, if the disappointment is the result of permanent internal factors, as in the Big Guy's case, it's time to change your course. Either way, you can turn the most devastating disappointment into a shining success. What could be nicer?

# 55: Inner Vision, Outer Limits

| How to: | Improve your motivation by lifting for yourself |
|---|---|
| **Key ideas:** | ⚬ *Internal orientation* – focusing on the process of the sport: skill development, personal progress, and enjoyment, rather than the end result |
| | ⚬ *External orientation* – focusing on other athletes' performances, and rewards and records, instead of your own effort and execution |

At 6'-2" and 310 pounds of muscle, Bill Kazmaier is one scary-looking dude. He's a genetic marvel who has "trained like a mad dog" for years, and the combination has produced results that speak for themselves. Bill has more muscle on his forearms than the average guy has on his legs, but beyond that, he has performed at unreal levels in the strength world. Bill's been a world champion and a world-record holder in powerlifting, he's won the World's Strongest Man contest three times, and along the way he's excelled in everything from Highland Games events to old-time strongman lifts. Underlining Bill's status, if you plunk him down in the midst of today's top strength athletes, years after he retired from competition, he still draws attention like a magnet. As one guy told me, "Kaz always has been and always will be The Man."

Recently, I asked Bill what he thought was the number-one mistake that people made in their training. After reflecting on the question for a few moments, he said, "Lifting for others." He went on to explain that "people have to lift for themselves, not to impress somebody or to beat someone in the gym or wherever."

Research psychologists who study motivation in sports have found that you can divide athletes along the lines of whether their goals focus on external things like winning or on internal things like mastery. Athletes in the first group will measure their satisfaction in terms of such signs of success as win–loss records, medals, and prize money. Athletes in the second group will measure their satisfaction in terms of such internal things as progress and task mastery. Clearly, the Kaz advises adopting the perspective of the second group, but what does the psychological research have to say?

For starters, the second style—focusing on the process of the sport, rather than the end result— appears to have a strong influence on one's staying power. This is because focusing on the task itself tends to make the sport more enjoyable, and it makes the training itself rewarding, rather than something that has to be endured in order to reach some other goal. The upshot is that athletes with a task orientation tend to have a long-term, often lifelong, relationship with their sport, while those who focus on externals tend to move on to something else as soon as they quit winning. It's been estimated that the attrition rate across sports tends to run at about 90 percent for kids as they go from their early teens to their late teens. If you've been training for a while, you know how people come and go in your gym. Since hard, consistent training is the single most important determinant of your progress, anything that has even the remotest influence on your staying power in the gym should be recognized as a vital training tool. When your psychological perspective has such a major impact on whether you even roll into the gym or not, it shouldn't take a rocket scientist to figure out which orientation will put you on track for the long haul.

The internal focus makes the whole activity much more enjoyable because it focuses on the process of what you're doing—not on the result. Thus, for example, if you were doing high-skill lifts like squat snatches, the internal focus would have you revel in the movement itself, whether you were lifting an empty bar or world-record poundage. An external focus would emphasize how much you were lifting—anything less than the world record would ultimately be seen as not just too little but as a sign of failure. If you were a bodybuilder, an internal perspective would be to take pleasure in each rep as a vehicle for stimulating progress, while an external focus would be to see each rep as a toll that had to be paid if you were going to beat so-and-so at the next contest.

Remember, the internal focus views each workout as rewarding in itself, rather than something that must be endured. That might not sound like much, but imagine the growing power of a technique that makes training something you look forward to, rather than a dreaded means to a desired end. Approach your workouts with this attitude, and cultivate enjoying the process of training.

Coaches, parents, friends, and other significant people can have a powerful influence on whether an athlete adopts an external or an internal orientation. It doesn't have to get as extreme as a parent shouting, "Do you want that Coke contract or not?" vs. "That was a great run, wasn't it?" For example, if mistakes are evaluated harshly and the stars get all the attention, athletes will tend to develop an external focus. Another common element in an external orientation is pitting one athlete against another ("Joe's waiting to take your place if you miss this lift"). If effort and execution are stressed and all athletes are recognized as valuable, then an internal orientation will be encouraged. In this approach, skill development, personal progress and enjoyment of the process are all emphasized.

Finally, don't think that going for the process rather than the prize means you have to have a lackadaisical attitude about your workouts, expecting little from yourself and embracing mediocrity. In fact, you still need to set goals, strive for improvement at each turn, aspire to and revel in setting PRs, and in every other way attempt to constantly outshine yesterday's performances. The difference is that if you miss a record attempt or have a down day—as you most certainly will—it's not the end of your world but just another blip on the radar screen.

The unvarnished truth is that almost nobody has the genetic package of Bill Kazmaier or a star of similar caliber. You might train your guts out and still look like last week's road kill next to Bill, but if you listen to what he says, you realize that you stand on common ground when it comes to the great secret of successful training: the key to hitting your outer limits depends on adopting an inner vision.

# 56: In the Mood for Muscle

| How to: | Use your positive emotions to make your workouts more productive |
|---|---|
| **Key ideas:** | &#42; *Moods* – far more under your control than you might imagine and containing a strong physiological component |
| | &#42; *Stress budget* – whatever you spend on worrying will not be available for building muscle |
| | &#42; *Physiological reactions* – while maybe nearly automatic, you can control the intensity and duration of your emotions |
| | &#42; *Mood-management tools* – techniques for seizing control of and managing your mood |

Good, bad, happy, sad, positive, negative—the range of moods is almost endless. Is one mood best for building muscle?

"Of course not," you say. "Muscle isn't a mental thing. Muscle is about as real as it gets, and moods are some fuzzy idea psychologists dreamed up."

Moods, in fact, influence muscles. More to the point, your moods will be a major determinant of how much muscle you build, how fast you build it, and whether you like the process or not. Add to this the fact that your moods are far more under your control than you would probably imagine, and you have a powerful training tool. Let's lay out the program.

For starters, your mood influences whether you even make it into the gym. For example, if you're feeling sluggish, you'll probably be "too tired" to train, or if you're feeling discouraged, you'll probably feel that training isn't likely to be productive anyway, so why bother trying? If, however, you're brimming with enthusiasm, you'll probably have energy to burn and a sense of being able to accomplish pretty much whatever you like. If you want proof of that process, think about a time when, out of the blue, you got some great news and your overall enthusiasm and energy levels soared as a result. On the other hand, you know what a damper bad news can be—it just takes the wind out of your sails.

Your moods have a strong physiological component. These events that you think of as existing only between your ears are tied to myriad biochemical processes in your body. You know the line about how stress kills? That means a host of internal changes are triggered by a reaction to stress. Those physiological processes are most closely tied to negative emotions such as anger and anxiety.

Training in and of itself is a stress, and, in fact, it has to be if you're going to gain in size and strength. Too much stress, especially unproductive stress, however, triggers all the negative emotions, which will only impede your training progress because they squander resources that you could use for muscle-building purposes.

Think of yourself as having a stress budget: whatever you spend on worrying will not be available for building muscle. On the other side of the equation, certain positive emotions can not only help you get to the gym and give each workout your best shot, but they can also help you recover from your training. That's why some of the fabled Eastern European training systems specifically cultivate a tranquil, relaxed state of mind as a restorative post-training tool. In other words, if you focus on being calm and relaxed after your training, it will help you recover. Is that a deal or what? Relaxing and feeling good will help you grow.

While some researchers might argue that the physiological reactions are nearly automatic, we can learn to control such things as the intensity and duration of our emotional reactions. The process begins by understanding that we do not have to be slaves to our emotions. Put two people on a freeway, for instance, and have them both get cut off by another driver, and while one explodes with a string of vile epithets, the other might calmly say, "I guess he didn't see me." The first driver goes over the edge emotionally while the second keeps his reserves for a more productive purpose. Try to moderate your reactions to unexpected situations, realizing that 1) you can influence your response, 2) you'll benefit from staying in charge emotionally, and 3) giving in to the full force of your moods is a childish indulgence.

Interestingly, researchers have found evidence that we begin to learn some of our most basic lessons about emotional management when we're mere infants, and one of the striking findings is that even when we're only a few months old, we can catch the emotions of the people around us. Infants can become more passive, depressed, and a variety of other negative things as a result of being around mothers who are so inclined themselves. The flip side of this finding is the suggestion that we can, similarly, learn to seize control of and manage our moods.

First, remember that you're in charge, so if you're tempted to just blow up, give up, or in some other way throw in the emotional towel, remind yourself that you're in control. Talk to yourself and come to grips with the upsetting event in a level-headed manner. If you don't succeed immediately, try again.

Second, use some specific mood-management tools in your training. For example, if you tend to have trouble with the idea of going through your whole workout, coax yourself into the gym by saying that you're only going to do the first part. Similarly, try to structure your workout to best complement your emotional makeup. Some people like to build up momentum by doing all their favorite exercises first and then hitting the dreaded-but-effective ones. Other people prosper by getting the tough stuff out of the way first, and then they glide through the remainder. Don't be afraid to experiment and see what works best for you.

Third, remember that good old behavioral psychology principles apply here: act angry and you'll feel angry. Act calm and you'll feel calm. This is the reason that even though it sounds dopey to tell people to try smiling if they want to feel better, it really works. Talk about a free and easy mood elevator.

Fourth, bad-hair days will come around, but don't let them ruin things for you. When you're not on track for a peak performance, rather than caving in and quitting, cut the weights, shorten your routine, or follow some other plan that allows you to train productively. Doing a new personal best each day isn't realistic, but doing the best you're capable of that day is.

Fifth, remember that your moods are contagious, so if you want to be bummed out or unproductive, hang out with negative people. On the other hand, if you want to get some place, spend your time with a positive, productive crowd—you'll be swept forward on the wave of collective optimism.

Enthusiasm, optimism, purpose, determination, focus, control—the moods for muscle are many. Put them to use for yourself.

# 57: The Right Things

| How to: | Figure out what's really critical to your success |
| --- | --- |
| Key ideas: | ❧ *Engineering human competence* – helping make people good at what they are doing<br>❧ *Accomplishment* – doing the right things right to make progress and perform well |

At first glance, it would seem that the guy was doing everything right: he almost never missed a workout, his routines were taken straight from some star, and he could talk weights until the cows came home. Even his clothes and his general style in and out of the gym suggested that he was committed to his training and knew his stuff. There was a problem, however, and it was a big one: he hadn't made a lick of progress in around a year.

In the same gym there was another guy whose appearance, not to mention his training program and the way he did some of his movements, indicated that he not only didn't know the finer points of the game but probably didn't even know there were finer points and might not have cared about learning them if he did know they existed. On the other hand, he did have something going for him. Almost every week, it seemed, he made progress, and every few months he seemed to have transformed himself because the cumulative gains made him nothing like the guy he'd been before.

To a casual observer the situation might be attributed to genetics, secret sauce, or any number of explanations. To a student of human performance, however, the answers lay elsewhere because, as Thomas Gilbert learned, it's not what you do that's important. It's what you accomplish.

Gilbert's passion was human competence and, specifically, engineering it. He was devoted to helping make people good at what they were doing. Whether it was putting together widgets, whacking a baseball, or making what would seem to be abstract decisions, Gilbert knew that some people were good at what they did and some weren't. Fortunately for most of us, he didn't stop there. He developed a variety of analyses and techniques to help make underperformers more like the superstars in their fields.

One of the first things Gilbert figured out was that when we analyze people who are doing their thing—whatever it is—we usually make the mistake of focusing on just that: what they're doing, as opposed to what they accomplish.

Suppose we had a system for evaluating a variety of performance measures related to training. For instance, we might see how much someone knew about basic training principles: whether the person knew an amino acid from lactic acid; knew Mr. Olympia from an Olympic gold medalist; and so forth. As you're a reasonable person, this approach probably makes sense to you, and you can think of all sorts of ways to evaluate how much people know about training and how well they go about conducting their own. That approach, as Gilbert figured out, is all wrong.

If we applied the approach to our two fictional trainees, the first guy would do really well on the tests we developed and the second guy wouldn't. For example, the first guy can wax eloquent on everything from spider curls to squat snatches, talk protein synthesis like a college professor, and rattle off every Mr. Olympia in history—in order. The second guy knows how to do some basic stuff in the gym, has a clue about guys like Yates, Coan, and Suleymanoglu, but that's about it. If they got into a conversation about training, the first guy could make the second guy's eyes go glassy in less than a minute.

Beyond that, a knowing eye watching both in the gym would see that the first guy seemed to have a handle on what he was doing because he was doing lots of little things correctly—things that might be nuances the second guy had never even heard of. In fact, watching the second guy in the gym, it would be reasonable to conclude that he was still pretty rough around the edges.

These differences would seem perfectly reasonable and understandable if the first guy was the one making progress and the second was the one who was stalled out, but that's the opposite of the way things are. Why?

Gilbert would explain that we were misled because while the first guy was doing most things right, maybe even as many—possibly even more—than the second guy, he wasn't doing the right things right. The person who does the right things right makes progress, and the person making progress is the one we want to emulate.

Take a power clean. The first guy might be able to rattle off all the benefits of the movement. He can tell you the theory of the movement, with intricate biomechanical analyses. He can blab for longer than you'd like about who has done what in the movement. If you watched him train, though, you'd see there must be something wrong because, despite his apparently complete understanding of the lift, he can't handle his body weight to save his life, and worse, his top set has been the same for the past 11 months.

The second guy, on the other hand, can't come close to the first guy in any conversation about the power clean. When it comes to doing the movement, he certainly seems to grasp the basics, but he isn't even sophisticated enough to know about, let alone use things like a hook grip or a dynamic start, things the first guy does automatically. If you asked the second guy to describe what he was doing, he might say it was kind of like doing a vertical jump, only while hanging onto a barbell. His understanding might not impress you until you realized that he was mauling his body weight in the movement a year ago and now does 150 percent of his body weight. To add insult to injury, the second guy has gained 25 pounds of body weight in the past year, while the first guy has gained three-fourths of a pound, he thinks. Clearly, the second guy is the one to copy.

The moral of this story, per Gilbert's advice, is to remember that it's accomplishment, not behavior that counts. That's the reason two guys can be on the same squat program, and while one outgrows his clothes in less than two months, the second one doesn't gain a whisper. The first one might do 95 percent of the things right, but when it comes down to the last few critical things, the two part ways.

Don't worry that this sort of analysis is too complicated for you to apply to your own training— and your life in general—because it usually doesn't take a Ph.D. to see who's making progress and who isn't. The key is to always remember that most people might do most things right most of the time, but that's the road to mediocrity. The superstars, in all activities, figure out what's really critical to success, and that's where they shine. When it comes to the superstars and their performances, it's as if someone told them the secret: it's not how much you do right, it's whether you do the right things right.

# 58: It's Only Baloney

| How to: | Avoid selling yourself short or limiting your vision |
|---|---|
| **Key idea:** | ❧ *"I'm only . . ."* – excuse for aiming low in the challenges you face |

The doctor came out of the delivery room and told the man that he could save either the mother or the child but probably not both. As good fortune would have it, both lived, but the baby's arm was broken during the delivery, and in such a way that all the nerves in his left shoulder were shattered.

Despite a surgeon's best efforts to reconnect the nerves, the boy would face life with one arm that was a caricature of the other. His left arm was four inches shorter than his right. And even though he spent his first six years with his left arm in a heavy steel and leather brace and his first thirteen years in twice-weekly physical therapy sessions, his left arm was virtually useless. He would never be able to raise it over his shoulder or even straighten it out; he would never be able to clench or extend the fingers. In fact, learning to tie his shoes was one of the biggest challenges of his life.

But this kid was no whiner, so instead of cowering in a corner, he squared off with his challenges. For every insult he had to endure, he just got tougher as he fought back. When he was 14, he said, "I discovered that $42 was all I needed to erase the hated image of myself that faced me every night from the mirror . . . My left arm hung crooked by my side, practically without muscle." Forty-two dollars, you see, was the price of a barbell set he'd seen advertised in a magazine. Since his family could barely afford the dollar for each of his therapy sessions, he knew it was out of the question to ask for $42. What did he do? He saved the 10 cents he'd been spending on bus fare from the hospital twice a week, first by walking and then running the five miles. That, he said, marked the beginning of his athletic career.

He got the weights and put them to good use. It wasn't too long afterward that he began playing high school football, earning his eligibility by wearing a baggy sweater and keeping his arms behind his back so the physician wouldn't notice his gimpy left arm. He won a starting spot by always trying to hit harder and be tougher than any other kid on the team. The kid with the withered left arm was moving on up, and you might guess that he went on to a nice job in a local car dealership, married his high school sweetheart, and lived happily ever after, with his high school football letter proudly displayed in the family room of his suburban home.

That wouldn't be a half-bad story, but the real one is even better. The kid gave the track team a shot, and one day he threw the hammer. Even if you've never seen the hammer thrown, you might guess that it's a two-handed event, which it is. As with the shot put, the best in the world are among the most powerful athletes on the face of the earth. If the kid had been a cry-baby, if he'd said to himself, "I'm only a cripple," he'd have never made it this far, but he wasn't one to let his vision be limited by piles of "I'm only . . ." baloney. He stuck with the hammer, attacking the event with his characteristic ferocity.

Fast forward a few years to Melbourne, Australia, and the medal ceremonies at the 1956 Olympics. The reporters were yelling at the winner to raise his arms over his head for their vic-tory photos. The man raised his right arm, but even to that day—the day he climbed to the highest level in his sport—he couldn't raise his left arm above his shoulder. Harold Connolly may not have been born with two good arms, but that didn't keep him from winning the gold medal in the hammer throw. It didn't keep him from making the next three Olympic teams, either. If he had succumbed to the "I'm only . . ." baloney, he'd probably have been a bitter man hiding in some dark corner. Instead, there he was, standing with an Olympic gold medal around his neck and the world at his feet.

The "I'm only . . ." baloney has a long history. It's been both proffered as a reason for not taking on challenges and, conversely, rejected as so much drivel. For example, in the Old Testament, when Jeremiah was told that he'd been appointed as a prophet, he tried to wiggle out of his mission by saying, "I'm only a boy," which netted him the rebuke, "Do not say, 'I am only a boy.'" Jeremiah got the message and went on to work.

Every day we face challenges in many forms, not the least of which is how to tackle our training. Do we aim high or low? Do we sell ourselves short and excuse our crummy performances because we're "only 14," "only genetically average" or "only another middle-aged guy?" Do we use the "I'm only . . ." perspective to look for little from ourselves and then settle for even less? That's the easy way out, but it's also the formula for mediocrity. Face up to the fact that to do what it takes to move forward requires serious effort. That's why there are so many armchair experts and so few doers. If you insist on saying, "I'm only . . .," be honest and finish with something like "lazy," when it comes to training hard, or "scared," when it comes to lifting bigger and bigger weights, or "uncommitted," when it comes to making it to all of your workouts. Face up to the real reasons you might not be making the kind of training progress you'd like and then do some-thing about it, instead of hiding behind all those "I'm only . . ." lines. That's the attitude that paves the road to progress.

You might not be Harold Connolly or Jeremiah, but their examples teach us a lesson: Don't sell yourself short; don't ever limit your vision of what you can do; don't ever say, "I'm only . . ." because that's nothing but baloney.

# 59: Innovation in Iron

| How to: | Be creative to make your training more productive |
|---|---|
| **Key idea:** | *Creativity* – uses an uncommon approach and offers a suitable solution to a problem |

One of the great myths in training, and in many other human endeavors, is that progress is made inch by inch, ounce by ounce; this implies that if you're on the right track, you can be assured of holding a steady course to your goal. It's an enticing idea. Unfortunately, all the evidence indicates that the concept is little more than a fairy tale. In reality, progress in the weight room, just as in other activities, tends to come—when it comes—in leaps and bounds, and the path upward has more dips, twists, and level spots than most people would ever believe.

That might leave the impression that progress is less under our control than we would like. Don't worry. This realization can point us toward more productive ways to search for the keys to progress, even if they tend to be off the beaten path. For example, one of the most fruitful ways to boost your gains is also one that's very rarely mentioned: be creative in your training.

Back in the infancy of modern weight training, the prevailing view was that the best way to make great gains was to do tons of different movements, many of which, as you'd guess, involved fairly small muscle groups. Along came a guy named Mark Berry, who said something like, "Nope. That's not how it works, boys and girls. Concentrate on just a few movements involving major muscle groups, and the results will blow you away." Berry was considered a bit of a birdbrain because of that screwy notion, but when he made a convert in a small Midwestern town, the weight world was turned on its ear. Berry's follower was a fellow named J. C. Hise, and he reported that by following Berry's suggestions, he managed to gain 29 pounds in a month. That was back in the 1930s, when most people training with weights were happy to gain a few pounds in a year, so you can appreciate the revolutionary impact of Berry's innovative training concepts.

Hise, by the way, was no creative slouch himself, and among his many enduring contributions to training is the cambered squat bar—a bar that is slightly curved in the middle. It sat on the shoulders much more comfortably and securely than a regular straight bar, allowing one to squat that much harder and make that much more progress. How'd Hise get the idea? The story is that his brother bent Hise's lifting bar while working on his car. The rest, as they say, is history. Hise's invention, by the way, is a perfect example of the widely accepted definition of creativity: it's an unusual, appropriate response. In other words, creativity uses an uncommon approach, and it has value because it offers a suitable solution to a problem.

Arthur Jones came along in an era when the pendulum had swung over to the side of doing a nearly infinite number of sets, and free weights were the dominant tool in any gym. Before Arthur Jones, a state-of-the-art gym might have a lat machine, a leg extension–leg curl machine, a hack squat machine, a Smith machine, and something for doing standing calf raises. Most gyms would have a lat machine and maybe a leg extension–leg curl machine. By 25 A. J. (after Jones), the weight world was so vastly altered that gyms were defined by their machines—machines for every conceivable purpose. Free weights, where it all started, became the exception in many clubs.

Similarly, for decades and decades it was accepted and practiced as a nearly sacred concept that you lifted weights three days a week—Monday, Wednesday and Friday. Along the way there were side trips to split routines of different types, but the basic rule of thumb remained the same— three training days a week, each followed by a rest day, with two days off at the end of the week. Then the Bulgarian weightlifting coaches said something like, "Hey, coal miners work hard every day, and so do all the other laborers in the world. Why do these pantywaist weightlifters think they need so much rest?" You've probably heard the stories about how the Bulgarians train six days a week, with multiple training sessions each day, as a result of that analysis. The first time I heard about how they trained, I was so stunned by their dramatically different approach that for days, if not weeks and months, I went around muttering, "It must be a mistake. They can't really be doing that." But they were, and in the process they produced athletes who blew up world record after world record.

The moral of the story is that creativity and innovation aren't limited to the world of art. They're just as applicable in the world of science and the world of weights—and the rewards can be incredibly rich.

"So, that's easy," you say. "I'll just cruise along the creative side of the street from now on and plan on getting bigger and stronger than ever."

That's certainly the right idea, but it's not as simple as it sounds. First, most people aren't very creative. That's one of the reasons innovation is so rare and so special. Second, it's one thing to say you want to follow the creative path, but it's quite another, and much tougher, to actually do it. Most of us need a tremendous amount of social reinforcement and, conversely, have little reserve for dealing with skepticism and criticism—especially when we're doing something that's different from what 99 percent of the population is doing. That tends to undermine a lot of efforts to follow a creative path.

The good news is that research has demonstrated that great intelligence and great creativity don't have the high correlation most people assume. In other words, some really creative people are sharper than tacks, while others are dumber than doornails. To be sure, one of the most cre-ative trainers I know gives the impression of having a room temperature I.Q., but his ability to generate creative training concepts would obliterate a room filled with blue-ribbon sports scien-tists. More good news comes in the form of research indicating that creativity can be fostered environmentally—in other words, if you're given opportunities to be creative and are reinforced for your efforts, you're likely to have your creativity enhanced.

Creativity and innovation are at the heart of each of the big steps forward in building size and strength. New ideas, usually considered revolutionary at the time, lead to major breakthroughs, producing results nobody ever thought possible before. Put that idea to work in your own train-ing: follow the herd for mediocre results, but be willing to strike out on your own if you want something really special.

# 60: Histrionics Don't Help

| | |
|---|---|
| **How to:** | Save your energy for lifting big weights |
| **Key idea:** | ✪ *Yerkes–Dodson Law* – up to a certain point, increasing arousal improves performance, after which continued arousal produces an increasingly diminished performance |

Some years ago I trained in a gym that had a front room for the bodybuilders—big, carpeted, filled with machines and mirrors; a side room for the aerobics classes—spacious, light and airy; and a back room for the weightlifters—small, dank, and stuffed with three lifting platforms. The front room was all spit and polish, and the gym owner was always doing one of two things: vacuuming the rug or polishing the mirrors. Occasionally he did a third thing: cursing whoever had sneaked in the chalk and sullied his janitorial jewel. By contrast, the back room was unkempt and always smelled of Tiger Balm or dirty socks, and if you'd forgotten your T-shirt or sweats, you could probably find something on the floor that would fit. As you might guess, people often dressed up to use either the front room or the side room, but dressing down would have been more appropriate for the back room.

For the most part, the regulars got along whether they were in the bodybuilding, weightlifting, or aerobics segment. It was just accepted that each group had its own goals and its own way of doing things. The weightlifters were only interested in how much they could lift—their domain was moving big weights, and some of them were pretty good at it, with more than one having represented the United States on world championship or Olympic teams. One day when they were minding their own business—wearing torn-up, smelly clothes, getting chalk every place, dropping heavy weights from arm's length overhead, etc.—they heard the most agonizing sounds imaginable issuing from the bodybuilding room. It sounded as if some brave soul were enduring torture during the Inquisition. The lifters piled out of the back room to see what Herculean labor was taking place in the land of chrome.

What greeted them was not a primitive—like themselves—bouncing around armloads of big plates on each end of the bar. Instead, they saw a handsome young man doing flyes with a pair of 15-pound dumbbells. On each rep he made sounds that suggested imminent death. The lifters went back to their 400-pound clean and jerks without uttering a peep, even though there was some feeling that the kids in the child care center probably could have out-repped the young bodybuilder.

Such histrionics in the weight room aren't limited to situations like that one. Undoubtedly, the biggest group of actors these days comes not from the bodybuilding end of the spectrum but from guys who see themselves as lifters. That group spends so much time and energy talking about how hard they train, you wonder how they ever have any time and energy left to actually lift anything. They don't just talk the talk; they drop to the ground, gasp for air and give the groan of death with the best of them. Have them do a few reps on a machine, and they'll give you a display of physical agony you're unlikely ever to see in such truly punishing events as, for example, the Tour de France, the Ironman Triathalon, or the Olympic marathon. In fact, this group has such capable actors, you'd think the WWF would be able to find more than one future superstar within its ranks.

"So, what's the big deal?" you ask. "Doesn't that just get them psyched up for a better performance? Isn't that why all those powerlifters bang their heads on the bar before they squat or have their coaches give them a smack in the chops before they come out for a lift?" It's true that grimacing, grunting, and groaning, even as they're tying their shoes, can be considered a freedom of expression thing—much like the color they wear. As for improving their performance, you're dead wrong. In fact, in most cases all those shenanigans will only take the edge off their efforts and are essentially energy leaks.

The idea of the Yerkes-Dodson Law is that up to a certain point, increasing arousal improves performance. At that point, however, continuing to increase arousal produces an increasingly diminished performance. The law also tells us that optimal arousal levels are lower for more complex tasks than for simpler ones. Basically, there are a lot of times when fueling the emotional fires makes for a less than blazing performance.

How do you feel after a stressful day, even if you were glued to a chair the whole time? Tired, right? That's because jacking up your emotional system isn't just a psychological process; it has correlating physiological effects such as an increased heart rate, sweaty palms, and so forth. The net effect of stepping up your emotional output is that it places demands on your body— keep it up for a while, and you'll be tired, whether you actually do anything or just continue getting psyched up.

That last principle explains the reason top performers, as opposed to the actors, know exactly when to hit the emotional accelerator. They know that hitting it too soon is a waste and will only diminish their performance. Correctly timed, however, hitting the gas will help them shoot forward in a very big way. Research has demonstrated that top performers seem to have this ability to know when to fire up their emotional systems while those with lower performances seem to get over-aroused at all the wrong times.

At the 1996 Olympics there was a weightlifter who had gotten plenty of pre-competition ink, and what he said was less than modest. When he came out to lift, he was already rocking and rolling: he stirred up the crowd, he hit some poses for them, he exhorted himself to lift the world. Instead of producing the phenomenal performance the naive might have expected, he didn't even lift as much as some guys who were half his weight. There was another guy who, having already locked up the gold medal, came out for a world-record attempt and was greeted by a tremendous surge of support. The lifter indicated with his hands that he would like the crowd to please hold it down.

Lest you think the second lifter was half asleep, close observers could see that when he started to pull on the barbell, he tripped some internal switch, and after everything was done exploding, he was standing up with the bar overhead and the record in his pocket.

Don't be fooled into thinking that big groans lead to big gains or that the game is to see who can mouth off the most about how hard he works or how much he suffers in training. Save your energy for actually moving some iron, and your results will speak, if not shout, for themselves.

# 61: Understand Overload

| How to: | Manage the overload principle for greater gains |
|---|---|
| Key idea: | ✎ *Overload principle* – to make progress, you have to do more than you're used to |

You may well know this story, but even so, it's worth repeating. Once upon a time in ancient Greece there was a fellow named Milo who began carrying a calf on his shoulders. Each day the calf grew, increasing Milo's burden. The result was that Milo ended up developing such tremendous strength that, among other things, he became a six-time Olympic wrestling champion. Years later it would be recognized that Milo's training program embodied the principles of overload and progressive resistance that lie at the heart of systematic weight training for increased size and strength.

In the late 20th century most people would say that overload has become a fact of life, even if you don't lift weights. Overload is a two-edged sword: it can cut you to ribbons, leaving you bloodied and beaten, just as easily as it can carve a path to your goals. Because of that, we need to come to grips with the overload principle, with the goal of learning how to manage it.

In its most basic form the overload principle means that to make progress, you have to do more than you're used to. That's a polite way of saying that gaining requires effort. Don't stop there, however, or you'll give up before you get started or just end up pounding your head against a wall.

If you ask the average person if he likes to struggle and strain while lifting heavy weight, he'll look at you as if you were an idiot. "What kind of fool do you take me for?" he might ask. If you need further proof that most people, being reasonable, actively avoid lifting heavy things, see how many takers you get the next time you have to move or just have to get your sofa bed from the downstairs living room to an upstairs den. On the other hand, people who lift weights actively seek out heavy objects—or at least they should. The bottom line is that unless you can actually enjoy your training at some level, you should consider spending your time elsewhere.

The second point is that just because something is harder, doesn't automatically make it more productive. There are plenty of things that can make your training more painful but won't do much to encourage your progress. For example, I once heard of a guy who used to dip his hands in oil before he deadlifted "because it made it harder." Sure, it made it harder, but was it more productive? If you whacked yourself on the head with a ball peen hammer a few times right before you trained, your workout would be harder and, in all likelihood, less productive. Learn to separate harder from better.

You also need to avoid the trap of feeling overwhelmed. For example, if you already lead a hectic life and are trying to add a demanding training program, the effort might seem more than you can handle. As a result you throw in the towel and don't train. That might be acceptable for some people, but it doesn't work for you because a little voice keeps whispering that you should be training, that it would be so nice to get bigger and stronger, etc. The result of wanting the benefits of training but not actually training is frustration. In that case you need to figure out how to make training a regular part of your life.

A proven strategy for getting into the gym is to choose a time that works best, acknowledging that it isn't perfect. That done, you always give training top priority in that time slot, to the point where you automatically say, "Sorry, but I'm lifting weights then." As simple as the approach sounds, it's remarkably effective, and it has the added advantage of developing into a positive habit—the longer you do it, the easier it is to keep doing it.

"Okay," you say, "that's manageable, but how about this business of always doing more? I'm not trying to be a wimp, but you can't really expect me to just keep lifting more and more." That's a valid concern because the direction that you should do more than you're used to doesn't simply mean that you just keep slapping a couple of more plates on the bar and somehow grinding out the same number of reps you used to do with less weight. It will work some of the time, under certain conditions, but it's not a universal solution. In fact, one of the most common and misguided pieces of advice along those lines is the notion that if you make the plates small enough, you can keep making straight-line progress forever. If you believe that, I've got a great deal for you on the Golden Gate Bridge.

Fortunately, there are alternatives, such as increasing the volume or the velocity of your training, or changing the exercises you do or their order. Variety not only keeps you fresh mentally, but it also poses new challenges physically. The best part is that novelty can trigger progress in ways that are a lot less painful than packing more weight on the bar, and it offers infinitely more options.

Overload doesn't have to be a dirty word, and it doesn't have to be something you try to avoid. Accept it as a key to making continued progress, learn to manage it, and you won't just make great gains—you'll have a good time doing it.

# 62:  From Iron to Gold

| **How to:** | Build your sense of accomplishment while building your strength |
|---|---|
| **Key ideas:** | &bull; *Self-efficacy* – the belief that you can do something, your sense of competence |
| | &bull; *Cognitive events* – things that take place in your brain |
| | &bull; *Effective performance* – accomplishing things, meeting goals, mastering situations |

Everyone knows the story about the 97-pound weakling who, after getting sand kicked in his face, buys a set of weights, transforms himself into a muscleman, and lives happily ever after. It's a nice tale, but as you might guess, it's only half the story.

The physical transformations that result from solid weight training are nothing short of remarkable: sunken chests begin to swell, shoulders thicken, arms and legs start to bulge through your clothes, and weights that once seemed daunting become warm-ups.  That's only the beginning. The psychological changes are even more dramatic.  You also stand up straighter, with your feet more firmly planted on the ground, and you look the world straight in the eye.

At the heart of this magical regeneration lies a solid training program.  Most of the really productive programs rely on the so-called basic movements, along with sound nutrition and adequate rest.  Although it's sometimes glossed over, the key to making progress on the training side is to keep increasing your load.  In the simplest form, that means your training weights must keep going up, and as many trainees know, one way to help make that happen is by setting goals.  Those two elements—setting and achieving goals—may not sound like much; however, they not only drive your progress on the physical side, but they also fuel your psychological transformation.

A little more than two decades ago, Stanford University psychology professor Albert Bandura published a paper on what he called "self-efficacy" and suggested that it was at the root of behavioral change.  Self-efficacy is something like a belief that you can do something, and Professor Bandura, a mighty figure in academic psychology circles, explained that whatever its exact form, psychotherapy works by altering one's level of self-efficacy.  In other words, there were myriad psychological treatments that had, as a common mechanism, the ability to influence a person's belief that he or she could do something.

"What's this got to do with lifting weights?" you ask.  It turns out that building your biceps and pushing up your squat poundage give you the opportunity to cash in on this vital mechanism, meaning that you'll not only get bigger and stronger, but your whole life will change for the better as well.

Even though Professor Bandura was focusing on cognitive events—things that take place between your ears—he pointed out that effective performance was the best way to influence this sense of self-efficacy. Simply put, accomplishing things, meeting goals, and mastering situations pave the royal highway to a Herculean mind-set. Michael Aleksiuk recently wrote a book called *Power Therapy*, in which he explained that we increase our sense of competence when we achieve goals that are meaningful to us. The value of this boost is that we become empowered, or gain increased ability to act in ways that improve the quality of our lives.

Coming back to the weight room, the archetypal program for transforming pencil-necks into musclemen is the 20-rep-squat program. Those who successfully follow it have clearly defined goals, which they kill themselves to achieve. Although it's nothing short of a baptism by fire, it's possible for all who are sufficiently motivated. The payback is that they not only remake their bodies in a month or two, but they also acquire a lifelong sense that they can accomplish some pretty tough things. That's what puts some added spring in their stride; that's what self-efficacy is all about. And because it's portable, permanent, and legal, it borders on the magical.

Years ago, *IRONMAN* founder Peary Rader regularly extolled the benefits of the classic 20-rep-squat program. One of the points he made was that besides adding some serious beef to countless bodies, the program seemed to have the ability to change people from hard gainers to easy gainers. In other words, people who previously lifted weights with nary a tangible result could now make good gains on a variety of programs. That suggests some pretty powerful stuff going on, and Peary explained it in terms of bodily transformations that seemed to be permanent.

It's an especially interesting idea in light of the psychological concept of self-efficacy. In fact, some of us would say it's the psychological conversion that really blazes the trail here. In other words, many people who have trouble gaining are hindered by their own negative, self-limiting thinking: "I can't do that because I'm a hardgainer." This leaden mantle melts away in the fires of hard-won accomplishments, freeing the person to raise his or her sights, which in turn lead to greater progress. Stated that way, it might not sound impressive, but what we're really talking about is the "open sesame" to size, strength, and success in life in general.

When you lift weights according to the tried and true formula of setting goals and achieving them, you reap amazing benefits, not the least of which is building yourself into the embodiment of muscle and power. And as dramatic as those benefits are, you also end up with a set of psychological benefits that can take you just about anyplace you'd like to go.

# 63: Blowing by Bad Workouts

| | |
|---|---|
| **How to:** | Take a bad workout in stride—and make something of it |
| **Key ideas:** | ❧ *Permanence* – degree to which an event is something that always happens or something that happens from time to time |
| | ❧ *Pervasiveness* – degree to which you regard your situation as something specific or something general |
| | ❧ *Personalization* – whether you explain events by using internal or external explanations |

How many times has this happened to you: you're all ready to have a terrific workout and what you get is a bust. Perhaps you came in raring to go because your last training session made you think that you were on your way to becoming a living legend. Perhaps nothing dramatic was happening lately, but at least you seemed to be solidly plodding along toward your goals. Or perhaps you had a rough time the last several times you hit the gym, and despite your best intentions, this latest workout, just like its predecessors, was a flat tire.

What you do next is crucial not only to your immediate progress, but also to how much progress you will ultimately make in the sport. In fact, the way you handle this situation may be representative of the way you handle potentially discouraging situations in life. There really are just two fundamental reactions: you can keep going, or you can quit. Let's see what determines which way you go and lay out a strategy for blowing by bad workouts.

The typical advice for managing bad workouts focuses on physical things. For example, the usual explanations are that you've been overtraining and should back off, or that your diet is poor, or that you need to use a certain supplement. To be sure, a host of physical factors have powerful influences on the quality of your training, but if you really want to understand the heart of the issue, look to the psychological, not the physical, world.

Consider two very different reactions to a bad workout. In one approach you conclude that you always have bad workouts, every routine you've tried has been a failure, and you can expect nothing else, since you're genetically challenged. In another approach you conclude that even if this last workout wasn't so hot, you've been cooking with gas lately, or even if you stank on one part of it, other parts actually went very well.

Research psychologist Martin Seligman and his colleagues have been exploring the reasons some people quit in the face of adversity and others continue to march forward. Why, they asked, when faced with a discouraging situation, do some people just treat it like a bad-hair day and continue taking care of business while others are completely devastated by it?

To help explain such phenomena, Seligman's group suggested three critical dimensions: permanence, pervasiveness and personalization.

When you have a lousy workout, do you tend to view it as something that always happens or as something that just happens from time to time? This is what permanence is all about, and it's key to the way you deal with misfortune: people who throw in the towel believe that permanent causes underlie their problems, while people who keep on trucking believe that their problems are only temporary. Thus, the quitter's view of a bad workout is that he or she *always* has bad workouts. Conversely, the person who sees the bad workout as an occasional thing can take it in stride and doesn't get derailed.

Pervasiveness has to do with whether you regard your unfortunate situation as something specific or something general. For example, one person might say that he or she has tried everything and nothing has worked, but another might say, "I gain a lot better on an abbreviated whole-body routine than I do on six-day splits." People who quit see negative situations in broad, universal terms, while people who keep plugging away put limits around the negative situation, controlling the damage rather than letting it flood into other areas.

Personalization has to do with whether you explain things by using internal or external explanations. For example, if you explain a bad workout by talking about your limited potential, that's an internal explanation—you look inside yourself for the cause of the problem. On the other hand, if you explain a bad workout by noting that you simply had a bad day, nothing more and nothing less, you are using an external explanation.

The next step is to use these dimensions to help frame a productive response the next time you're faced with a bad workout or any other discouraging situation. First, be sure to view the problem in the narrow frame it deserves—for example, think in terms of this workout, not training in general. This will help you look at the occasional bad workout as just that: occasional and not something to get discouraged about. Second, when one part of your workout goes south, it's tempting to throw in the towel, but don't. In fact, if you quit at this stage, you're digging your own grave. Reduce your weights and/or reps and even change your routine, but keep going, and chances are you'll leave the gym with a feeling of success, even if one aspect of your workout didn't turn out as planned. Third, look outside yourself for explanations of why things went wrong, rather than trying to attribute them to your internal characteristics. Of course, this doesn't mean you should avoid taking responsibility where appropriate, but it does mean that you shouldn't call yourself hopeless when, for example, a bad workout might easily be due to a particularly stressful day at work.

When you're in it for the long haul, bad workouts come with the territory. The way you handle them, however, is up to you: they can either leave you broken down and in despair, or you can learn to blow right by them.

# 64: Insights From Injuries

| | |
|---:|:---|
| **How to:** | Not let fear of injuries take the edge off your training |
| **Key ideas:** | ✎ *Avoidance behavior* – when your fear makes you avoid things or reach out in a very hesitant manner |
| | ✎ *Approach behavior* – when you jump right into an activity without fear and go for it |

We're all trying to do things perfectly, so it makes good sense to always study perfect examples, right? That's usually true, but sometimes we can also learn a lot by studying things that have gone wrong. Consider injuries, for example.

Nobody wants to get hurt training or competing, but unless you're uncommonly lucky, something is bound to go wrong at some point. Don't worry. We're not claiming that you can count on having a catastrophic accident, because that's actually very unlikely, but just as you'll probably pick up a cold here and the flu there, chances are that you might tweak a body part or two along the way when you're physically active. The important thing is what you do from that point forward.

Let's start with a couple of extreme examples to get a sense of how this injury thing might play out. Two people are roughly the same age and body type. Both think they're knowledgeable about good training techniques; both have been training for years. One, however, tries to be scrupulously aware of proper technique, taking progress in small, measured steps, avoiding movements he considers likely to cause injury. The other is also concerned with technique but, from a lifting-efficiency perspective, is perfectly happy to take big jumps in search of personal records and relies on lifts the first fellow wouldn't touch with a 10-foot pole. If the first person has a byword, it's *caution*; for the second, it's *go-for-it*.

You might think that the first person has a long history of training uninterrupted by injury, while the second has probably paid the price for his apparently riskier training style. Ironically, the opposite is the case. The first person has injured himself so regularly one wonders if he can comb his hair safely, while the second usually trains without incident, giving the impression that he must have a score of guardian angels. Tellingly, the men respond to injuries very differently. The first backs off from training completely, while the second always finds a way to keep training.

Their differences start in the mind. Consider the primordial emotion of fear. Among other things, fear can narrow your psychological perspective and tighten your body. Fear naturally makes you avoid things, and while you might think that means complete avoidance, it also includes reaching out in a very hesitant manner—hence the term avoidance behavior.

Lack of fear, on the other hand, encourages what psychologists call approach behavior, which is just what it sounds like. Someone afraid of the ocean might avoid it altogether or maybe just dunk a toe into it; someone who's not afraid literally will jump right in. The irony is that by holding back, you often set yourself up for injury, while letting go would allow for smooth sailing. Although you may not want to admit to fear, you can exhibit the same behavior and call it control: a mind-set in which you must regulate everything meticulously vs. a more easygoing, come-what-may attitude.

It's commonly believed that even though power cleans are inherently dangerous, they're much safer than full squat cleans. In fact, even though the injury rate among those who perform power cleans properly is negligible, people are more likely to develop aches and pains doing power cleans than full squat cleans. The probable reason? Power cleans require you to hit the brakes in the descent phase of the lift—which sounds like the prudent, controlled style preferred by the first person described above. In contrast, on a full squat clean you ride the bar down to a rock-bottom squat before ascending, in what would appear to be the nearly reckless style of the second lifter.

What can happen on the power cleans is that you get a jolt by hitting the brakes, which is even harder if you begin the lift unnaturally tense, and it's the jarring impact that produces the aches and pains. While the second approach might seen foolishly kamikaze-like to the first lifter, it's executed in a relaxed style, which allows you to move fluidly and take full advantage of the body's natural elasticity. As a result you lift bigger weights with no pains afterward.

A closely related but more subtle way these two approaches produce very different outcomes stems from the fact that most injuries occur on the lifts you miss, not the lifts you make. That might sound screamingly obvious, but many people miss a vital implication: when you're hesitant, when you hold back, when you're fearful, you're actually more likely to miss a lift and, therefore, more likely to injure yourself than if you attack it full tilt.

In competitive situations, you can easily find patterns that closely parallel those outlined above. For example, at a recent Olympics a B-session lifter was attempting a weight that, although modest by international standards, obviously was very daunting to him. The result was an amazing scene, which included the lifter crawling around on all fours and lying on his back groaning and gasping, looking to all the world as if he had suffered the most grievous of injuries and would soon expire. An hour later, incidentally, the fellow was right back to being his normal self. In contrast, 1993 World's Strongest Man winner Gary Taylor once had a 900-something-pound tire fall back on him, pinning him to the concrete floor. Taylor lay there cracking jokes with those around him, even though when they lifted the tire off him, his foot was pointing at a right angle, instead of straight ahead. Everything in his knee had been so severely torn that it looked as if a giant had grabbed him with one hand above the knee and one below and twisted with all his might. Taylor's next stop was emergency surgery.

You don't need examples as strikingly different as these to understand that a lot of people really don't like lifting, or they're afraid of it, or they see that they can't compete at the level they'd like, or they're afraid to really try because the outcome is uncertain. In all of those cases, injuries—both real and imagined—are the likely outcome, and once a person is injured, withdrawal is the order of the day. On the other hand, if you really love training, embrace the idea of giving competition your best shot, and are not unduly burdened with thoughts of what might go wrong, you're actually less apt to get injured, and if you do, you'll probably take it in stride.

# 65: Don't Worry—Work Out!

| | |
|---|---|
| **How to:** | Reduce your anxiety and feel better with a good workout |
| **Key ideas:** | &#10086; *Anxiety* – general feelings of uneasiness not tied directly to a single event, unlike fear<br>&#10086; *Free-floating* – characteristic of anxiety that tends to engulf you although its roots go beyond a specific external source<br>&#10086; *Drive* – quality of anxiety that arouses you and primes you to do something with nervous energy |

It's a gnawing sensation in your gut, and even if you can't put your finger on exactly what's causing it, you know the results: you're uneasy, agitated, and apprehensive. You can't concentrate, you can't relax, you can't seem to do much more than worry. Welcome to the club—you're anxious.

Fear is a familiar idea. For example, you're dangling off a cliff by your finger tips; a hulking Rottweiler is growling and coming toward you; you're alone late at night deep in the woods and you hear a strange sound—what else are you going to do in those situations but be afraid? Fear, unlike anxiety, has a specific external source. Anxiety, on the other hand, might have its roots in something specific, like taking a test in school, getting bad news at work, or reading about one world crisis or another, but the overriding characteristic of anxiety is that it's general and not tied directly to a single source. Hence, psychologists often refer to anxiety as "free-floating," which means that while it tends to engulf you, its roots go beyond a specific external source. Another characteristic of anxiety is that it's widespread—everyone is afflicted, from teenagers with concerns about self-image and social acceptance to middle-aged executives pondering the meaning of their lives. Everyone is subject to bouts of anxiety, and have no doubt about it, anxiety can be very uncomfortable.

Anxiety is often seen as the result of stress, and what's important to realize is that this emotional response is at least partially under our control. For starters, we all need to understand that our emotions and our behaviors are related. For example, in response to such stressful emotions as anxiety, some people might cry, others might overeat, and so forth. Some, the smartest of them all, hit the weights.

Without going into excruciating detail, in classical psychological theories anxiety was seen as a "drive," which meant the affected person was aroused and primed to do something. Unlike a depressed person, who slides into lethargy, anxious people are wound up—they might pace, talk incessantly, or fidget. Rather than just letting the nervous energy deplete your resources and make you feel lousy, why not channel this energy into a constructive activity, like working out? Instead of letting anxiety buffet you hither and yon, seize it as an opportunity—consider it bonus fuel for a workout.

Even if you accept the idea as sound in principle, it's sometimes hard to implement. Here are some suggestions to help you make it a success. First, make sure that you begin your workout with easy movements and easy weights—this is not the time to decide you want to learn how to do squat snatches or go for a PR in the clean and jerk. It is, however, a great time to do spot-perfect squats, curls, or just about anything else you like. Aerobic exercise is also very well-suited for periods of anxiety.

Pick an initial movement that you like, especially if you're particularly anxious. Try to block out everything but training, and consciously move slowly through a warm-up routine that's even more systematic than the one you usually use. Actively cultivate a sense of measured purpose— it may be the world's rattiest gym, but try to get in the same frame of mind you would assume in a great cathedral.

If you do things right, your mood will improve noticeably and quickly, but don't think about it; instead, just focus on your training and let your thoughts and feelings take care of themselves. As you start to feel better, you can hit the gas a little harder in your workout, and you can begin to stretch a little in terms of letting your workout evolve toward heavier weights and tougher movements, but don't push for that type of finale. What's vital is that you start gradually and end by notching up a rock-solid workout that leaves you feeling better and more energetic. If you're more of a lifter than a bodybuilder, remember that missed lifts make you feel bad and successes make you feel good. Therefore, be sure that you choose weights with the idea of virtually 100 percent success; save your misses for another day.

Be sure to finish the workout by reinforcing what just happened. Acknowledge how good you feel and what a good workout you had, and that the good feeling is the result of the good workout. Go have your favorite protein drink, knowing that you'll be bigger and better tomorrow.

When the United States surgeon general officially tells the world that exercise "appears to relieve symptoms of . . . anxiety and improve mood," you can bet that the idea is no longer the exclusive domain of the lunatic fringe. So the next time you're anxious, do yourself a favor and hit the gym—tap the nervous energy, focus it on your training. Chances are better than good that your mood will improve almost on the spot, and the longer term results of your training will make you feel even better. Don't worry: work out!

# 66: Regarding Rules

| | |
|---:|:---|
| **How to:** | Get the information—the rules—necessary for productive training |
| **Key idea:** | ❧ *Standard procedure* – in a pragmatic sense, the universal principles or rules that govern training progress |

Two guys start training at the same time, and after a year, one of them is noticeably stronger and has muscles he never knew he had before. He's thinking that this weight stuff is a pretty good thing. The other guy gains about 30 pounds of muscle, completely outgrowing two sets of clothes, and as a result of his training, his strength and muscular mass bear absolutely no resemblance to their former levels. He's amazed, and so is everyone else who's seen the transformation. The difference can't be attributed to genetics or anything else complicated—it's a simple matter of knowing the rules and following them.

Rules, in general, can get a bad rap. We might think of them as being artificial—perhaps even things that are made up by someone who needs to impose his will on others. In such cases, rules are not only unproductive, but they make a lot of people so angry that they almost go out of their way to break them. Some people are repelled by rules as a concept because they associate all rules with this sort of senseless decree. On the other hand, there's the kind that we call social convention—things that might make society work more smoothly but that are neither vital nor universal. Etiquette provides examples of that type of rules.

When we talk about rules here, however, we're not referring to either of those two types. If you strip all the emotional baggage from the word, rules are nothing more or less than the standard procedure for doing something, not in a social sense but in a pragmatic sense. In other words, we're not talking about what time your gym closes or how you're supposed to share a certain piece of equipment. We're talking about the universal principles that govern training progress, whether you're in Chicago or Calcutta, training 50 years ago or right now. So, while it's nice of you to put your dumbbells back in the rack when you're done, what we're really interested in is whether you're paying attention to things like overload, progressive resistance, and recuperation, the factors that make the human body grow bigger and stronger. Rules, in this case, contain the seeds of your progress.

It's clear that you can't follow a rule if you don't know it exists, which is the reason highway patrolmen probably hear so much of "I didn't know this was a 55-mile-per-hour zone." And while it might sound simple, discovering the rules—the information—necessary for productive training takes some skill and effort.

Even though we're surrounded by ever-increasing amounts of information, it always takes some effort to get, and it varies enormously in quality. On the Internet, for example, you can find everything from material written by someone whose expertise is recognized around the world to training advice from someone whose primary motivation is to see his name on the screen. The first person can explain even something like the basic construction of barbells with precision, while the second thinks that collars and sleeves on a barbell are the same thing.

Sorting through the mountains of information isn't easy, but if you're motivated to succeed, you'll read, ask questions, and always be on the alert for good advice. As a general rule, look for consistent threads when you're evaluating training advice, and you'll go in the right direction. Thus, for example, if a routine has stood the test of time and if it tends to work for a wide variety of people, it's probably a better bet than one that's put forth by only one person—especially if that person has either a vested interest in the information he's providing or some other motivation for saying, "The rest of mankind is wrong; only I know the truth."

If you can't muster the energy to learn the difference between push presses and triceps pressdowns and which is the better choice for building overall size and strength, it doesn't seem likely that you could ever put forth the effort required to make serious progress. In fact, if rolling up your sleeves to learn the basics is too daunting, then instead of putting your head down and training hard in search of results, you'll probably train haphazardly and spend most of your time and energy searching for either the magic combination of supplements or the trainer who can put muscles on a mushroom merely by blinking.

Knowing the rules, however, is no guarantee that you'll do everything right. For example, you may know that you're supposed to do a set to failure, but that doesn't mean you won't dump the bar when you're still capable of three more reps. You may fully understand that you need to get enough sleep to recover properly, but that doesn't mean you'll automatically manage your social life to allow for that. You may mouth all the familiar lines about how vital it is to be consistent in your training, but that doesn't mean you won't make a habit of taking time off to nurse some sore body part or another.

In some ways it should be easier to learn the rules—get the information—because that's a cognitive activity, and you can sit down or even lie on the couch while you're soaking up information. The second part, following through, might seem tougher because you have to actually walk the walk—it's the physical component of the process. Fear not, though. If you're highly motivated, you'll look forward to taking the required steps. You'll lust after gains, and you'll know that if you follow the rules, you'll make maximum progress.

# 67: A Little Help From Your Friends

| | |
|---|---|
| **How to:** | Choose friends who will help your quest for strength |
| **Key ideas:** | ❧ *Peer pressure* – a fundamental way your friends affect your thoughts and behavior |
| | ❧ *Group opinion* – people go along with what the group thinks to an amazing degree, even when the group opinion is sheer folly in the face of simple physical evidence |

Training, diet, attitude, and genetics are the primary factors that determine just how far you'll get in your quest for muscular size and strength. What's nice is that all but the last are under your control. And what's even nicer is that with a little help from your friends, you can improve your performance in each of those areas, producing maximum progress. "Muscles from Mike?" you're thinking, wondering how your best friend, for all the good he does, can possibly influence how big your biceps get or how much you bench-press. Here's how it works.

Friends give us a frame of reference: through their eyes we see ourselves as accepted or rejected. They make us feel like successes or failures; they can just plain make us feel good or bad. Further, they give us our ideas about what's good, bad, and in between. Some psychologists suspect that our overall personalities are largely the result of our friends' influences, each of which can have a dramatic impact on where we go in our lifting careers and just how fast we get there.

Peer pressure, a fundamental way your friends affect your thoughts and behavior, is powerful, but because it surrounds you, it's easy to overlook. When you flip through old family photos and see how oddly everyone dressed 30 years ago, just remember that all those people with the bell bottoms and the Nehru jackets were making fashion choices based on what their friends accepted and rejected at the time. Those same social influences are still at work today, although it's harder to see them while you're in their midst.

We constantly get cues of approval and disapproval from the people around us, and nearly all of us shape our behavior accordingly. Early research in social psychology attempted to demonstrate that the way we describe how we feel is largely dictated by what we can infer from the people around us. Other research in social psychology demonstrated the amazing degree to which most people conform to the group opinion, even when that opinion is sheer folly in the face of simple physical evidence. So much for the idea that most of us are free spirits who independently blaze trails to our individual goals of glory.

When you add to those influences the idea that your friends, much more than your family, might shape your overall personality, it's easy to see that the friends factor is something that can work either for you or against you in an extremely powerful way. It only makes good sense to understand what's going on and use it to your best advantage.

If you remember this phenomenon—that your friends shape your physique—you've got a potent tool and can put it to good use. Forewarned is forearmed, so you're already ahead of the game with just the knowledge that the crowd you hang out with influences your lifting. It will help you anticipate and deflect negative influences they might have on you, and that's tremendously beneficial. Suppose your best friends live on greasy burgers, fries, and soft drinks and wouldn't consider consuming calories from any other sources. You may be able to build some mighty muscle on that diet, but it's going to be tough. Similarly, suppose your friends like to stay out all night, couldn't find the local gym if their lives depended on it, and think bodybuilding, weightlifting, and all associated activities are strictly for the birds.

Sure, you can succeed in that social environment, but you've loaded the dice against yourself. Consider how much easier things would be for you if your friends shared your passion for training, walked around with thermoses filled with protein drinks, and considered their workouts to be a veritable institution in their lives, like going to church on Sunday morning. In that sort of social setting you can concentrate on the difficult business of lifting.

It's even better if your friends share the key attitudes or personality characteristics you need for success in lifting or any other activity. Ideally, your pals set goals, are willing to work long and hard to reach them, and aren't unduly discouraged in the face of setbacks. They neither give in to endless whining and hand-wringing nor pat each other on the back for the most mundane of achievements. Imagine a guy who could be world champion in at least a couple of strength sports—he's got all the physical equipment for the task and the basic mental hardware as well. The only thing missing is the emotional glue that makes everything stick together, and if you ask people who've known him a long time why he hasn't risen to greatness, they'll explain that he learned to set his sights low from those around him and always had an excuse for why things went awry—as they inevitably did. It's sad, but this is a true story you can find repeated time and again.

If your friends just aren't into this lifting thing, are you doomed? No. Success in any venture requires individual effort, so in the end it's always going to be up to you to make it to the gym or not, put in a good effort or not, eat right or not, and so forth. You may not be able to count on your friends to directly support your efforts, but if they don't disapprove of what you're doing, you're way ahead of the game. And if they pursue a passion of their own with the same type of zeal that you have for your lifting, you can still support each other by modeling the personality factors that lead to success.

People have risen to all kinds of glory, personal and public, from the most unlikely settings. What they've usually done, however, is stick to their course while they worked not just on their goals, but also on getting themselves into a more favorable environment. That environment starts with your friends. Even if things aren't perfect right now, keep your eyes on your goals, ever alert to fellow travelers who either help or hinder your quest.

# 68: Grappling with Gratification Gremlins

| How to: | Avoid short-term distractions and stay on the path to your long-term goals |
|---|---|
| Key idea: | ❧ *Delay of gratification* – the process of giving up a smaller reward right now for a bigger reward in the future |

Suppose you're fairly typical when you start lifting weights: you weigh less than 150 pounds, your arms are about 12 inches, your chest is about 34 inches, and if you tried to squat 135 pounds, we'd be calling 9-1-1. From those humble beginnings you plan to do some big things: maybe you want to be a professional bodybuilder or win the World's Strongest Man contest, or perhaps you've set your sights on an Olympic gold medal or two. Whatever your long-term goals, the chances are better than good that there's a vast piece of territory between where you are now and where you want to end up—and all along the way there will be a series of nasty little gremlins whose mission is to lure you off your chosen path.

Psychologists talk about "delay of gratification," which is the process of giving up a smaller reward right now for a bigger reward in the future. Just think of it as choosing between a small cookie now or waiting for two big cookies later. The cookie example is actually a pretty good one. As infants and little children we are challenged to learn how to delay gratification. Some people are better at it than others, but successful people in all walks of life tend to have developed their skills in that area. If you want to get the most from your training, you should too.

Nearly all of us face a gap between where we are and where we'd like to be. That gap is what sets the stage for us to be tempted by those gremlins.

Ever notice how the one piece of a doctor's advice everyone in the world is quick to accept relates to lifting heavy things—actually, not lifting heavy things. Maybe someone's an overweight, junk-food-eating, cigarette-smoking, couch potato, but, by golly, as much as he'd like to help you move that piece of furniture, he'll solemnly tell you, "My doctor said not to lift anything heavy." It's a good thing remote controls are so light. The challenge is that you're caught up in an activity that's completely based around lifting heavy objects.

"So what?" you say. "I like lifting weights and, besides, I have a goal." That's great, but don't completely dismiss the idea that you're involved in an activity that most people, most of the time, find unpleasant, and it's easy for the gremlins to lure you off your path. For example, don't you think there's a big avoidance factor in a lot of injuries? After all, how can anyone expect you to train if you're hurt? Having an injury is a legitimate reason to skip training. More subtle, but part of the same process, is all the attention paid to the dangers of overtraining: not only is it the rationale for training less, but anyone who follows that school of thought can walk around feeling like an enlightened being. Whatever the exact nature of the temptation not to train, the effect is the same: a smaller short-term reward (e.g., going to a movie) is accepted instead of holding out for a larger long-term reward (e.g., moving a step closer to that state title).

To some extent, it's true that sticking with your training is just a matter of toughing it out, but there are some basic strategies gleaned from psychological research that can make your task easier.

When research psychologists test (torment?) little children with delay-of-gratification research, one of the most prevalent findings is that keeping the temptation out of sight is a powerful aid to keeping the kids on track. Put the cookies in a five-year-old's face and see how long most can wait, compared to putting the cookies in the next room. The same principle works with big kids too. Try to distance yourself from whatever is bedeviling you when you should be training. That approach doesn't always lend itself to something as simple as physically picking up the tray of cookies and moving it, so you need to develop additional skills. Foremost among them is distraction—anything that keeps your mind off whatever is tempting you not to train. For example, one reason so many people like to listen to music while they train is that it can help squash the little voices whispering, "Let's go to the beach," "My back is sore," "I really need another rest day." Some people like to count each rep as intently as possible for similar benefits, and others like to feel the muscles working as fully as possible. Others, even more imaginative, see themselves in their minds' eye winning world championships and breaking world records with each set.

Another basic approach to stifling the gremlins is to make the temptation more abstract and less tangible. A little kid might not be able to get beyond the mouthwatering sweetness of a chocolate chip cookie, but you should be able to consider it a source of empty calories coming from a small pile of bleached flour with some artificial dyes and flavors thrown in. Similarly, instead of focusing on thinking about how pleasantly you could be spending your time instead of sweating away in the gym, think about the alternative activities in bland, neutral terms. For instance, instead of thinking of yourself as being entertained by a hit sit-com, try thinking of being bombarded with electrons as you waste your time and your life on the opiate of the masses.

At the same time work the flip side of the equation. For starters, focus on short-term goals as the way to fulfill your long-term aspirations. Thus, instead of focusing completely on that world record you plan to break, take satisfaction from the way each set you do today moves you a little closer to that overall goal. Similarly, instead of getting caught up in your hoped-for results, try to focus on the act itself. For instance, don't fantasize about being interviewed on network TV following your Olympic victory but, instead, develop a sense of pleasure and satisfaction from actually doing your training lifts.

Once upon a time, someone got the notion that all we needed to do in order to achieve happiness was eliminate our inhibitions, and that progressed to the idea of just letting it all hang out. Now it's practically taken as gospel that if we could only achieve total spontaneity, not only would our true selves emerge, but we would also fully realize our capabilities. The funny thing is that one of the cardinal characteristics of successful people, in just about any pursuit, is that they have developed the ability to control their impulses—they've learned how to manage the delay-of-gratification gremlins, gladly trading a Camaro today for a Corvette tomorrow.

# 69: Self-Canceling Combinations

**How to:** Keep from pursuing conflicting goals and getting nowhere

**Key idea:** ❧ *Focusing illusion* – when considering goals, you may focus on something that's actually inconsequential or you may exaggerate its benefits and how much it will change your life

"I want to get huge, shredded, strong—I want it all." It's a familiar refrain, and it would seem that with a little creativity and a lot of effort, it's possible to pull it off. As you know, however, appearances can be deceiving. As much as you might like to believe you can have everything, you can't. In fact, the best way to get nowhere is to try to get everywhere at once.

It's easy to see why you can be led down the path to the everywhere–nowhere syndrome: every day images of everything from pro bodybuilding victories to Olympic gold medals are around to tantalize you. One moment you may be captivated by someone winning the World's Strongest Man competition, and the next you may be thinking triathlons. Left, right, up, down: add them all up and you land just where you started. That's the problem with trying to combine too many things or, more important, things that work in opposition to each other. It's those self-canceling combinations that can really block your progress.

Let's oversimplify things just to illustrate a point. To get bigger, you need to consume more calories than you burn; to get leaner, you need to consume fewer calories than you burn. Thus, when you simultaneously want to get bigger and leaner, you should eat more calories than you need and eat fewer calories than you need. That's the classic self-canceling combination—whatever you do in one direction is offset by what you do in the opposite direction, so you end up where you started. It certainly is possible to simultaneously increase muscle mass and decrease fat, but the point remains that some goals are easier to combine than others, and some goals are largely mutually exclusive. It's the mutually exclusive goals that you need to learn to manage, not just for your physical progress, but also for your peace of mind.

At the heart of these conflicting goals is the unwillingness to make choices—after all, if the game show host only lets you choose one of three possible doors, your decision automatically requires you to give up the other two. In real life, with nobody enforcing rules like that, you want to try to open all three doors—at once, no less. Part of the problem here is just knowing, or not knowing, what you want most. You can argue that one of the best ways to figure out the answer to that question is to give things a try, to see how they work for you.

The first thing to realize is that no choice, no matter what you think, is going to be perfect, and as long as whatever you choose isn't lethal, you can probably correct your course if you want to. Most people stumble in the first part of the process because it's too easy to get fooled when we consider things like potential goals. Research psychologists talk about "focusing illusion" when people make judgments. You may focus on something that's actually inconsequential, or you may exaggerate how much something will change your life. For example, you may think that if you can add five inches of muscle to your upper arm, your whole life will change for the better, but what you may find is that having a bigger upper arm means just that: your upper arm is several inches bigger than it used to be. You didn't get smarter, better-looking, more merciful, or anything else that's good in the process—your arm just got bigger. Sometimes that's exactly what happens, and you can imagine the cold showers awaiting all the commercially ambitious Olympic gold medalists who don't end up on a Wheaties box or with a Coke contract.

The point is not to denigrate any goal you may have but to make it easier for you to pick your goals by realizing that nothing is perfect—and that the concept works in both directions: whatever you give up isn't likely to be the be-all and end-all any more than whatever you choose is. Once you realize that, you can lighten up on yourself a little and use the breathing room to pick one goal or maybe a couple that go together. You may decide to train for size and strength at once, but combinations such as simultaneously trying to gain weight and run a faster marathon don't mix.

The next part of the process of avoiding self-canceling combinations is to understand that timing really is everything. The example of trying to eat more and less at the same time may sound idiotic, but a surprising number of people actually try to do it. You can, in fact, productively eat more and less, but it's a matter of timing.

Back in the 1950s a young stalwart named Bruce Randall decided that he wanted to become the strongest man in the world. Bruce started off weighing about 200 pounds, and in the course of his run to the top, his body weight went past the 400 point. As you might guess, Bruce consumed a lot of food along the way, and he used the same progressive techniques at the table that most people reserve for the gym: day by day he consciously ate an extra chop, drank an extra glass of milk, and so forth. By following that program, Bruce gained more than 200 pounds and got very strong in the process. After a while, he decided that being so huge wasn't going to be a way of life for him. He changed everything around, progressively reduced the amount of food he ate, and 32 weeks later found himself weighing 183 pounds. Later, Bruce went back up to about 225 pounds and won the Mr. Universe title. Sometimes you can come pretty close to having it all, but only if you pay attention to the timing: Bruce Randall did end up going to some very different places, making his mark in each, but he did so in a very organized manner, taking the journey one step at a time.

In a world that has a lot of compelling choices, sometimes it's hard to pick one while giving up another. The way out, you think, is to mix a little of this with a little of that—a reasonable approach, as long as you avoid self-canceling combinations.

# 70: Happy Hour

| How to: | Look forward to your workout and see it as a ticket to a better life overall |
|---|---|
| **Key ideas:** | 🙠 *Optimizing human experience* – making us the best we can be |
| | 🙠 *Resilience* – being able to bounce back from set-backs |
| | 🙠 *Optimism* – expecting good things to happen |

It's amazing how pumped up people get about their training while they're reading their favorite muscle magazine—why, they're going to blast this muscle to oblivion and bang out PRs like there's no tomorrow, and when they're done training, the gym is going to feel as if a tornado just swept through it. Then, when the next workout rolls around, they have these aches that mean maybe they need more rest, and you know, overtraining is a perilous thing, so they either bag the workout completely or do something better suited to a shy kitten than a hungry tiger. While everyone likes progress and big gains, an awful lot of people seem to dread training. That dread leads to skipped workouts or lackadaisical training, and the net effect is to slow down or completely stop progress.

We're here to reverse the pattern: we want to show you how to put a little rocket fuel in your training. The first step is to learn to enjoy your training. We want you to think of your next training session as something more like happy hour than going to the dentist. The choice is yours.

Suppose we wanted you to take a dim view of your training. Suppose we wanted you to come up with an excuse for skipping it altogether or approaching it with the half-hearted hesitancy that's certain to produce half-baked results. How could we engineer that? Probably the best way to set the stage for that type of failure would be to convince you that your efforts would be largely for naught. We could tell you that you probably have limited potential, that the price you have to pay for progress is dear and nearly requires deals with the devil, that most of what you hear about training is rubbish, and so forth. Such statements prime you for failure by undermining your sense that you could make gains—and that, of course, isn't the ticket to embracing your training.

Now let's see what we can do to fire up your enthusiasm for training. The first thing would be to convince you that your efforts would pay off, so we'd want you to believe that if you train smart and hard, you'll make progress. The funny thing is, that's true. Howard Gardner, the Harvard

University professor who created the theory of multiple intelligences, says he learned that no matter how great or small one's talent pool is, he or she can make steady progress with regular work. Does that sound applicable to your training? You bet. Shake off the naysayers, and embrace the idea that progress is yours for the taking, one workout at a time.

The next step in the process is to quit viewing your workouts as painful intrusions or bothersome events you could just as well do without. Instead, view your training as a great opportunity. For starters, training is going to give you bigger biceps, mightier PRs, and all the rest of the things that drove you to the gym in the first place. It's the first step in what might make you a world-record holder or an Olympic champion, but even if those outcomes are uncertain, done right, it's guaranteed to make you better than you were yesterday.

One of the secrets to effective training is that you should finish your workout feeling better than when you started—proper training gives you a nearly instantaneous return on your investment. In fact, the process is so powerful that you can often completely turn around a bad day or a blue mood by banging out a good workout. If you start your workout feeling good, you should leave it feeling even better.

Effective training does more than add inches to your arms and pounds to your power cleans: it teaches you key lessons and skills that will help you in all walks of your life. A standard advertising ploy in the old days of muscle-building involved stories of a 97-pound weakling who was a total loser, but when he started to lift weights, he turned into a veritable Hercules, and the world lay at his feet. Commercial ballyhoo aside, the core of those stories has a tremendous amount of truth in it.

Research psychologist Martin Seligman has championed the idea of developing psychological theories and techniques for optimizing the human experience: instead of just focusing on how to cure man's psychological ills, Seligman wants to start putting some major effort into learning how to make us the best we can be. And one of the keys in the process, according to Seligman, is for us to learn to be both resilient and optimistic.

Resilience means being able to bounce back from things, and optimism means expecting good things. What better place to cultivate those than in the gym? Your training can teach you to bounce back from a lousy day, a poor start, a bad set, or even one bad rep—it can teach you that what began poorly can end on a very high note. Your training can prove to you that there's every reason to expect good things because it can provide tangible evidence that you can transform your body and your spirit. What's more, the lessons that you learn in the gym will carry over to all phases of your life. One of the big benefits a lot of people get from their training is the sense that they control their destiny, that effort pays off, and that near-miracles can be expected. Those are things they learned in the world of muscles, but they also apply them to the rest of their lives.

Training, if you talk to some, sounds like a gruesome activity that's confusing, involves many hazards, has limited payback potential, and generally should be avoided—which is what many people do. Others take quite a different view: they look forward to their workouts, seeing them not just as opportunities to move toward their muscular size and strength goals, but also as tickets to better lives overall. Needless to say, people in the second group are on to something big: they've discovered a happy hour that's the real deal.

# 71: Perspectives for Progress

| | |
|---|---|
| **How to:** | Use an outsider's perspective to boost your insight into your progress |
| **Key ideas:** | *External factors* – explanations that don't have anything to do with you or your personality |
| | *Internal factors* – explanations that are related to you and your personality |
| | *Armchair climber* – person who loves the gear and wants to be associated with climbing, but who almost never actually climbs |
| | *Dissociation* – stepping back and looking at yourself as an outsider would |

"Where to go?" "How to get there?" These are two of the toughest questions you can ever face, whether in terms of your training or your life as a whole. How many times have you wished you could really pinpoint your goal(s), thinking that it would then be pretty easy to figure out how to get there? Now that you're no longer trying to win the Mr. Olympia, the World's Strongest Man contest, and an Olympic gold medal in weightlifting all in the same year, you need some serious suggestions for how to start making progress.

Chances are you're no dummy, so you've given your training and the rest of your life a lot of thought. You've considered this, weighed that, pondered the other, but you still aren't coming up with clear answers to the big questions of where and how.

That will take some effort on your part, but with what I'm about to teach you, you'll be able to get a whole new view of things. Simple as the technique sounds, it will probably shed some light on what have been deep dark corners filled with all sorts of mysteries.

I recommend that you start considering things from the perspective of an outside observer. For example, when you don't do squats, even though you know they'll make you grow like nothing else, you come up with a list of reasons, such as, "My knees are bad," or, "I'm too tall to squat." Somebody else is likely to think things like, "He's lazy," or, "He's just a wimp." When you explain your own behavior, you tend to think in terms of external factors—things that don't have to do with your personality—that, in this case, make it impossible for you to squat effectively. Somebody else, however, tends to think in terms of internal factors—things related to your personality—and they're seen as the source of your inability to squat effectively. That distinction often characterizes how we explain our own behavior vs. the behavior of others: we tend to explain our own behavior in terms of external factors, and we tend to explain other people's behavior in terms of internal factors.

While that's an oversimplification of what research psychologists have learned about how people explain behavior, the crux of the matter is that we tend to use very different explanations depending on whether we're dealing with our behavior or somebody else's. And that's what creates the opportunity to add a little horsepower to our self-analyses—it gives us a way to potentially boost our insight.

Most people have a big gap between what psychologists call their ideal self and how they see themselves. This gap—wanting to be Mr. Olympia, for example, but knowing that you're 135 pounds of skin and bones—creates dissatisfaction, which can motivate behavior that moves you toward your goal but can also lead to distorted perceptions. In fact, it's important to realize that your view of yourself isn't necessarily accurate. For example, one research study found that more than three-fourths of the high school girls in the study felt they were overweight, even though almost all were normal.

People may also not want to recognize things about themselves that are obvious to everyone else: they might think that if only they didn't suffer from their infernal headaches, for example, they'd not only be Olympic champions, but they'd also have the entire world by the tail. To the rest of the world, the headaches seem more imaginary than real and not much more than a thinly veiled excuse for doing little, risking less, and reaping almost nothing. Years ago, when rock climbing was far from a mainstream activity, the sport attracted more than a few people who loved the gear and wanted to be associated with climbing, but because they got very uncomfortable if there was any air under their heels, they'd almost never actually be seen climbing. Hence, they were dubbed armchair climbers. If you ever wanted to hear some unlikely excuses, you could just put a bunch of those guys at the base of a climb; yet if you asked one what his hobby was, he'd most likely say, "Climbing."

Similar distortions can occur in the Iron Game. Few of us are immune to the pressure of thinking highly of ourselves, and few of us would think that we're stupid about our training, even if everyone else does. That's how we get into trouble assessing our own training and why it's so beneficial to step back and try to look at ourselves as an outsider would. Psychologists call that dissociation. You can start by asking yourself some pretty tough questions.

For example, you know that your training is both smart and hard, but the outsider, being a rude little beast, asks, "How much has your bench increased this year?" Or, feigning sincere interest, "How much muscular body weight have you added in the past three months?" Or worse yet, "Just what do your arms measure, anyway?" You might prefer to not hear—or answer—those questions, but go ahead. It's only you talking to yourself. Tell the truth, and that's the first big step in the right direction. If you can come to grips with the facts that 1) you want to power clean 300 pounds, 2) you've been stuck at a little under 250 for nine months, and 3) if you keep doing everything just as you've always done it, you'll still be power cleaning 250 nine months from now, you'll be able to make a change and crash through that plateau.

When you have a problem, it's usually pretty helpful to talk to a friend, not just because it feels good to get it off your chest, but also because your friend, not being so close to the problem, may be able to give you insights that have escaped you. Psychologists can offer compelling explanations for how differently we view our own and other people's behavior, which helps us understand why there can be great value in getting an outsider's view of things. You don't need the $50 explanation or even another person, however, because you can do it for yourself. Take a moment to step back and look at yourself as somebody else might. It may be scary at first, but if you take the plunge, you'll be happy with your progress.

# 72: Two for One

| | |
|---|---|
| **How to:** | Use two techniques for boosting your ability to move forward toward your goal |
| **Key ideas:** | ❧ *Foot-in-the-door technique* – an approach which builds on getting you to agree to a small request before moving to a bigger one |
| | ❧ *Two-stage process technique* – an approach that overreaches at first, eliciting a "no," then rebounds to a scaled-down request that nets a big "yes" |

Tough cookies that we are, we don't like to fool around, do we? When we set a target, we go right for it. We grab it by the jugular and that's that. Or is it? Let's be honest here and talk about all the times when you set out to reach point A and stopped, stuck, five serious steps short of your goal. What I want to propose is a psychological technique that will help you avoid that. Specifically, we're going to discuss how to boost your ability to move forward. This technique relies on a psychological strategy that's been proven to improve the chances that people will do what you ask them to do. Instead of focusing on other people, though, we're going to unleash its power on you, and we're going to release it in the gym.

The idea of charging forward certainly has its place, and sometimes it's an impressively effective strategy. The problem is, of course, that sometimes it not only doesn't help you make progress, it actually leads to reversals. A carefully structured two-stage process can really get maximum mileage out of each step forward.

Experimental social psychologists have studied factors that influence how likely someone is to go along with a request. For example, a psychologist might be interested in seeing how many people are willing to contribute time or money to a charitable cause. As a general finding, rather than just asking directly for whatever is desired, a more effective method is to approach the problem in two steps.

There are two basic ways this can work. Suppose we really want a small contribution, but rather than asking for it directly, we first ask if you think it's important to help people in trouble. The idea is that it's pretty easy to get you to agree to that, which tends to soften you up for the second part, asking for a contribution. Because the approach builds on getting you to agree to a small request before moving to a bigger one, it's often called the foot-in-the-door technique.

A very different tack also relies on a two-stage process. Suppose we want to get a contribution, but this time we start with a much larger request: would you be willing to volunteer to work in the local office one Saturday a month for the next year? That's a pretty beefy request, so you're likely to explain that you'd like to offer your services, but you just won't be able to. Since, in fact, it was just a set-up, we smile and nod and ask, "But could you make a small donation?" and you hand over some money without even thinking twice about it. That approach, because it overreaches at first, eliciting an almost certain "no," rebounds immediately to a scaled-down request, which nets the big "yes."

"Sneaky people, these social psychologists," you mutter. Take heart, because what we have here is the guts of a system that can get you bigger biceps and a new PR in the squat. Here's what you do.

It's been a lousy day—just about everything has gone wrong, and you're tired and stressed out—and the last thing you want to do is train. To make things worse, it's a heavy day: the thought of all those plates on the squat bar is almost enough to make you skip the gym altogether. Applying this devious psychological technique to yourself, you say, "This is what I'll do: I'll go to the gym, but all I'm going to do is stretch a little, just to loosen up my shoulders. Maybe it will make me feel better." After a few minutes of stretching, you decide that you can handle the warm-up sets that were scheduled for today's first exercise: power snatches. You take them one rep at a time, and before you know it, the warm-up sets are history and you smoothly progress upward through all of your work sets. About an hour later you've finished the whole workout, including some heavy squats. "Hey," you think, "this foot-in-the-door stuff is a real kick in the pants. It works—I just had a dynamite workout on a day when I felt worse than yesterday's road kill." One point for the first two-stage approach option.

Here's a good scenario for the second approach. You're trying to power clean 250 pounds—it's a nice round number, it's more than your best friend can do, and it's got enough plates on the bar to look like something. There are only two problems: your PR is 235, and even though you've done 235 more times than you can count, the thought of 250 scares you silly. It just plain breaks your will, so your body could never succeed with it. No problem, because you're armed with a brain, and one of the secrets locked inside it is the psychological technique that uses a big "no" to set up a big "yes." So you begin to focus on 275—you think about the pair of 45s on each end of the bar, thick ones, and that fat little 25 keeping them company. You'd like to be Marine-tough on this one, but when you ask yourself, "Can I do this?" you answer, "No way." Your brain sends down the next message, "How about 250?" and without thinking, you say, "Sure." Before you know it, you've got yourself a nice and new PR.

So there you have it—two ways to get a "yes" in the gym and out. They're lab tested and psychologically secure, but even better, they're free and portable, and really do work. Two for one—consider it new math for better results.

# 73: Make Friends with Fatigue

| | |
|---|---|
| **How to:** | Get a great workout even when you're tired |
| **Key ideas:** | ❧ *One-less-rep training* – staying at least one rep on the easy side of the comfort line when you're tired |
| | ❧ *Lost opportunities* – holding back when you train because of fatigue |
| | ❧ *Runner's high* – neurochemical assistance you receive from your body when you train that reduces discomfort and increases your sense of well-being when you're done |

At a recent international strongman contest, a 6-foot, 300-pound, muscle-laden competitor came charging out of the gate like an enraged bull: nostrils flaring, fists clenched, arms spread, he lunged for the start line, mowing down anything and anyone in his path. About two minutes later he was stopped in his tracks as effectively as if someone had cracked him over the head with a two-by-four. Physically and mentally, he was a broken man, and the dramatic change was wrought by a foe familiar to all who train: fatigue.

"Fatigue," Vince Lombardi observed, "makes cowards of us all."

Consider such classic examples as marathoners or triathletes crawling toward the finish line, disoriented, losing control of their basic bodily functions, and it's easy to understand why fatigue has the power to scare us. Most people will never experience the bone-deep exhaustion of ultimate aerobic efforts or the fiery trials of over-the-line anaerobic work, but we're all familiar with fatigue in one form or another. It isn't just an uncomfortable state; in the extreme case, it causes such intense pain that, being smart critters, most of us avoid it if at all possible. That sounds perfectly rational, but it's the first place things go wrong.

The avoidance behavior is very powerful, and for people who train, it has the initial impact of stopping them cold. Lifting weights or running, for example, is going to make you tired, right? Being tired is unpleasant, right? Churning those two pieces of information for a millisecond, your brain flashes the message, "Don't train!" and if you're susceptible to the suggestion, you head back to the couch. Thus, a lot of workouts never even get started because fear of an all-too-familiar by-product of training—fatigue—makes us hit the brakes before we leave the starting blocks.

Those with stronger wills, more motivation, or thicker skins might get over this first hurdle, but don't think they're home free, because a bigger trap is lurking. Fear of fatigue can cause us to hold back in our training, and as soon as discomfort appears, we call it a set or, worse, a day. Call it one-less-rep training—meaning you stay at least one rep on the easy side of the comfort line. Just like not training at all, training that's too easy isn't productive, so once again, fear of fatigue limits your opportunities and cuts into your ability to succeed. Workouts like those are truly lost opportunities, so what you need is a method to counterbalance your fear of fatigue. What we want you to do, at some level, is to make friends with fatigue. Here's how you do it.

For starters, fatigue isn't all bad. How many times have you felt better after a workout than before? Your answer should be, "Almost always." Training should be viewed as an investment because you have to make an effort, take a risk, and hope that your reward is something greater than your effort. This is how things work in the training world, and all who throw in the towel before the workout starts or who soft-pedal their efforts deny themselves the chance to feel good that day and in general, not to mention specific rewards like getting stronger and more muscular, having more endurance, losing fat, and so forth. The lesson you have to learn is that things that make you tired initially can also make you feel better, often much better afterward, so there are times when you have to put on the blinders, block out the fear of fatigue, and just march forward.

The knowledge that you'll feel better after training can help you get started on your workout, but how about the next step, working through the pain barrier? For one thing, it's important to remember that you're not running this gauntlet naked and alone. Our marvelously engineered bodies give us neurochemical assistance along the way, both reducing the physical discomfort and increasing our sense of well-being when we're done—that's what the much ballyhooed "runner's high" is all about. Knowing this can help take a little of the edge off the fear of fatigue, and the biochemical process itself will help reduce the discomfort normally associated with fatigue.

The next step in the process is to try to relax and remove yourself a little from the whole process. Try to detach yourself and make it an experience that, as much as possible, you're observing from the outside. Quit focusing, for example, on just how tired you are, how this and that ache, and how much worse everything is going to feel in another three reps. Instead, try to concentrate on the process of churning out your reps and executing your lifts correctly, not on the negative feelings associated with fatigue. Try to get into the rhythm of your training, going as much as possible on autopilot.

Finally, learn one of the biggest secrets of all by harnessing the ability of fatigue to relax your mind. This point is very rarely appreciated or discussed, but it's a powerful training tool that can become a tremendous ally in your quest for progress. The mind is the most important thing you have going in your training, but make no mistake about it, it has to be managed. Out of control, the mind is like a drunken monkey, chattering, distracting, dysfunctional. Our minds can make too much of a new PR, even though the additional weight on the bar is physically negligible.

Once a little fatigued, the mind relaxes somewhat, and that's why you can sometimes get your best workouts when you enter the gym a little tired. A small dose of fatigue is sometimes all that is required to manage the monkey, which allows your body to extend itself to new levels of achievement. So while it might be tempting to write off your training each time you're a little tired, doing that probably causes you to miss some of the most productive workouts you could have.

Fear of fatigue hampers training by stopping it in its tracks or by restricting its progress. Turn things around by coming to a better understanding of fatigue. Put it on your team, and make it work for you. Make friends with fatigue.

# 74: Setting Up to Succeed

| | |
|---:|:---|
| **How to:** | Prepare for your training before you work out—and get more out of it |

| | |
|---:|:---|
| **Key ideas:** | ❧ *Planned vs. instinctive training* – a formally-structured routine will usually help you reach your goals better than doing whatever you feel like doing that day |
| | ❧ *Constructive self-talk* – positive instructive guidance you give yourself during your workout |
| | ❧ *Mental rehearsal* – relaxing and then forming mental images of yourself succeeding with a specific lift |

If you've never been to a top arm wrestling contest, you might not understand that what takes place *before* the actual match often takes more time than the match itself. For example, some top competitors pace back and forth, getting fully crazed before they approach the table. Others charge the table, ramming it like angry bulls—full of steam and fury—only to maybe back up for another run at the table. And approaching the table is only one small aspect of getting set up, because as any veteran of arm wars will tell you, there are a lot of details to manage, since the position of everything from the tips of your fingers to the top of your shoulders can affect the outcome of the match. Because there's so much to attend to and because these preparatory steps can be so vital, a lot of high-level matches take a long time to get set up, and then might be over in a flash.

This is something like how your training should be, because no matter how intense your training schedule, it probably takes a relatively small part of your overall day, but as in the case of championship arm wrestling, what you do in the surrounding time has a critical impact on your in-gym results.

For starters, you know that training without recovery is a ticket to nowhere, so one of your top priorities is to make sure that in between training sessions, you've supplied your body with the nutrients and the rest it needs to rebuild from the last workout. This sounds simple, but a lot of people wonder why they aren't gaining, even though they consume about 35 grams of protein a day and always get five hours of sleep a night. Take the time to learn enough about nutrition so you can develop a plan you can have confidence in, and then stick with it. Similarly, get a handle on how much sleep you need for proper recovery and then make sure that you get it. If you cover these two bases, you'll be well on your way to succeed from one workout to another, but there's more to a good plan, and it's the things that follow that can dramatically increase your progress.

The first rule is that while spontaneity offers some significant benefits, when it comes to training, a certain rigidity usually produces better results. I know a guy who used to own what was probably the most famous lifting gym in the U.S., and he used to say that "Six o'clock was when Ken walked through the door," because one of his top lifters was so punctual that you could set a watch by his arrival. This sort of rigidity would help Ken never miss training, because he knew that at six, he'd be in the gym. Period. It also meant that he could plan everything, like when he would eat, work, and sleep, plus he would even be able to predict just how many people might be squatting that night, so rather than being caught by surprise, he could focus on the business of training. In contrast, if his workouts took place whenever he happened to land in the gym, a lot of factors that might have been predictable would now be in flux, causing him to waste time and energy in the gym.

Just as a rigid schedule helps you get to the gym and be more productive once you arrive, a planned routine will usually help you reach your goals better than what we might politely call instinctive training. Thus, while formally-structured cycling programs, for example, will never produce systematic results forever, one reason they can work exceptionally well for at least a while is because they require very specific lifts each workout, as opposed to your simply doing whatever you feel like doing that day. This is an important point, because sometimes it is just this task specificity, as opposed to the particular cycle, that is the real engine driving your results. I once asked an extremely knowledgeable lifting coach if he let his lifters back off on a bad day, and he asked, in turn, "Can you change your schedule at the Worlds or the Olympics?" Sometimes you just have to learn to dig deeper, even when you don't feel like it.

In the same way that you should be careful to get the proper nutrition and rest in between workouts to facilitate recovery, you need to husband your resources in between workouts, so that you can hit each training session full blast.

I know a guy whose daily work can involve periods of fairly heavy labor, but because he's nutty about his training, he consciously tries to schedule things so that his heaviest work is either done after he has trained or on a rest day. As an example of micro-managing your daily physical activity to facilitate your training, another guy alternated which hand he used for holding his toothbrush, thinking that would help him keep his arm development more balanced. While this second example is pretty extreme, the general idea of conserving your physical resources is intuitively obvious.

Less obvious, but in many ways more important, is the need to do the same thing cognitively and emotionally. Ideally, you want to keep your mind quiet and focused and your emotions on an even keel, especially in the hours leading up to your workout—all the nervous energy you don't waste, for example, getting angry, talking, or worrying, can be put to use squeezing out extra reps in the gym—the reps that will force progress if you make them, or leave it as an unfulfilled promise if you fail.

Finally, the real drivers of your progress are firmly rooted in your motivation and your confidence levels, so anything you can do to boost them in between training sessions will have a dramatic impact on your actual training. Reading about training or a star you admire will help provide cognitive fuel to motivate your training, and you can further reinforce this by looking at photographs and videotapes. Use this information to create appropriate mental images of yourself succeeding, and as the basis for creating constructive self-talk ("Keep your back flat . . . squeeze . . . keep going!"). If you're really serious, take the time in between workouts to go through formal mental rehearsals, relaxing first and then forming mental images of yourself succeeding with a specific lift, for example, you have planned for your next workout.

When you get right down to it, your actual gym time is pretty brief, and what you get out of it will largely depend on what you did before the workout even began. Starting today, don't make your training a random walk. Take the time and make the effort to do things right. Get set up to succeed.

# 75: Knocking Out Nuisances

| | |
|---|---|
| **How to:** | Deal with daily annoyances so you can get on with your training |
| **Key ideas:** | ❧ *Doer* – person who jumps right into things instead of talking about it; says "can" instead of "can't" |
| | ❧ *Dissociation* – process of selectively diverting your attention away from, for example, unpleasant situations |

Consider all of those wonderful vitamins—little nutritional spark plugs that can fire up your body in this terrific way or that. One's good for your bones, another helps you recover, another boosts your endurance, and so on; each seems as if it can do something really good for you and all you have to do to realize the benefits is swallow the little beasts. The only problem is that each of those vitamins is in its own little jar, and opening each of those jars can be a nuisance. You know that, and figuring that you already have enough annoyances in your life, you usually skate right by the vitamins, letting your mighty army sit idle and unused on your shelf. That's the problem with nuisances—they keep you from doing some good things.

If you stop to think about it, what could be more of a nuisance than lifting weights? For starters, getting to the gym requires a commute for most people, and if you skip that by training in your garage, for example, the temperature might be anywhere from 25 to 95 degrees—meaning that you'll either freeze the whole time or will soon be sweating so much that you can practically swim where you had been lifting. Once in the gym, things don't really improve because you have to get changed, and you know what a pain that is. If you're an Olympic lifter, or training for another sport, you probably do a fair amount of stretching before you start to lift. The list seems endless: one nuisance after another, and you haven't even begun your actual workout yet! No wonder most people train not at all or half-heartedly at best.

The same situation occurs in many other walks of your life, and how you deal with nuisances will largely determine whether or not you can create a string of successes or if ten years from now, you will still be whining about this impediment or that. So whether you're planning to get to the Olympics, the Olympia, or some point in between, it's going to be to your advantage to learn how to deal with daily annoyances.

Before beginning a difficult mission, it's productive to first develop an appropriate mind set. For example, if you're about to begin a marathon, you should steel your nerves for a long haul; if you're about to try a heavy lift, you tighten your belt first, figuratively as well as literally. To deal effectively with nuisances, you want to be a doer. Doers jump right into things, rather than sit around and talk about them. Doers say "can" rather than stewing about reasons for "can't." And while doers don't have to be spinning dizzily like whirling dervishes, you're not likely to find them glued in place or moving like molasses—after all, they have places to go and things to do.

A related element in your battle plan has to do with excuses—you know, the convenient little tool that always makes some ache pop up right before it's time to hit the gym. Funny how that works. You know all the familiar excuses, and probably at least a couple of unique ones, and deep in your heart you know when you're pulling one out, rather than taking care of business.

When Tommy Kono started training, he didn't fit anybody's image of a budding superman. After all, the *wunderkind* sported a 29-inch chest and a 9-inch arm. Who would have guessed that he would go on to set more than two dozen world records in weightlifting, win gold medals in two Olympics (plus a silver in another), and garner a string of physique titles as a side venture? Talking recently about his progress as he went from an ordinary kid to a superman, Tommy summed up an essential point by saying, "The day you start to make excuses is the day you will quit making progress." Remember that, no excuses: easy to say, hard to do, an incredibly powerful concept that applies just as much to not getting sidetracked when your shoelace breaks as it does to why you're not living up to your potential.

In addition to being primed for action and not getting bogged down with excuses, successfully managing nuisances requires that you know when and where to put your attention. The mind is a wonderful tool, but powerful as it is, its force can be destructive when not used properly—just like a chainsaw.

As a corollary to the idea of being a doer, it's important to understand that many nuisances not only exist, but also grow simply because you procrastinate in the face of them. Think about it: each time the thought of some annoying person, thing, or event crosses your mind, you waste time and emotional energy. Do it a lot and the waste is significant. Each time the thought crosses your mind and you fail to solve the problem, it's as if you're borrowing money—you'll get by for the moment, but you will be repaying what you borrowed with interest. A standard piece of advice for managers who are trying to be more efficient is to only handle each piece of paper that crosses their desk once. In practice, since most people shuffle the phone messages, memos, and reports from place to place before finally taking the required action, this simple strategy can produce huge time savings. Do the same thing with the nuisances in your life: try to deal with them on the spot, so they don't waste any more of your time and energy than necessary.

While some annoyances can be smashed in their tracks, many are just little things that are best dealt with by ignoring them. For example, rather than dwelling on the fact that this or that little thing has gone wrong or is imperfect, why not try to focus on something else? When you have to wade through some mindless activity you really don't like, whether it's driving to the gym or going through all the preparation before you can actually begin to lift, why compound the problem by focusing on it? Instead, turn your attention to something else—maybe think in a constructive way about a problem you are wrestling with at work or at school, make plans for the weekend, or just daydream. The key is to focus your attention on something other than the annoying situation you have at hand.

Psychologists call this process of selectively diverting your attention *dissociation*, and it can be a very effective strategy for dealing with a host of unpleasant situations, including pain. It's not a cure-all, but selectively distracting yourself from little annoyances can help you glide over the bumps and potholes waiting along your way.

This whole notion of not granting nuisances false importance is probably the single most important element in your overall strategy. After all, the concept of making mountains out of molehills is better saved for your training itself.

# 76: Brains Fuel Gains

| | |
|---|---|
| **How to:** | Put your intelligence to work to boost your might and muscle |
| **Key ideas:** | ૹ *Adaptation* – making the best of what you have at hand |
| | ૹ *Shaping the environment* – taking an active role in making things better suited to your purposes |
| | ૹ *Selecting a new environment* – if adapting and shaping don't work, you may have to move elsewhere |

Back in the early and mid-1950s, Canada's Doug Hepburn was widely regarded as the strongest man in the world—he packed around 275 pounds of powerful, shapely muscle on his 5'-9" frame, and there wasn't much he couldn't do when it came to strength. Although not as widely known, Hepburn is also something of a thinker–artist, who seems likely to have been just as comfortable in a beat coffee house as he was at the World Weightlifting Championships, so woe to anyone who assumed this mountain of muscle was a moron. Pity, for example, the newspaper reporter who once asked Hepburn, "How's it feel to be all brawn and no brains?" to which Hepburn replied, "I wouldn't know. How does it feel to be neither?"

Brains and muscles aren't mutually exclusive; they are interrelated, and everything else being equal, the person who is smarter about his training will have more muscle and power to show for it. To put this idea to work for your training, let's take a look at how a leading view of human intelligence can help you boost your might and muscle to new levels.

The study of human intelligence has a fairly long history that is filled with more than its share of controversies. It's easy to get everyone to agree that people differ in terms of such characteristics as height, but it's much tougher to get them agree that people also differ in what we call intelligence. Part of the difficulty is that it's clear that there seem to be different ways to be smart, and not the least important is how well you can function in the real world, as opposed to how you might perform on an intelligence test. Muscle and power live in the real world, so we're most interested in talking about being smart in the real world.

Yale psychology professor Robert Sternberg, who is a distinguished researcher in the field of human intelligence, sees three cognitive mechanisms as instrumental to real-world functioning. The first is *adaptation*, which means making the best of what you have at hand. The second is *shaping* the environment to make it more like what you would like. The third is *selecting* a new environment. To understand how these mechanisms can help or hinder your training, let's apply them to one of the most common training problems: the not-so-small question of where you should train.

Fabled Iron Game author John McCallum once wrote about how he had trained hard, but had never made a lot of progress until he happened to be stationed on a Navy ship whose entire "gym" was one very heavy, fixed-weight barbell. In the face of this situation, McCallum's training took a 180-degree turn, and instead of doing his usual myriad upper body movements, he began doing nothing but squats, whenever he could get a couple of guys to hoist the barbell up on his shoulders, and dips in between some exposed pipes. Sometimes he threw in a few dead-lifts for good measure. The result was that McCallum suddenly started making the fastest gains of his training career because he had inadvertently stumbled onto the time-honored system of using squats to force overall gains. Of course, most people faced with McCallum's dilemma on the ship would have tossed in the towel as far as their training goes, probably whining about what they didn't have. McCallum, however, by adapting to the situation, by being smart about making the most of what he had at hand, made great gains. For the record, it should also be pointed out that McCallum was a member of the Mensa Society, so don't think this brains and muscles thing is mere fiction.

Shaping the environment means that you can and do take an active role in making things better suited to your purposes. Consider, again, the dilemma of where to train. Arnold Schwarzenegger has often cited how he was inspired both in bodybuilding and in his life in general by the example of Reg Park, a leading figure in bodybuilding who went on to additional success in Hercules movies and commercial gym operation. Park began his bodybuilding career in his parent's garage, and before you think that we're talking about a spacious affair with lots of square footage dedicated to young Reg's bodybuilding efforts, consider that the family car had to be pulled out of the garage to make room for Reg each time he wanted to train. Similarly, years ago in *Iron Man* magazine, an enthusiastic and creative trainee named Michael Salvatti wrote an article describing how he had made equipment that allowed him to train very heavily in his bedroom. He had specially designed equipment that made use of the furniture already in the room, so rather than being hindered by these "obstacles," he turned them into his allies in his quest for a gym.

At the other end of the spectrum, a few years ago I met a fellow who lived in Africa who never let lack of "a proper gym" keep him from training hard and heavy. Not having the standard equipment, he did bench presses, for example, on a thick plank lying on the ground. "That's okay for a beginner," you might say, "but I'm already too advanced for that." This guy, you should know, competed in some high-level international strongman competitions where he did well enough to get invited to the prestigious World's Strongest Man contest.

Sometimes adapting or shaping won't work, and the smart move is to get mobile. When U.S. Marine Tom Gough decided to make a comeback in weightlifting, he needed to train in a gym that was oriented toward Olympic lifting, and one that had a suitable coach. Mike Burgener's gym was the closest thing to fit the bill. Being only about a 20- or 30-minute drive from Camp Pendleton, the commute should have been pretty manageable, but the wrinkle was that Gough didn't have a car. So he took a two-hour bus ride, and then walked uphill 2-1/2 or 3 miles to

Mike's gym. If he were lucky, he'd get a ride back to the bus station when he was done. He did this several times a week. Things got harder for Gough when he finished the School of Infantry at Camp Pendleton, because his next stop was 29 Palms—now, instead of a bus ride part of the way to Mike's Gym, he had to hitchhike a distance that took 2-1/2 or 3 hours to drive; sometimes it took Gough eight hours to make it hitchhiking. Gough stuck it out, and his next stop was the U.S. Olympic Training Center, which led to a berth on the U.S. weightlifting team at the 1996 Olympic Games. If Gough hadn't been smart enough to train in Mike's Gym and tough enough to do what it took to get there, he wouldn't be an Olympian today.

Use your brain when it comes to your training—adapt, shape, and select as necessary for gym decisions and every other facet of your training, and your reward will be greater progress. Smart isn't just for school: brains fuel gains.

# 77: Urgently Upward

| | |
|---:|:---|
| **How to:** | Understand that you are shaping your future with today's workouts |
| **Key ideas:** | ➤ *Progressive resistance* – increasing the weight from one workout to the next |
| | ➤ *Overload* – doing more than you're easily capable of doing |
| | ➤ *"Making" progress* – being fired up, trying really, really hard, and putting in a lot of effort |

Ask any ten people what to do when your workout starts to make a bad hair day look good: "bail out" is what at least nine of the ten of them will probably say. In fact, it's taken as a sign of prudence, if not downright wisdom, to back off when things don't feel right, and heading for the door is seen as a perfectly acceptable response. After all, everyone knows that Rome wasn't built in a day, and that progress is best coaxed, not forced, right? So it's foolish, not to mention unproductive, to beat your head against the wall, right? Wrong.

Like some other myths kicking around gyms, this idea of backing off in the face of adversity has become popular—not because it's productive, but because it's the easy way out. Who wouldn't embrace the idea that whenever you hit some rough waters, you can turn around and head back to shore? The only problem with this approach is that while it might leave you sitting fat and happy on the beach, you'll never be able to accomplish all that you might have, because to maximize your gains, you need to have a sense of urgency—on each rep, in each workout. Let's see how it works.

On paper, the idea of backing off on a bad day makes a lot of sense, but so did the idea that the earth is flat. After all, why struggle today when tomorrow will bring another day, and with it the hope that things might go easier? The best way to understand why this approach sells you short is both to consider the nature of making progress and to put performance in the context of high-level competition. First, let's look at progress.

Everyone knows the story of Milo of Crotona, who carried a calf on his shoulders in ancient Greece. The idea was that because the calf was gaining weight each day, Milo had inadvertently launched the lifting business in using the principles of progressive resistance and overload. Most people can handle progressive resistance, especially in the abstract, but overload isn't such a warm and friendly concept. Overload demands that you do more than you're easily capable of doing—it's just like your junior high PE teacher screaming at you to keep doing more push-ups because until you do more than you can easily, you're not going to make progress. That hurts, doesn't it? And because we don't like pain, we'll do our best to avoid it.

Enter the bad hair day in the gym, and prepare for the double whammy. Everything feels like it weighs a ton, so the pain factor is worse because on top of the physical distress you're suffering, there's the mental anguish that fifty feels like a hundred. Thus, you'd not be far off target to say that these off-days add insult to injury. No wonder we'd all like to run and hide from them.

Back to Milo, who by now is lugging around a bull on his shoulders. Everyone likes the story at this point—Greek kid makes good, becomes a muscleman, wins a pile of Olympic gold medals. If he lived now, he'd be on his way to the movies and have a string of infomercials as back up. And while everyone likes to embrace where he landed, they forget the steps that took him there: all those workouts when Milo got out of bed and felt like saying, "This stuff is a bunch of . . . ." Well, you get the idea.

There was a time when only a couple of men in the world had closed the infamous IronMind No. 3 Captains of Crush® gripper. When this elite group expanded to the point of including an entire handful or two, the No. 4 gripper was developed, and it became known around the world as the gripper that nobody could close. Then along came a guy from Tennessee, Joe Kinney, who mashed the beast. Kinney hardly fit the stereotype of what people were expecting: he bought his vitamins at a feed store, didn't even weigh 200 pounds and, my goodness, he was about forty years old at the time. Since then, Joe has been swamped with requests from people looking for magic routines and secret formulas for improving their grip strength. Being patient, Joe tries to explain, you have to be fired up to try hard, really hard, that it all takes a lot of effort; and when he gets frustrated by someone looking for an easy route to the top, he might shake his head and mutter under his breath, "Why do you think they call it *making* progress."

That's the real key to the riddle of gains: you have to make them, and the main ingredient is the mental fire that comes from a sense of urgency. You have to do it *now*.

In our digital society, where first FedEx and then faxes have become slower than we'd like, it's easy to get lulled into thinking that we're primed for doing things right now, but actually our technological advantages put us behind the eight ball on this urgency business, because having a real sense of urgency harkens back to our primal roots. Turn back the clock, way back, and see the world as being divided into predators and prey. Each morning the predators wake up to the reality that if they're lazy or slow, they'll die from hunger. Each morning the prey wake up to the reality that if they're lazy or slow, they'll die from being eaten. Talk about a motivator: acting full force each day was about the only thing that kept you alive.

Next, consider high-level athletic competition, such as the World Championships or the Olympics. Guess what? If you're scheduled to compete at 5:00 p.m. on March 12, that's when you're expected to show your stuff—whether you feel good, bad, or indifferent at that particular moment. That's precisely why some truly international-level coaches don't buy into the back-off-on-a-bad-day philosophy. Is that what you'd do at the Olympics? Of course not, so why not prepare yourself right now to deal with the situation at hand in the very best way you can?

And that's where you really are right now: what you do at this moment is going to determine what you become next. So begin to treat each rep as if it's the most important one in your life, as maybe being the last one you'll have a chance to do before the axe falls, and you'll be on track for making serious progress. To become the best you can be isn't a matter of looking for shelter from the storm. Instead, it requires that you develop a sense of urgency where you act with the knowledge that the future is just a blink away, and you shape yours by what you're doing at this very instant.

# 78: It's Only Mental

**How to:** Gain use of the most powerful training tool in the world: your mind

**Key ideas:**
- *Mental power* – mental events are not only very real but have a profound effect on decidedly physical events
- *Dumbing-down* – bringing things down to the lowest common denominator, the lowest level

An athletically-muscular guy stands over a barbell that is about twice his body weight: his goal is to snatch it, which means he has to rip it from the ground to arm's length overhead in one complete movement. Not a mean feat of strength by any stretch of the imagination, but something he has done many times. When he misses on his first attempt, both he and his coach look disappointed, but not unduly alarmed. When he misses on the second attempt, they both show real concern. When he misses the third time, he's out of the Olympics, bringing home no medal instead of the gold they had figured was his for the taking. People who knew the lifter understood that he was fully capable of making that lift, so they shook their heads and said, "It's only mental," as if that somehow made the disaster something less than it was.

We could examine this comment from more than one perspective, but what we would like to focus on at the moment is the idea that being mental makes something less important or less powerful than something that is, say, physical. What we'll do is illustrate with several examples how, in fact, mental events not only are very real, but also have a profound effect on decidedly physical events. "Cute idea," you say, "but I'm looking for another 25 pounds of muscle on my body and another 100 pounds on my PR deadlift." Then you really had better read on because what we're about to discuss could make the difference between meeting your goals or getting comfortable with always doing less. That's all.

One of the most vivid examples of mental power comes from the world of voodoo—not the muscle-building-hype variety, but the real thing, where victims of spells literally die based on their belief that this is inevitable after, for example, an enemy points a bone at them in the wrong way. Powerful stuff, this notion that an idea can kill you, and maybe this is a little too dramatic for you, so maybe you don't believe it or think it's an isolated case of mind over matter. The truth is that there are many, many documented cases of sudden death, evidently from psychological causes, and they are not limited to "primitive" cultures, or even to people with their propensity for over-active imaginations: the phenomenon has even been demonstrated in the laboratory with rats. And while the results are anything but clear cut, at least some studies have shown a link between psychological factors like optimism or pessimism and both the likelihood of getting cancer and the outcome once you have gotten it. Once again, it's "just" the mind that is intervening here.

Flip over to more common occurrences and consider the tales—both real and apocryphal—about a frail but frantic person lifting an enormously-heavy object off a loved one to save his or her life. Or ever known someone who's always too busy to do this or that, or maybe is incapacitated by this ache or that pain, but invite him to dinner, let alone to be your guest on a month-long cruise or a European vacation and *voilà*, time's available and the pain has vanished. Miracles like this happen every day, proving, if you only care to see the evidence, just what a powerful force your attitude and outlook can be in even the most physical of situations.

The point in all of these examples is to show how extremely powerful the mind is, fully capable of whisking emotions and behaviors from one end of the spectrum to the other—what you think is even capable of killing you. We also want to caution you against dismissing these examples as simply being cases of weak-minded individuals, which you certainly are not. If you are tempted to make this mistake, pause for a moment and take a close, honest look at yourself. There is no easier way to understand the power of the mind than to consider fear: are you claustrophobic, for example, or maybe agoraphobic, or maybe acrophobic, just for starters? Good luck telling a claustrophobe trapped in an elevator that the fear he experiences is "only mental." The point is that the mind is extremely powerful, so you want to both acknowledge its influence and strive to continually harness it for better performance.

To understand how what you think fundamentally shapes what you get from your training, let's start with goals: some people don't have any, so where they end up may or may not be a place they like. Other people have it down to a nit. For example, a few years ago I met an up-and-coming young salesman in Germany who told me his career goals, each of which was tied to the specific BMW model he hoped to be driving at that stage of his life. Or perhaps you knew a kid who since fourth grade spewed how she was going to Harvard Medical School when she grew up and planned to do post-doctoral research in oncology at Stanford.

Most of us aren't quite that focused quite that early, but that's no excuse not to try, starting right now. What are you attempting to do in the next year? Maybe drop 15 pounds of fat or maybe add that much muscle? Are you trying to get stronger, or don't you care? Next, back off from these longer term goals and define some milestones: if you bench 225 right now and hope to do 300 in a year, don't leave your progress to chance. Instead, don't just plan your workouts, but establish intermediate goals, such as 250, 275, and so forth. And even if you can't figure out the rest of your life right now, at least figure out something, and then stick with it. Just as accomplishments will feed further accomplishments, indecision and failure will fuel more of the same, so don't be afraid to grab the bull by the horns and start making decisions about where you would like to end up and how you will get there.

Media people talk about dumbing-down, bringing things down to the lowest common denominator, and while that can be a good way to sell a lot of some things, it's not the road to achievement and success. Similarly, you can always strive to do less and less and set your goals lower and lower, but why cheat yourself out of what you can become? Interestingly, while some putative experts in building strength and muscle advocate less and less training, a fundamental principle evident in the training regimens of the world's top weightlifters is that their training loads are always increasing—and they lift heavier and heavier weights as a result. Just remember that while you were training two or three times every two weeks, the athletes who will win gold medals at the Sydney Olympics were probably training two or three times a day. Go ahead and mumble about genes, supplements, or whatever else you might choose, but the truth is that the body can adapt up as well as down, which is why there is a very strong correlation between effort and results. A friend of mine said he is so tired of people calling him up for training advice and having them whine, "But I can't train that often because I'd be too sore," that he screams at them (expletives deleted): "Why don't you just not train at all—then you'll never be sore!" Don't sell yourself short by convincing yourself that you can only do less and less. Why not put some energy into convincing yourself that you can do more and more?

"It's only mental," is about like saying "it's only gravity"—the concept might be abstract and lend itself to complicated intellectual musings, but in the end, it's about as real as a rock in the road: you can ignore it and risk a crash, or you can acknowledge its presence and then successfully deal with it. Mental events aren't mere ghosts, and the sooner you get rid of the idea that something is "only mental," the sooner you'll gain use of the most powerful training tool in the world, your mind.

# 79: Cut Loose With Creative Juice

| How to: | Think for yourself to come up with different, better ways of training |
|---|---|
| Key ideas: | ▪ *Creativity* – being highly educated or intelligent are not pre-requisites for being creative<br>▪ *Brainstorming* – coming up with many new ideas without censoring or monitoring them |

In a monkey see, monkey do world, there tend to be a couple of leaders and many followers. For example, Company A makes a slick new food supplement—the stuff works, tastes good, and has a catchy name to boot. Ethics and self-respect aside, Company B promptly imitates Company A, coming as close to the real McCoy as they dare, trying to stay just this side of federal court. Company C comes out with a knockoff of Company B, and before too long, Company A has inspired a host of imitators, all dumbly playing follow the leader with Company A. Same thing happens with training: someone finds something that works, at least for himself, and before long, half the world is moving in lockstep with him. That's business as usual, which is fine if that's all you want, but what if you don't want business as usual? What if you're looking for something optimal, as opposed to just well-accepted? What if you want to think for yourself, instead of just being another copycat?

Back in the 1930s, there was young muscle magazine editor named Mark H. Berry. At that time, the standard way to train was to do a myriad of different movements, almost none of which was heavy. Berry was marching to the beat of a different drummer, because he began advocating very hard work on just a few movements, and the principal one in his book was heavy squats. Berry was widely ignored or ridiculed for his ideas, but then along came a guy named J. C. Hise, who wanted to prove that Berry's theories were all wet, and he figured the best way to do it was to follow Berry's recommendations. As a result, Hise gained about thirty pounds in a few weeks, and Berry, instead of having yet another thorn in his side, had gained a poster boy par excellence. Together, Berry's theory and Hise's practice turned bodybuilding and lifting on its ear, and it has never been the same since.

Incidentally, don't think that Hise was short of imagination himself because, for example, when he needed squat racks to follow this program, he solved the problem by cutting a couple of tree limbs, leaning them against a strong fence, and resting the barbell in conveniently-located forks or big nails pounded into the tree limbs. Oh, the power of imagination.

"But I'm no Albert Einstein or Leonardo da Vinci," you say. "How can you expect me to be creative?" Let's see how it works, because you might not be so hopeless as you think.

First, it's been well-established that contrary to what you might think, being brainy and being creative don't necessarily go together. Happily, people with average intelligence can be extremely creative. Also, being highly educated is not a prerequisite to creativity. So, just because you don't happen to be a Harvard Law School graduate doesn't mean that you can't come up with some mighty creative thinking as far as your training goes.

Second, creativity comes in many forms. Most people, for example, think fine arts when you mention creativity, but any sphere of human activity can be touched by a creative influence, and your training is no exception. Who would ever have imagined that someone would come up with an entire training system that was based around lifting heavy barrels, but now, thanks to Steve Justa having done exactly that, strength nuts all over the world would be hard pressed to imagine not having this type of training program.

So take heart and believe that you can think for yourself and come up with different, better ways of doing things, which is just what we want you to do with your own training. The key to the whole thing is to encourage yourself to start trying to think of things creatively.

If your training has been going nowhere for a while, instead of just telling yourself that you're genetically challenged so stagnation is to be expected, or that you will just try harder in the future, step back and give some hard thought to just what you are—and are not—doing. To facilitate this process, take a cue from creativity researchers, and learn to be very supportive as you generate new ideas in your brainstorming session. This means that you should be more concerned with coming up with new ideas than you are with monitoring them; you specifically do not want to screen your ideas, so that you only come up with "good" ones.

Of course, this is opposite of how many, if not most, of us were socialized. We have generally learned that it is safer to say too little than it is to say the wrong thing and be criticized for it, so we lean toward heavily censoring our thoughts. It's a related process that encourages people to stick with the pack, no matter where it goes, rather than strike out on their own. This is precisely what stifles creativity, so we encourage you to suspend judgment as you come up with new ideas, and to try to develop at least a reasonable comfort level when operating in solo mode.

You might start with your goals and examine whether they should be changed. Maybe it's time to gain weight, or build your strength, or reduce your body fat levels as a way to try something different—after all, if you don't like where you are, you might as well move along and try something new. Once your goals are established, consider your training schedule. If you have always trained four days a week, maybe it's time to try three, or maybe six. Some people make progress training as little as once or twice every week or two, and others train two or three times a day, virtually every day, so there is a lot of latitude for finding or developing the schedule that works best for you. Next, evaluate your workout routine. For instance, if your core workout has always involved certain key movements done in a standard order, maybe it's time to throw out the baby with the bath, and rewrite your program on a blank sheet of paper.

You'll also want to look at the related factors such as diet, rest, and attitude, while always remembering the things you might have taken for granted, such as where you train. In your quest for greatness, don't be afraid to turn your world upside down and inside out. Also, don't overlook the potential power of seemingly minor adjustments. For example, adding a half hour nap or actually using your favorite protein supplement might be all it takes to significantly boost the quality of your training. Finally, as you examine each of these areas, to help fuel your thinking, remember to consider not just what you do, but also what you don't do—some of the things you're not doing, or should stop doing, might open the door to the next level of gains.

Following the herd will always be the preferred route for most people, but when it comes to gaining the biggest benefit from your training, the wise thing to do is to be creative and think for yourself. So while the wannabes will always be busy blindly copying and following someone else, the leaders of the pack will be off on point, scouting the territory beyond.

# 80: Soar With More

| | |
|---|---|
| **How to:** | Crank up your training when progress stagnates |
| **Key ideas:** | ɪ♠ *"Less is more"* – idea of focusing attention on doing a limited number of basic movements |
| | ɪ♠ *Unproductive movements* – exercises that are a waste of time and energy and don't contribute to your progress |
| | ɪ♠ *Overload* – asking your body to do more than it's used to, and it adapts by getting bigger and stronger |

Once upon a time, in the not too distant past, the idea that less training could produce more results was a fairly novel concept—hard as that is to believe, now that the whole "less is more" concept has become such a cliché. But why wouldn't it become popular? Who wouldn't love to train less and gain more? Who wouldn't love a legitimate reason to back off when it comes to something as strenuous as lifting weights? The only catch is that there really aren't any free lunches, and gains are usually proportional to effort. In short, while less can produce more, it's more likely that less produces less and more produces more. Confusing? Let's unpack the concept and see how, more or less, all of this applies to making progress.

The "less is more" approach starts with the idea that instead of doing a zillion movements—which might produce overtraining and limited gains—one should pick a limited number of basic movements, things like squats and deadlifts, and focus one's attention on them. The next step along these lines is to make sure that not too many sets are done, and that there is plenty of recovery time in between workouts. Things are still fine to this point, but one thing leads to another and before too long, three workouts per week go to two; then it's one every four days and before too much longer, it's maybe three workouts every two weeks, and so on. After a while, you wonder whether any of these guys ever train at all.

There is a definite seductiveness to this approach because the idea of getting more for less is inherently appealing, but the drawback is that most people who jump on this bandwagon are usually settling for much less than they have to, often without even realizing it. Misunderstanding the process usually begins at the first stage, when the training program is cut down from many movements to just a few. When progress continues, or even accelerates, this is often misinterpreted as a sure sign that training less is the wiser way to go when, in fact, what is really happening is that the person is just dropping a lot of unproductive movements. And so while one person might do five sets of four different lifts, all done with the intention of increasing, say, his power clean, another person might come along and just do five sets of power cleans. When the second person makes more progress than the first person, it's easy to conclude that this proves the dangers of overtraining when it might just show that the other four movements were a waste of time and energy.

This is an important lesson, because the history of progress in both bodybuilding and lifting is pretty much a history of training more, with greater results. For example, when bodybuilders and lifters started to do multiple sets, progress exploded, and while decades ago the standard routine for most of the world's top lifters was based on training three times per week, many of the world's top lifters today train three times a day. And lest you think this increase in training frequency is being done by reducing training intensities, consider that some of the top lifters who train the most often are also the ones who train at close to 100% intensity levels most of the time.

"But I'd never recover . . . I'd always be injured," the less-is-more extremists would say. Could be, but not necessarily. First, our bodies adapt to stress, which is exactly why we coax them to get bigger and stronger by overloading them—we ask them to do more than they are used to, and they adapt by getting bigger and stronger. This also means that we can increase or decrease our ability to withstand rigorous training based on what we do. Thus, how hard we can train effectively is elastic, and it goes up or down depending upon what we think and do. And just as we can condition ourselves to train less and less, we can also condition ourselves to train more and more.

Second, ironically enough, it's often the case that more frequent training is the best way to avoid injury because the body is more likely to be properly loosened up and primed for the lifts we want it to do. Ever notice how your worst workouts usually come after your longest layoffs? How many people who train during the week and take the weekend off find that Monday's workout is the toughest of all, even though they should be the most rested for it? In a more extreme case, some of the hardest-training Olympic-style weightlifters virtually never take layoffs because everything from soreness to injuries only increase when they come back from a layoff.

The final point about doing more comes back to the idea that properly performed training is like a good investment: it returns more than you originally put in. Thus, the person who has hit the level of reasonably good overall conditioning might run several times a week, lift weights hard a few days a week, do plenty of other work throughout the day, and still have lots of energy. At the other end of the spectrum, a poorly-conditioned person who keeps reducing his training load might even complain that he's tired the day after an arm workout. Part of the difference is in the mind, but all the effects are felt in the body.

Talk to even the most demanding of all coaches in the Iron Game, coaches who are famous for putting their lifters on routines that are so hard that even veteran lifters stare at the programs in disbelief, and you will quickly learn that the key to being able to train at this level is to gradually increase your training load. Think of this process as being analogous to adding weight to the bar: you don't go from benching 50 pounds to 500 pounds in a hop, skip, and a jump, but rather in a long series of usually small, often irregular steps. You add five pounds here, ten pounds there, and so forth, over many, many hours of training. The same process applies to boosting one's overall training intensity and volume—the operative word for your increases should be "slowly."

And as with just about everything, successful implementation of this entire process begins between your ears, because while you might not be able to completely will yourself to each level of success you would like, you can certainly think your way down to a level of reduced expectations and general passivity that will ensure the most mediocre of results. Believe that you can succeed, and then act accordingly.

None of this emphasis on turning up the heat is to say that you can't get tremendous results from abbreviated programs, or that even just a little training isn't infinitely better than no training at all. What is vital to understand is that when your progress stops, instead of always thinking in terms of how you are probably overtrained and need to back off, think instead that you are stagnating because your body has become used to your current training load. At this point, the correct response isn't to back off, but instead to bump up the ante. So if you want to soar, try doing a little more.

# 81: Hostile Help

| How to: | Use adversity and criticism to your advantage in training and competition |
|---|---|
| **Key ideas:** | ⚬ *High-skill task* – performed better in front of an audience of hostile strangers than in front of a supportive, friendly audience |
| | ⚬ *Psychological aikido* – the ability to use your attacker's energy to neutralize his assault |

You learned it as a little kid—home court advantage is nothing to be taken lightly. Maybe your first taste of this thing was at a piano recital or an elementary school play where you had the place packed with supporters. Spanning two generations, just about everyone but the family dog was there, plus a couple of neighbors, and you even knew that a bunch of the other kids' parents were rooting for you too. So how could you lose? How could you do anything but perform at your very best under these circumstances?

And consider the opposite situation. It's the World Weightlifting Championships and you're expected to have a tooth-and-nail battle with a national hero and you're in his country. To make things more colorful, your country and his have a long history of border disputes, ethnic clashes, and the like. And since cultural niceties in his country do not include restraining oneself when expressing one's political and cultural preferences, every time you come out to lift, the crowd boos, shouts, and curses you—to the point where a riot seems inevitable—and all of this continues throughout each one of your lifts. Hardly the conditions for success, right? How could anyone expect you to succeed in an adversarial environment like this?

Recent psychological research has shown that as comforting as it might have been to have had your grandmother at your side during that solo, this really isn't the way to always produce the top performance. In fact, the research shows that hostile audiences can actually bring out your best. Let's take a brief look at the research and see what it means in terms of your training and competition.

Research psychologists, for example, have studied skilled performances and what happens when you have either hostile strangers or family and friends in the audience. Common sense would dictate that you would obviously do better in front of the supportive audience, and you would probably also think that this effect would be more pronounced with a high-skill task than a with a low-skill task. In fact, the research indicates the opposite, so even though the people who had the support of friends during their task experienced less stress than the people who had to perform in front of hostile strangers, this second group produced better performances and got through the task faster. Talk about turning a negative into a positive.

Explanations for this pattern of results suggest that, perhaps, when you face a friendly crowd, you might simply choke in the face of the pressure to try to please them. When you're facing a hostile crowd, however, you might feel as if you have nothing to lose and as a result, you might take risks that can pay off in terms of better performance. Some people might also be able to simply draw on the negative energy generated by the hostile crowd, harnessing it and using it to adrenalize their performance and produce better results.

Think about how this can work for your own training, starting with the whole idea that you might either face apathy or outright criticism for training in the first place. Sure, you could fold in the face of this adverse social environment, but knowing what you do now, you think, "Hey, I can put this to good use. They already think I'm nuts, so what's at risk? Nothing. So I might as well keep banging away in the gym." And so you do.

The gains come along, a little progress here, a little more there, maybe even a big chunk here and there once in a while. Before too long, the bug has bitten, and you'd like to compete—part of it is just to see what you can do, but part of it is also to see how you stack up next to everyone else. As things turn out, the right contest at the right time is coming up and you decide to enter.

On the day of the competition, you feel as if you're in the middle of the arena, and you're just awaiting the emperor's signal to decide your fate—it's not quite that dramatic or quite that hostile, but you're sure not in the thick of things with your best friends. They might not be throwing chairs at you, but if words and looks could kill, you'd already be pushing up the daisies.

But you don't let this get under your skin because you know that you might be able to use this situation to your advantage, and just to throw the hostile audience a curve, you politely smile, bow, and wave to them before ripping a lift in a way that leaves even you stunned. You act as if you do this every day, sometimes maybe even before breakfast, and they go silent. They don't know quite what to make of you, but they're sure it's not good. On the other hand, you know that you have a secret—the knowledge of using their hostility for your own good— and you also know that the moment is yours, so instead of jumping the planned 5 kilos, you go for 7.5 on your second attempt, smoke it, and then repeat the process for your third attempt. You're definitely in the zone that day.

This is just how things went on the first lift, but it presages the second because they just about tear down the house when you come out for your opener, but once again, you think to yourself, "They hate me. So what? I'll show them!" and you figure you might as well go for it, so you just pull out all the stops. You move your opener up 2.5 kilos, smoke the weight, and nail your second and third attempts, getting two personal records and a state record in the process. By the time the contest is over, you have their hero on the ropes, and even though the fans might still hate your guts, you not only won the whole enchilada, but you used their hostility to help you do it. This time when you smile and bow, you know that you really owe them a lot, even if they don't have a clue as to how they helped you. Neat trick.

View knowledge of this psychological phenomenon like having an ace up your sleeve, quietly lurking there, always ready to be deployed when needed. Or think of it as being like psychological aikido, knowing that you have the ability to use your attacker's energy to neutralize his assault. Maybe even better, walk around with the quiet sense of confidence that comes from knowing that even when you hit choppy water, you have the skills to keep sailing toward your goal.

# 82: Grow With the Flow

| How to: | Use your emotions to improve your performance |
|---|---|
| **Key ideas:** | ◆ *Flow* – occurs when you get absorbed in your task, forgetting about yourself and your surroundings, and emerge having outdone yourself or performed at a top level |
| | ◆ *Entry into flow* – the height of using your emotions to improve your performance |

Olympic-style weightlifters compete on two lifts: the snatch and the clean and jerk.  For simplicity's sake, think of the clean and jerk as lifting the barbell from the ground up to your shoulders first, and then getting it overhead—the sophisticated version of what you probably did the very first time you grabbed a barbell.  On the snatch, however, the barbell is lifted from the ground to arm's length overhead in one movement—not likely to be the first thing you would naturally try to do with a barbell and not even something that might easily be pictured, but when you see the movement or learn how to do it yourself, you can't help but be impressed with the lift.  Jim Schmitz, who has coached multiple U.S. Olympic weightlifting teams, describes the snatch as involving things like power, speed, flexibility, balance, and courage.

Although the snatch is such a complex lift that the average person would find it difficult to do a decent one with just a broomstick, the world's top lifters can snatch a serious amount of weight.  For example, guys who weigh around 200 pounds can snatch over 400, and the best of the big boys snatch over 450.  Despite the numbers involved, there's an interesting thing about making a PR in the snatch—whether it's a world record or something well below your body weight, chances are that it will feel light.

"A PR feels *light*?" you ask.  "How can that possibly be?"

The answer lies in the phenomenon psychologist Mihaly Csikszentmihalyi calls flow.

Flow is what you've probably experienced any time you have outdone yourself or at least performed at a top level.  Sure, you might have been doing something like working your way up a technically tough rock climb or performing a complex surgical operation, but you might also have been doing something as routine as waxing your car.  What happened, though, is that you got lost in your task and became so immersed in it that you entered an autopilot mode and probably didn't even realize what you were doing until you were done, and then experienced something like waking up—you probably had a sense that you had at least figuratively speaking been someplace else during the task. Ironically, while you were unaware of what you were doing, you were performing at the very top of your game. Nice trick, huh?

Daniel Goleman, who has developed the idea that happy, successful people exhibit emotional intelligence, considers entering the flow to be the height of using your emotions to improve such things as performance because beyond your emotions not interfering with your performance, they augment it. Before you dismiss this as trivial or as a given, consider how frequently and pervasively your emotions work against you, cutting into, for example, your training and reducing the effectiveness of your workout.

Lifting weights, in case you hadn't noticed, has the curious distinction of being a chosen activity that involves something most people consciously try to avoid: lifting heavy objects. Given that most people will go out of their way to avoid lifting heavy things, it shouldn't come as any wonder that it's easy to either talk yourself out of training altogether, or talk yourself into training at half-throttle. "I haven't recovered from my last workout," "I might be injured," "Overtraining is the curse of mankind," are the kinds of thoughts that trigger the emotional responses that are certain to undermine your workouts. If you want to degrade the quality of your training even more, make sure that you are, for example, anxious, have been fuming about something for hours beforehand, or just plain are having the emotional counterpart of a bad hair day.

On the other hand, if you want to understand the power that positive emotions can impart to your training, consider the days when you came to the gym feeling just great and how you sailed through your workout. Even more dramatic, perhaps you have had the experience of being in the middle of a mediocre workout when suddenly you received some good news, or maybe hit a lift you didn't expect to make. As a result of the sudden change in your emotional state, your entire workout turns on a dime, and you blast through the rest of your training like a person possessed.

Flow isn't something you can find in a bottle or a jar, but you can learn to structure your activities to increase your chances of hitting it, and the benefits will amaze you.

For starters, intense concentration seems to help entering flow, which at first might seem odd since one of the characteristics of flow is forgetting about both yourself and your surroundings. In fact, this makes perfect sense, since to really focus on a task, you have to become oblivious to your surroundings and run through the required activity without thinking about it. Once I was taking photographs of some of the world's top weightlifters as they were in their final preparation for the World Championships, and because the training hall was dark, I asked the coach if I could use flash—something that is usually forbidden in competition, among other reasons, for fear that it will distract a lifter and cause a missed lift. The coach said yes, go ahead, flash is no problem because, he said, his lifters had to learn to fully concentrate on their task of lifting the bar. They must have learned to do this well, because the team returned from the Worlds with a pile of medals.

Csikszentmihalyi has found that high levels of concentration and entry into flow are facilitated by tasks that are somewhat challenging—not too easy and not too hard. You can understand this pattern when you consider how your attention wanders when something is so easy that you get bored, and how you can feel defeated or overwhelmed when something seems out of reach. Thus, by adjusting the weight you are using, for example, you can fine-tune your workouts to optimize chances of entering flow.

Another characteristic of flow is that even though you are operating at peak performance levels, your brain activity is actually reduced. Because less cortical activity is required when you are engaged in familiar tasks, you can see the benefits of practicing, practicing, and practicing some more. When you are extremely familiar with something, the neural circuits are so well-oiled that the task becomes fully automatic. And if you ever think you've hit the point that you are so perfect that you don't have to practice any more, watch a world champion weightlifter drilling on the snatch and clean and jerk over and over again with extremely light weights, polishing a movement he has already performed countless times.

It's also easiest to hit flow when you're not too tired, so if you can, try to schedule your workouts for times when you're not absolutely drained, physically or emotionally. Conserve your energy coming into your workout, try to keep your emotions in check, and the fresh feeling you have at the start of your training will pave the way to a top-quality workout that, besides leading to progress, will make you feel even better when you leave the gym than you did when you entered.

Finally, because flow is all about concentration, do the little easily-controlled things that foster better focus. For example, yak before, yak after, but don't yak while you're training. Similarly, even though it's common to have loud background music in many gyms, the rule for maximum efforts in weightlifting is absolute silence. Learn to engage the power of quiet and put it to use in your own training.

Free, portable, and available to all, flow can help you grow.

# 83: Orchestrating Accomplishments

| | |
|---:|:---|
| **How to:** | Make what you do add up to big accomplishments, not busy work |

| | |
|---:|:---|
| **Key ideas:** | *Ectomorphs* – people who are small-boned and tend to be skinny |
| | *Mesomorphs* – people who are large-boned and tend to be heavily muscled |
| | *Accomplishments* – the *results*, not the details, of what you do |
| | *Expectations* – affect how hard you train and what your goals are, e.g., lower expectations mean that you are operating at a reduced level because you're aiming at a lower goal |
| | *Feedback* – maximize by using a training log, rather than relying on memory |

Two people lift weights, and even though an outside observer would say that they appear to be doing most things identically, it's also evident that one seems to be making quite striking progress, while the other one's rate of gains is someplace between slow and stagnant. If they're both doing nearly the same things, why is one's stock soaring north, while the other's plunges south?

The confusion is easy to understand given that both people started training at about the same time. Both could be described as somewhere between classic ectomorphs (small-boned and tending to be skinny) and classic mesomorphs (large-boned and tending to be heavily muscled). They are about the same height, started off weighing about the same, and even do workouts that would appear to be more similar than different.

Yet, for all they have in common, a year after both began training, one has gained 10 pounds of body weight, and the other has gained 30. One still hopes to squat 300 pounds some day, and the other is already looking at that as a goal for his bench press. And even though neither one is an upper body specialist, the second guy's arms are now two full inches bigger than the first guy's. In fact, on just about every measure, while the first person has definitely made some gains, they are minuscule compared to the second person's. What gives?

Let's start with why they appear to be doing pretty much the same things, yet their results are so different.

Suppose your favorite aunt, who does aerobics but doesn't lift weights, talked to both guys and watched them train. This is what she'd note: both concentrated on basic exercises. Both used pretty brief routines. Both knew that the big movements, squats especially, were the key to making gains in size and strength, and this is where they put their emphasis. Both tried to eat well.

At this point, it's easy to see why your aunt, and just about everyone else, would note the remarkable similarities in how these two guys approached their training, even if their results were as diverse as night and day.

Enter your favorite uncle, who does neither aerobics nor weights, but is a psychology professor who happens to be particularly interested in boosting human performance. Your uncle watches both guys train, asks each a few questions, and immediately says he can explain why one is doing so well while the other one flounders, and if you just pay him his customary, exorbitant consulting fee, he'll be happy to let you in on the secret. Since you're his favorite nephew, and you're struggling to save enough money for a new computer, he relents and tells you what's going on for free.

The first thing he explains to you is the distinction that people like him make between mere behavior and actual accomplishments. Thus, while two people might think of themselves as being equally busy day to day, one might have nearly nothing to show while the other racked up a host of accomplishments at the end of the day. In our example, your uncle explains, both guys are doing squats. In fact, both are using what appears to be the same squat program because both are giving it special treatment in their training and both are using the same set–rep scheme. That's the behavioral side, explains your uncle, and because what they're doing appears so outwardly similar, it's easy to be confused about the different results these two guys get.

The difference in the results, says your uncle, is what accomplishment is all about, and to understand it, you have to dig a little deeper. Accomplishment is the result of what you do, he explains, and in the case of these two guys working out, accomplishments include things like gaining size and strength. And even though these two guys are running through behaviors that might appear very similar, what they are accomplishing is wildly different. The difference in their accomplishments is what separates their results—one has gained very little after a year's training, while the other one has completely transformed himself.

You're not stupid, and you even like school from time to time, but at this point what you'd just like to know is how you become like the second guy. You're in the market for the missing 20 pounds of muscle, which includes things like a couple of more inches on your arms and some more big plates on the squat bar. So you ask your uncle to cut to the chase.

Your uncle explains that since you're the kid who thinks of 500 megahertz as limpingly slow, while he's the middle-aged guy who still appreciates the latent potential of a number two pencil and a legal pad, you will be happy to know that the crux of what separates these two guys can be explained in terms of information, what they have available and how they use it.

The first guy, who's gained only 10 pounds, works under the assumption that he should expect little progress, and that lifting weights is fraught with dangers that are to be vigilantly avoided. Dire among these dangers, for example, is doing too much and/or getting injured in the process. The second guy, the one who's gained 30 pounds, on the other hand looks at lifting weights as arguably less dangerous than crossing the street, and when done right, much more effective for such wondrous things as building bigger arms and scary levels of strength. And while the first guy would swear on a stack of Bibles that he gives his workouts his all, there are some huge differences between what he does and what the second guy does.

Both, for instance, started squatting with about the same weight, but while the first guy worried incessantly about his technique, not to mention the risks of squatting, and therefore has prudently guarded against adding weight too quickly to the bar, the second guy read a description of good squatting technique, noticed that even a five-year-old doesn't appear to find the movement hard to execute, and has since concentrated on adding plates to the bar, rather than obsessing about some nuance in technique or what might go wrong along the way. If the second guy has obsessed about anything, it's adding weight to the bar and never missing a workout, so it's not surprising that over the course of a year, he has done about twice as many workouts as the first guy, and his squatting weight completely outstrips the first guy's. And that's been a key to the difference in their overall size and strength gains.

These differences, your uncle explains, are tied to differences in expectations and feedback about how good their performance is. So, since the first guy has much lower expectations than the second guy, he's operating at a reduced level simply because he's aiming at a lower goal, unlike the second guy, who is always stretching to do more. Sometimes, your uncle notes, people might lack good feedback about how they are doing, and this is also a striking difference between these two guys. The first guy runs through his workout by memory, or on instinct, while the second guy approaches it as if it's carved in stone. Ask the first guy about his training weights, for instance, and he mumbles something about "the little black plates, you know the ones I mean?" while the second one spews numbers, trends, and week-to-week differences with the zeal of a market analyst and backs the whole thing up with a well-worn training log.

Finally, your uncle explains, the first guy is not to be ridiculed, because he really believes that he is trying the best he can. The problem is just that he usually trains with just that level of specificity regarding his goals, and the truth is that he could do much more than he does. The second guy, on the other hand, approaches his squats, for example, with the idea that at least under certain conditions, he can add five pounds to the squat bar each workout, even though grinding out the reps is a near-death experience. When the second guy comes in for his next workout, he's not just going to try the hardest he can, your uncle points out, he's going to take five pounds more than his last workout and then do whatever it takes to make his reps.

That's what it's all about, your uncle concludes: it's nice to do what appear to be the right things, but what really matters is whether you get the results you want, and that's the difference between mere behavior and actual accomplishment. "Set specific goals," he advises, "aim high, get plenty of concrete feedback, and never quit, and you're bound to succeed. That's what it takes to orchestrate accomplishments."

# 84: Cumulative Consequences

| How to: | Make slow, consistent, steady progress as the sure path to victory |
|---|---|
| **Key ideas:** | ✌ *Cumulative* – small differences day by day add up to huge differences down the road |
| | ✌ *Observational learning* – how you learn by watching those around you, "monkey see, monkey do" |
| | ✌ *Context* – knowing why you aspire to reach a particular goal |

Maybe you remember the children's story about the ant and grasshopper. While the ant toiled steadily, the grasshopper played and played. Days, weeks, and months went by like this—the ant worked while the grasshopper played—and by the time winter came, there was a huge difference between how each was prepared to face the coming months. Before you dismiss the story as mere pre-electronic kids' entertainment, take a moment to consider how powerful processes like this work in the gym, as well as out, and consider whether you're running your life in a way that will help you reach your goals.

Day one in the gym for just about everyone is a zinger: attitudes are great, effort is there, enthusiasm is bubbling over, and plans to conquer the world abound. A week later, things remain looking good, but a mere month down the road, attrition has begun to exert its influence. Three months into the training thing, a lot of the people who first walked into the gym are back on the couch, the remote within easy reach, and since they no longer go to the gym, they have a few extra hours each week for their favorite Internet activities: chatting and playing games. The people who are still plugging away in the gym are starting to morph by now: stomachs are shrinking and getting harder, chests are swelling, and weights that used to stay glued to the floor are, magically, light for curls. For all the outward changes in the people who kept banging away in the gym, the real magic seems to be going on under their skin because there's just something about the way they stand up and walk around. Whatever this thing is they seem to exude, it's positive, and they seem to be able to apply it to whatever they do—things related to lifting and things not.

What's happened, basically, is that the group that continued to train learned the skills necessary to succeed, while the group that quit learned the skills that make failure likely. Here's how it works.

Unless you're Paul Anderson, you don't just walk into the gym on day one and bang out honest squats with 400 pounds. Throw four 45s on each end of the bar, put the average person under it, and watch 405 drop them like a blow from a sledgehammer. On the other hand, virtually any guy who was lucky enough to be born remotely within the wide range considered "normal," can look forward to repping out with this same weight if only he trains wisely and diligently. And odd as it might sound, the wise part of this equation is the easy part; it's the diligent component that makes or breaks people.

Returning to our animal friends, it's not that the ant necessarily did anything incredibly dramatic on any one day. Instead, it was a diet of steady, consistent effort that rang the bell for him. Day after day, the ant plugged away while the grasshopper took the course of least resistance. It's like the one kid who saves a few bucks here and a few bucks there, and before you know it, he's bought a piece of real estate. And it was his small but steady efforts, not a windfall, that paved the way to his success.

It's the same thing with training, where slow and steady is the sure path to victory. Everybody tends to sense the truth of this, and all the ideas like meticulously planned training cycles and the use of micro-plates reflect the common belief in doing what you can to keep churning forward. The most important point of all, however, is to remember to show up, day in and day out, because small differences day by day add up to huge differences down the road. That's why devotion to duty leads to such rich dividends over the long haul. Even better, this type of conscientious effort carries an extremely valuable fringe benefit that is often overlooked—whatever you're doing becomes habit forming. Use this system correctly, and it means that by training steadily, for example, you not only reap all the direct benefits of consistent effort, but you also will find that it's easier and easier to get into the gym each time you're supposed to. Without dwelling on the negative, it's important to remember that this identical process works in the other direction just as well: each time you skip a workout, it becomes easier to skip the next one.

And while lifting weights is always going to be more work than staying in bed, there are things you can do to make it more likely that you hit the gym, armed for progress, rather than while away your life loafing on the couch.

Monkey see, monkey do pretty much tells the story of what research psychologists call "observational learning." Think we don't learn by watching those around us? Go spend ten minutes in a pre-school and watch what the kids do—a good chunk of their play will relate to imitating what they see grown-ups doing. More specifically, if you are surrounded by high-drive, achievement-oriented role models, chances are good that you will have learned the attitudes, skills, and behaviors to make headway yourself. And if you want some of this progress stuff for yourself, but are not naturally surrounded by successful role models, focus your efforts on 1) realizing how you control your situation, both present and future, and 2) trying to identify and surround yourself with the types of people, images, and activities that are most likely to produce success.

For example, just because your family might not model the most appropriate attitudes, skills, and behaviors for success, don't let that limit you—instead, adapt this approach to your world and establish a different set of reference points for yourself. Use your friends, find a mentor, identify a public figure, maybe a sports hero—the point is to go out and identify people who demonstrate what it takes to get ahead, and learn how they do things. Mentally surround yourself with these images, the ones that will take you forward. In the training world, every gym has a group that never misses training and another group that is always on half-throttle when it comes to their commitment. You know which group you should identify with. And with the help of your reference group and positive images, make sure that day by day, you march steadily toward your goals.

Along the way, try to keep the process enjoyable and use goals and sub-goals to motivate your efforts and help sustain you through the tough times. If you're struggling to boost your squat weight, besides thinking about the final big number you are aiming for, think about each five- or ten-pound jump along the way; think of how much more impressive the bar looks each time you slap on another pair of 25s; and how each time another pair of 45s goes on the bar, you've reached a major milestone. Pat yourself on the back each time you reach one of your goals, and then set your sights on your next one.

To make goal-setting even more effective for spurring progress, it is important to keep your goals both in context and dynamic in nature. The context part means that you need to always know why you aspire to reach a particular goal, so that it has some relevance and value that goes beyond just saying, "I squatted with 315 for 20 reps today." Maybe, for instance, you take particular pride in the fact that 315 means you had three 45s on each side of the bar, and when you started, just one was enough to make your knees shake—literally and figuratively. Or maybe you made a deal with yourself that when you hit 315 x 20, you'd buy a pair of real weightlifting shoes. Perhaps 315 x 20 was a marker that meant you'd have reached a size–strength point you wanted, for example, to play football. Use context to add flesh to your goals, and this will help you use your goals to motivate each of those workouts that mark a step toward your destination.

Keeping your goals dynamic is another twist that can help you stay on the course of progress. Let's say that you have a goal to power clean 225 pounds, but along the way you injure your wrist so you can't do power cleans at the moment. You could head for the sidelines, explaining to yourself and the world that your injured wrist makes it impossible to hit your goal, or you can come up with a modified plan. Maybe, if you try, you'd find that you can do clean pulls; or if even those are out of the question, you go to good mornings and a lot of squats. The point is that some people quit as soon as they get a hangnail and other people will find a way to train even when they're in a cast. You can guess who makes progress and who doesn't.

Progress in all walks of life is a wonderful thing, and what's especially nice is that even though the system isn't perfect, when you work hard, you have a pronounced tendency to go forward, which means that you control your destiny to a remarkable extent. And little steps, small and steady, will take you where you want to go, because where you end up is a consequence of your cumulative actions.

# 85: Advantageous Values

| How to: | Develop the values—thrift, investment, hard work, education, organization, and discipline—that are critical for success |
|---|---|
| **Key idea:** | ☀ *Values* – ideas that you hold dear and that steer your life |

Values—the things that you hold dear and that steer your life—might sound like a nice topic for school or church, with little bearing on might and muscle, but nothing could be further from the truth. Values sort out the winners from the losers, and in the barbell world, your values will determine, among other things, whether you make progress or not. Let's take a closer look, identifying the values that are critical to success, talk about them briefly, and outline how to put them to work for yourself.

Sometimes the best way to get a handle on solving a problem or to gain a better understanding of how something works is to change your perspective: if you're used to looking at something a certain way, it can be very productive to simply look at it from a different angle, or maybe cast the situation in a different context. For example, while it's fairly common to talk about what makes individual people succeed or fail, it's not so common to talk about why entire countries tend to succeed or fail, but that's exactly the subject of a new book, *Culture Matters: How Values Shape Human Progress*. Following our own advice, let's see what defines the formula for national success, and then try to apply it on an individual level—not just to your life in general, but specifically to the challenge of making progress in your training. Don't worry, we plan to keep this analysis simple and sweet.

As you might guess, among the values that appear relevant to success are thrift, investment, hard work, education, organization, and discipline, each of which is just as applicable for an individual lifting weights as it is for a country as a whole—even if you're not used to thinking of them in those terms. For example, each of us has finite resources, financial and otherwise, so making thrifty use of them means that what you have will go further. Consider money and how you can either spend a little here and a little there, ending up with little to show for it, or if you had a goal of gaining body weight, for example, you could focus your financial resources on the food and supplements that will help you reach your goal. And don't make the mistake of limiting your thinking about thrifty management to money: your time and your energy might be even more limited than your financial resources, so you can either use them prudently, for maximum benefit, or you can waste them.

Investment might seem hard to understand in terms of training, but think of it as the work that builds your foundation, as opposed to the superficial finishing work. Two guys can start training at the same time in similar condition and one could specialize on bench presses and curls, while the other might really push his squats. Short term, the bench press–curl guy is going to look as if he made the smarter choice, but as they go down the road a bit, it's going to be clear that the other guy, the one who took the time to invest wisely in work on his major muscle groups before specializing on his smaller ones, is headed toward a much bigger payoff. Just as with money: don't let lust for short-term gains blind you to what's best for long-term growth.

Hard work is really one of the biggest determinants of your success level, so if you spend a disproportionate amount of your life in bed or on the couch, don't expect to accomplish much. And while it's become fashionable in some training circles to wax eloquent about how hard you train, it's really like most things: it's the walk, not the talk, that matters, so button your lip, keep your head down, and save your energy for an extra rep or another five pounds on the bar. Let your efforts and your results speak for themselves.

Education isn't limited to how you did on your organic chemistry final—it's smart to learn as much as you can about whatever is important to you, and if that means getting bigger and stronger, you have to do your homework the same as you did for chemistry. Use the Internet, ask questions, read all the books and magazines you can find. You don't have to end up a walking encyclopedia, but if you take the time to learn a little about the field, you won't be surprised that a meat and water diet coupled with a lot of concentration curls won't help you outgrow your clothes.

Some people are busy all the time—just ask them, even though if you looked at what they had accomplished at the end of the day, you might fit the list on the head of pin. Other people might not build Rome in the same period of time, but they make a good start. The difference between these two types of people usually has little to do with talent, but instead depends on factors that are entirely under everyone's control, and chief among them is organization. If you spend two hours a day dispatching a task that a normal person can complete in ten minutes, you're not going to have a very productive life, and you certainly will find it easy to say that you just don't have the time to train. You'd be amazed at how many genuinely busy, productive people make training a regular part of their lives by either working out first thing in the morning or at lunch time—by being well-organized, they essentially grab some time that otherwise would be used less productively, and they use the time to train.

Discipline is the glue that holds everything together. In the example above, if you're disciplined, you might have to get out of bed early to train when you're supposed to, rather than sleeping late, and it's just as critical in each of the other areas we discussed. Discipline is what makes or breaks you along each step of this path: from thrift to investment to hard work to education to organization. In each case, just as with dieting, understanding how the concept works is the easy part; the challenge is having the discipline to do what's required, but as with a lot of things, you can learn discipline and you get better at it with practice. The danger is, however, that the opposite is just as true: if you practice an undisciplined lifestyle, that, and only that, is what you'll get really good at.

Nations are built one person at a time, so it's no surprise that successful nations are composed of successful people. Similarly, successful people are the result of distinct values—advantageous values—that are there for anyone to adopt, and they are as useful in the gym as out.

# Index

# Index

# Index